Snow White with the Red Hair

SORATA AKIDUKI

24

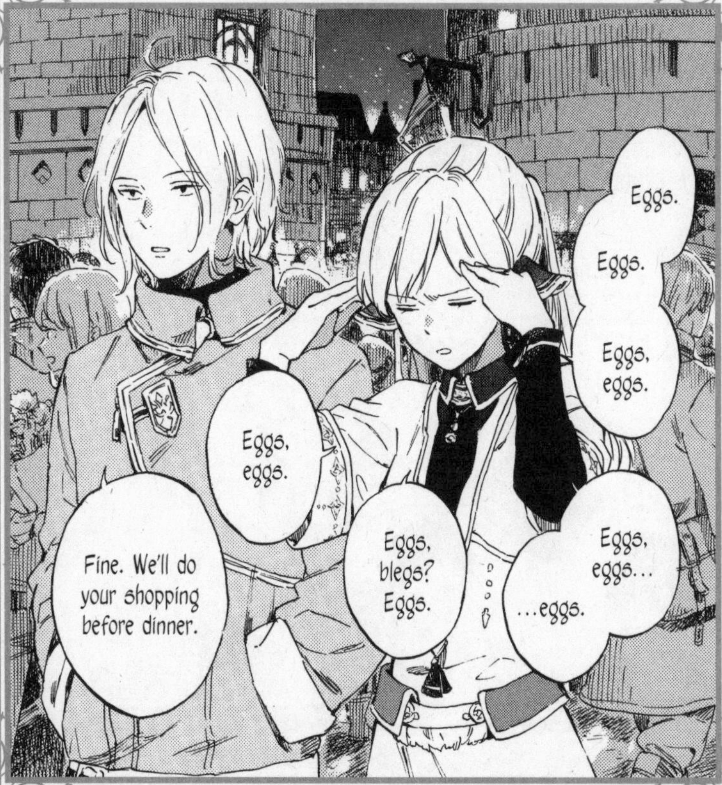
Eggs.
Eggs.
Eggs, eggs.
Eggs, eggs.
Eggs, eggs...
...eggs.
Eggs, blegs? Eggs.
Fine. We'll do your shopping before dinner.

THE STORY

Shirayuki was born with beautiful hair as red as apples, but when her rare hair earns her unwanted attention from the notorious prince Raj, she's forced to flee her home. A young man named Zen helps her in the forest of the neighboring kingdom, Clarines, and it turns out he is that kingdom's second prince! Shirayuki decides to accompany Zen back to Wistal, the capital city of Clarines.

Shirayuki has met all manner of people since becoming a court herbalist, and her relationship with Zen continues to grow, as the two have finally made their feelings known to each other.

"They say that red is the color of destiny."

SHIRAYUKI
Working as a court herbalist. Has feelings for Zen—feelings that he shares.

ZEN WISTERIA
Prince of Clarines and brother to the king.

RYU
Shirayuki's boss. A brainy kid who became a court herbalist at a young age.

OBI
Former assassin. Currently, Zen's knight and Shirayuki's bodyguard.

MITSUHIDE & KIKI
Zen's knights who double as his aides. They're good friends who share a strong bond.

After becoming a full-fledged court herbalist, Shirayuki takes a work trip to the northern city of Lilias with her boss, Ryu. When a mysterious illness starts spreading, they put their skills to use and figure out what's causing it.

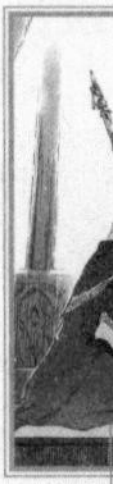

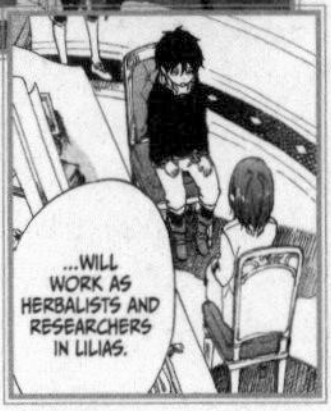
...WILL WORK AS HERBALISTS AND RESEARCHERS IN LILIAS.

Once back in Wistal, Shirayuki and Ryu are ordered to return to Lilias by the newly crowned king Izana. But this time, it's no mere business trip—it's a personnel transfer for two whole years. After arriving, the pair work with colleagues to neutralize the toxin of the glowing orimmallys—the same plant that caused the mysterious illness earlier. Their stunning success brings an end to that chapter.

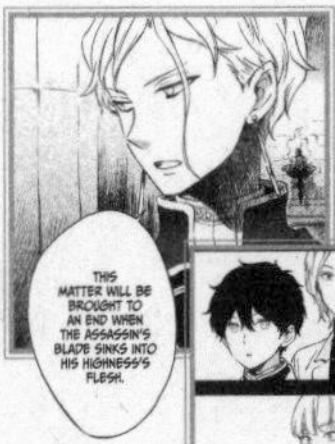
THIS MATTER WILL BE BROUGHT TO AN END WHEN THE ASSASSIN'S BLADE SINKS INTO HIS HIGHNESS'S FLESH.

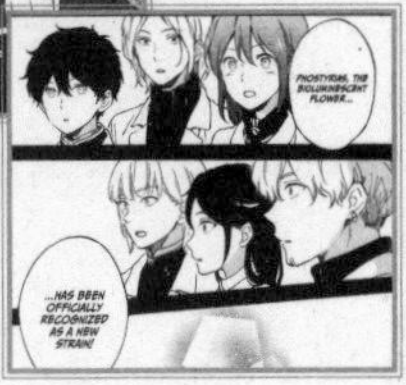
PHOSTYRIAS, THE BIOLUMINESCENT FLOWER...
...HAS BEEN OFFICIALLY RECOGNIZED AS A NEW STRAIN!

Elsewhere, Zen's life is threatened during a plot by Toka Bergat to wrench authority over the northern lands away from the crown. Mitsuhide dashes headlong into danger to defeat the would-be usurper in a duel. Afterward, Kiki accepts Hisame's proposal and the two become engaged, while Zen is assigned as an aide to his mother—the lord and warden of Wirant.

Meanwhile, "phostyrias," the nontoxic bioluminescent plant bred by Shirayuki and the Lilias group, is to be planted along the roads of the north. But to do so, Shirayuki, Obi, and Ryu need the permission of Count Eisetsu Lugiria. Eisetsu has a request of his own, however—for help rooting out a Toka Bergat sympathizer within his territory. While Obi makes contact with Tsuruba, a knight named Yozumi Elys asks Shirayuki to look into an unusual perfume. Soon after she confirms the perfume's unsettling effects, Obi returns with news about Lady Riella, a suspicious noblewoman who is expected to attend the Masked Knight's Ball. Together with Tsuruba, the group concocts a plan to infiltrate the party and find Lady Riella!

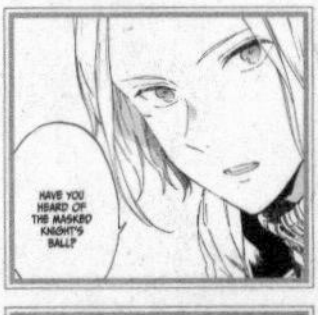
HAVE YOU HEARD OF THE MASKED KNIGHT'S BALL?

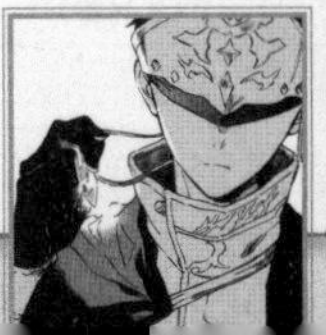

VOLUME 24
TABLE *of* CONTENTS

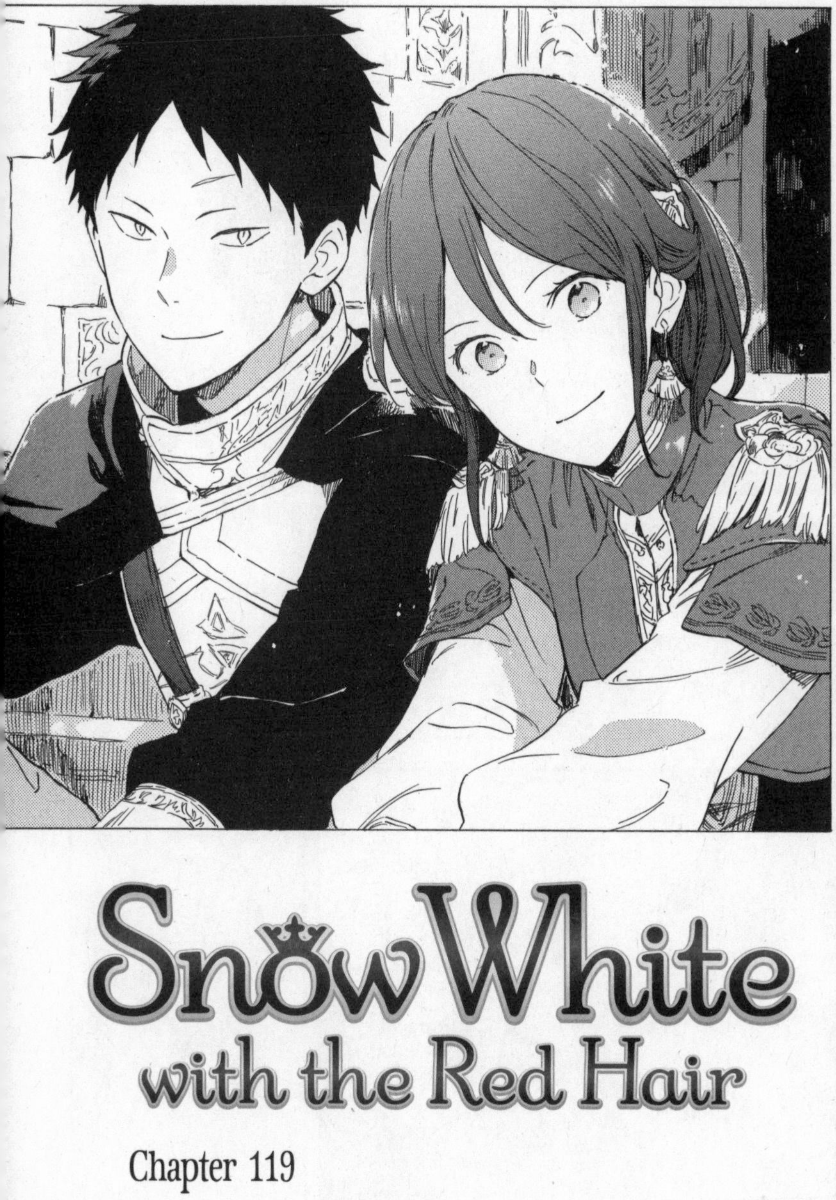

Snow White with the Red Hair

Chapter 119

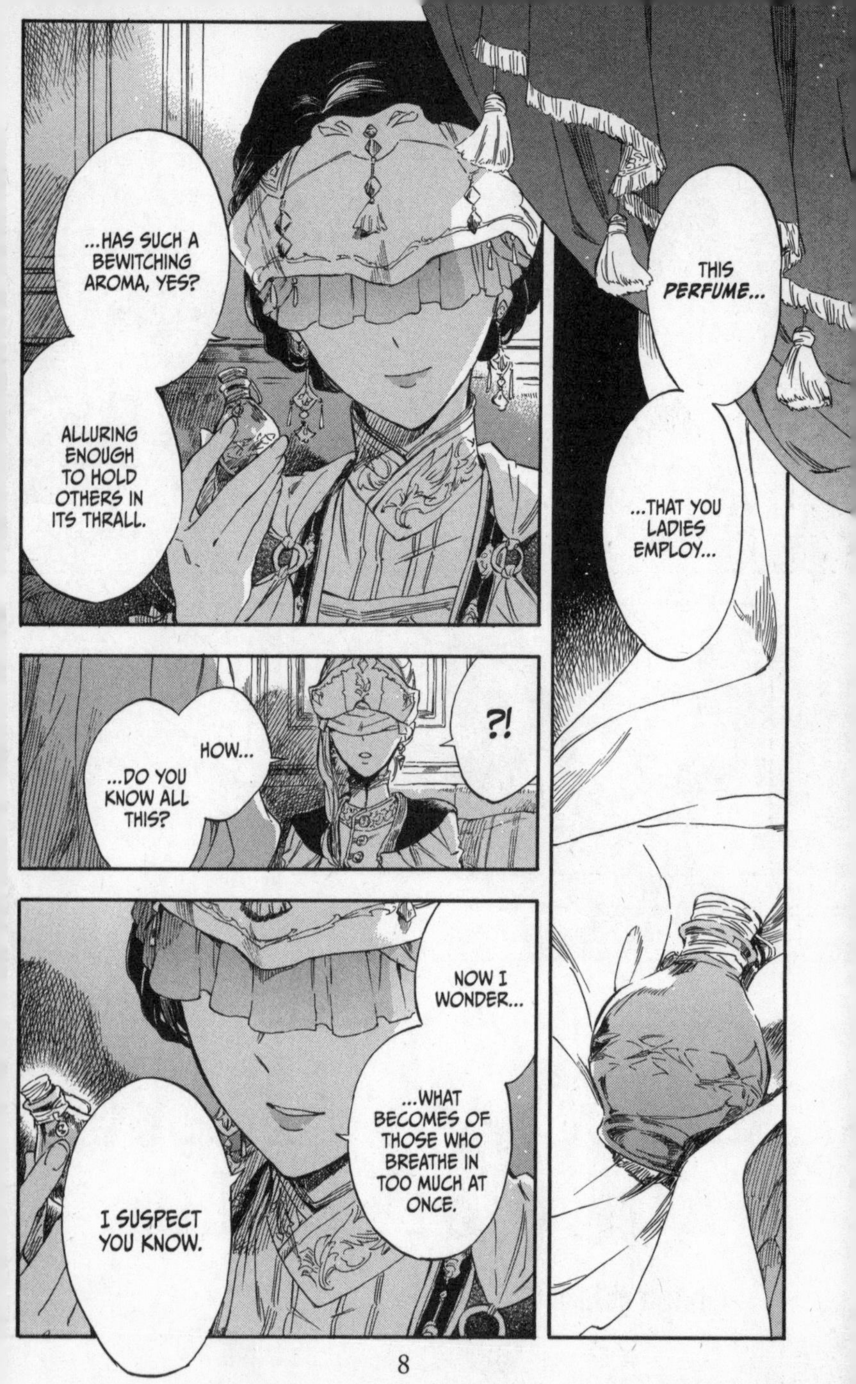
THIS *PERFUME*...
...THAT YOU LADIES EMPLOY...
...HAS SUCH A BEWITCHING AROMA, YES?
ALLURING ENOUGH TO HOLD OTHERS IN ITS THRALL.
?!
HOW...
...DO YOU KNOW ALL THIS?
NOW I WONDER...
...WHAT BECOMES OF THOSE WHO BREATHE IN TOO MUCH AT ONCE.
I SUSPECT YOU KNOW.

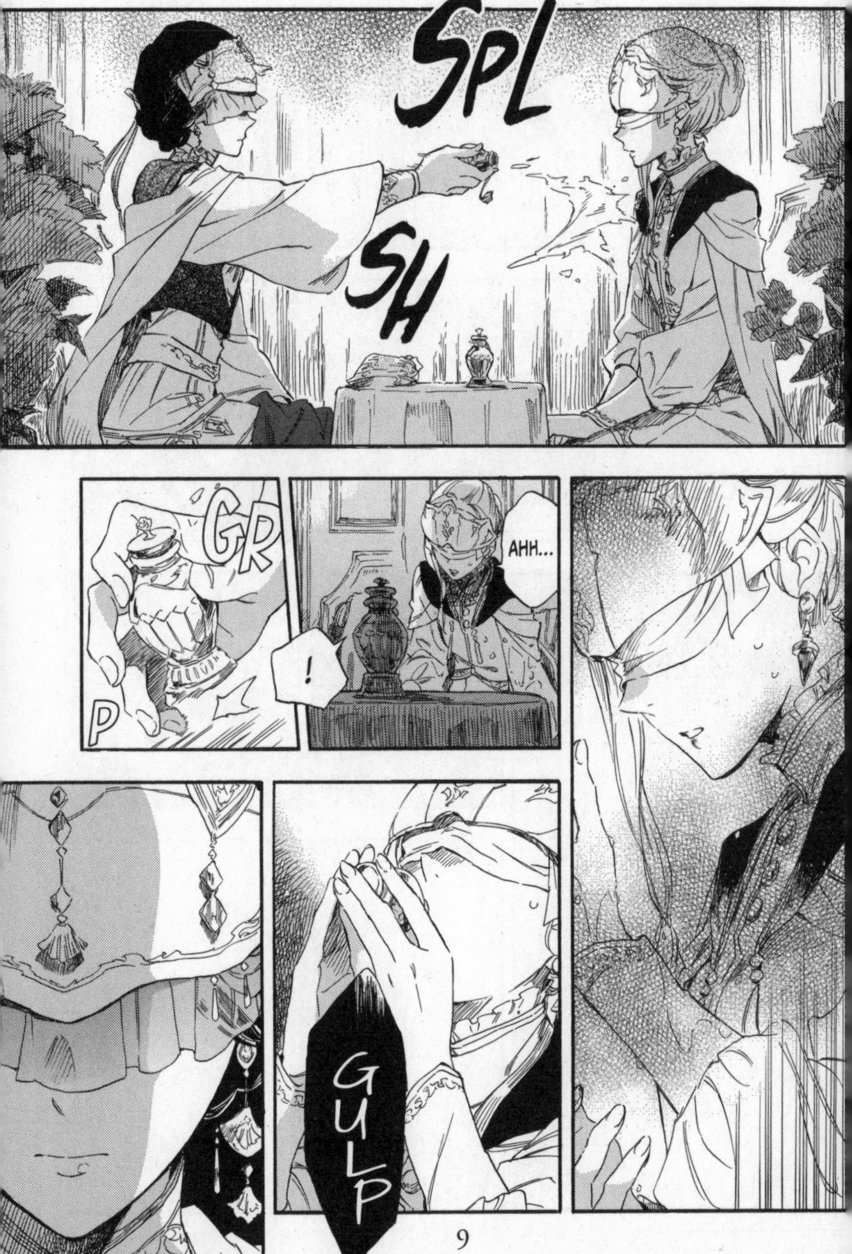
SPL
SH
AHH...
!
GR
P
GULP

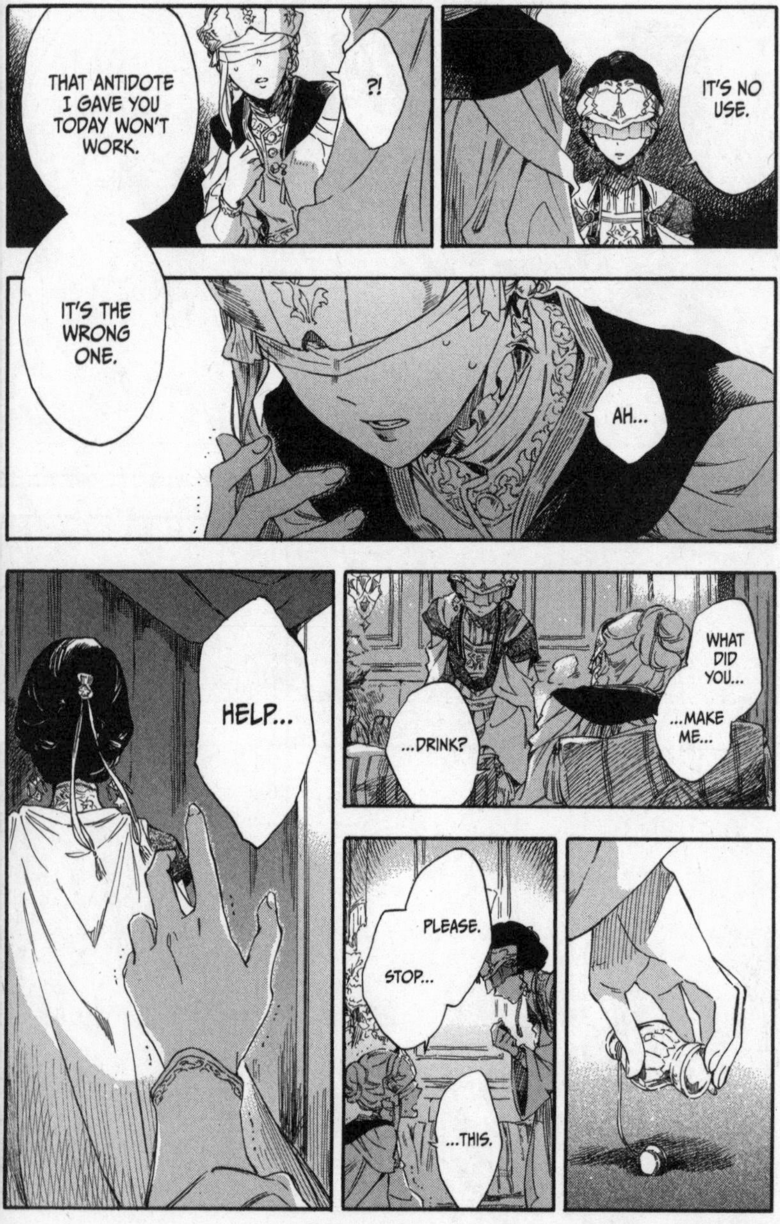
IT'S NO USE.
THAT ANTIDOTE I GAVE YOU TODAY WON'T WORK.
?!
IT'S THE WRONG ONE.
AH...
WHAT DID YOU...
...MAKE ME...
...DRINK?
PLEASE.
STOP...
...THIS.
HELP...

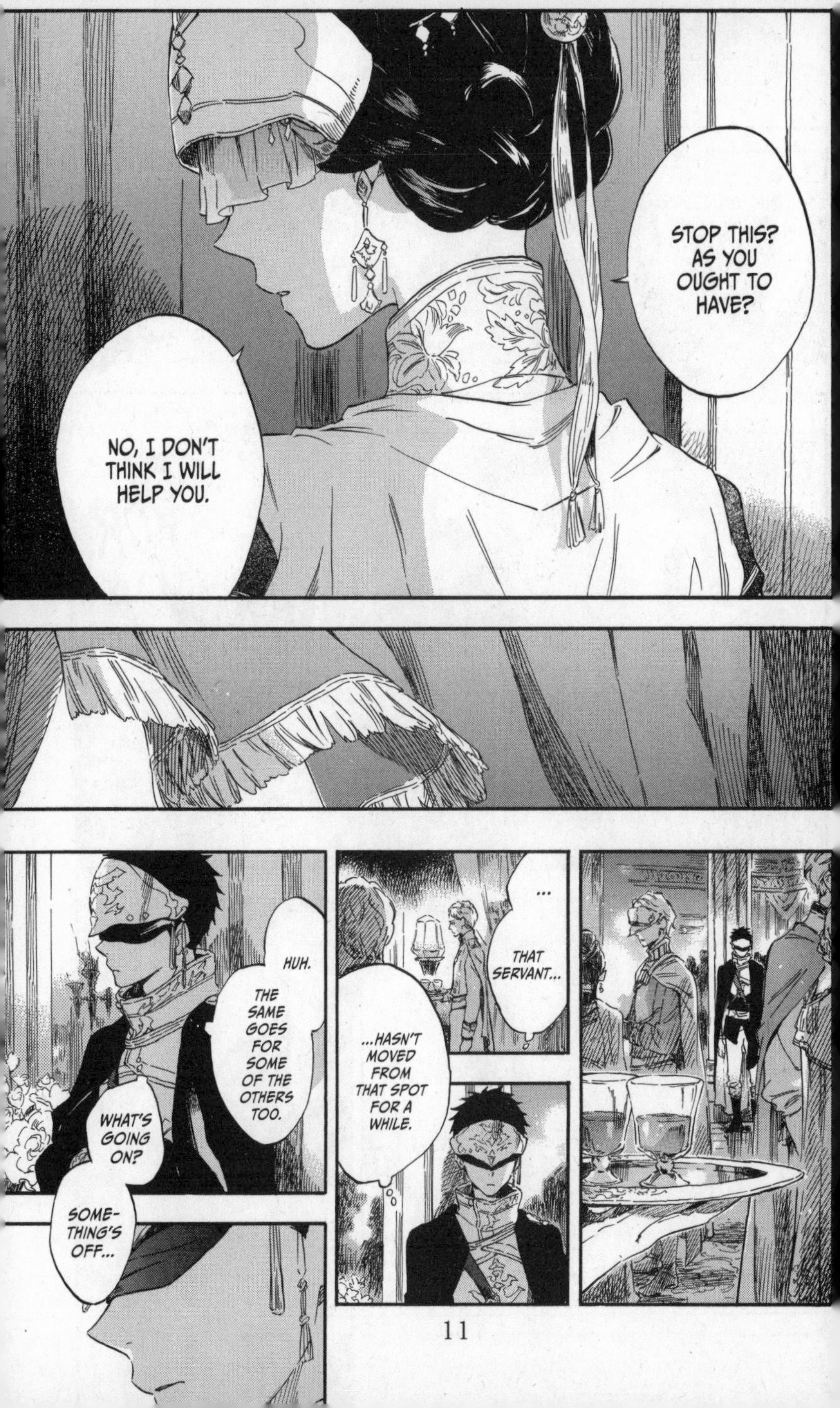
STOP THIS? AS YOU OUGHT TO HAVE?
NO, I DON'T THINK I WILL HELP YOU.
...
THAT SERVANT...
...HASN'T MOVED FROM THAT SPOT FOR A WHILE.
HUH.
THE SAME GOES FOR SOME OF THE OTHERS TOO.
WHAT'S GOING ON?
SOME-THING'S OFF...

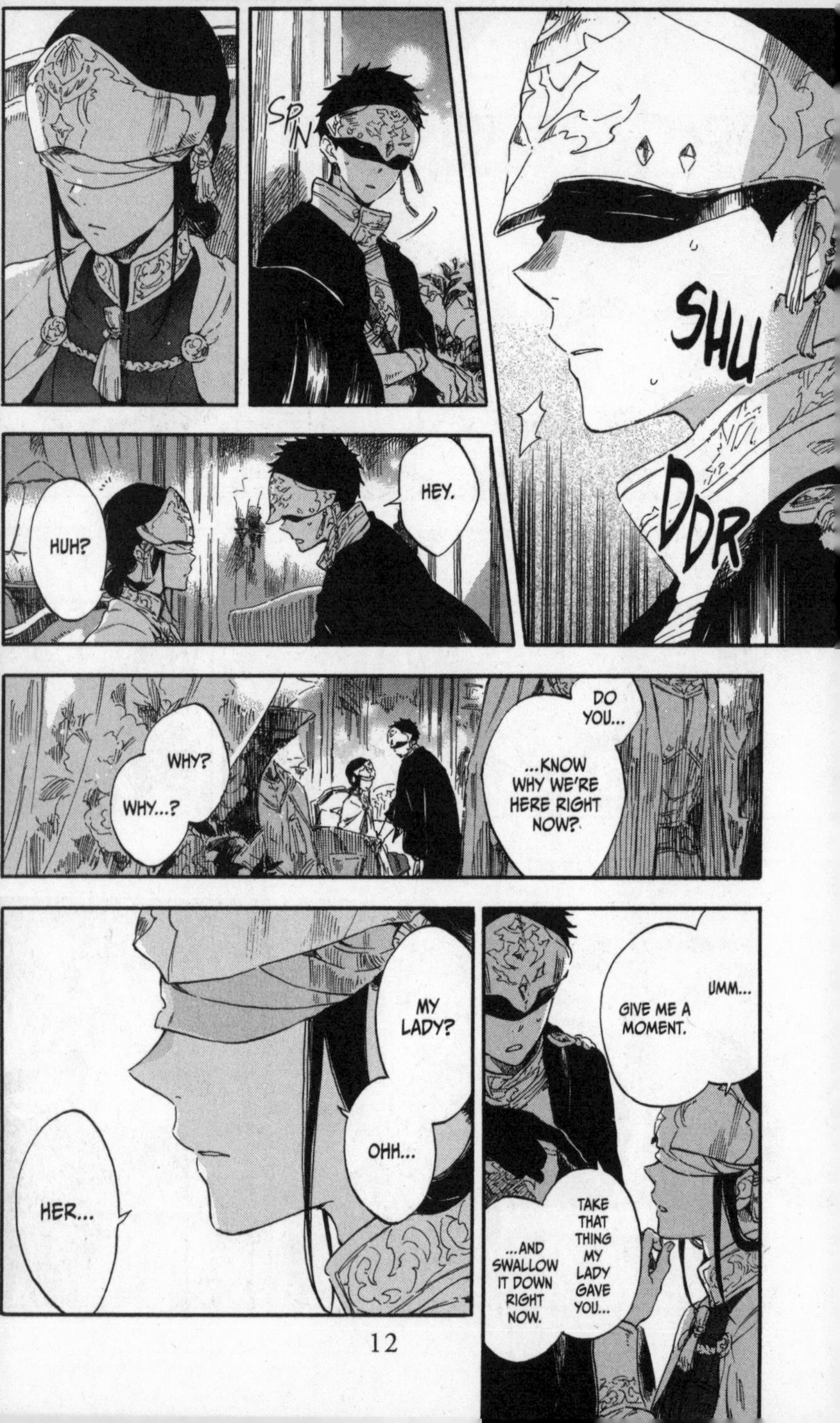
SHU
DDR
SPIN
HEY.
HUH?
DO YOU...
...KNOW WHY WE'RE HERE RIGHT NOW?
WHY?
WHY...?
UMM...
GIVE ME A MOMENT.
TAKE THAT THING MY LADY GAVE YOU...
...AND SWALLOW IT DOWN RIGHT NOW.
MY LADY?
OHH...
HER...

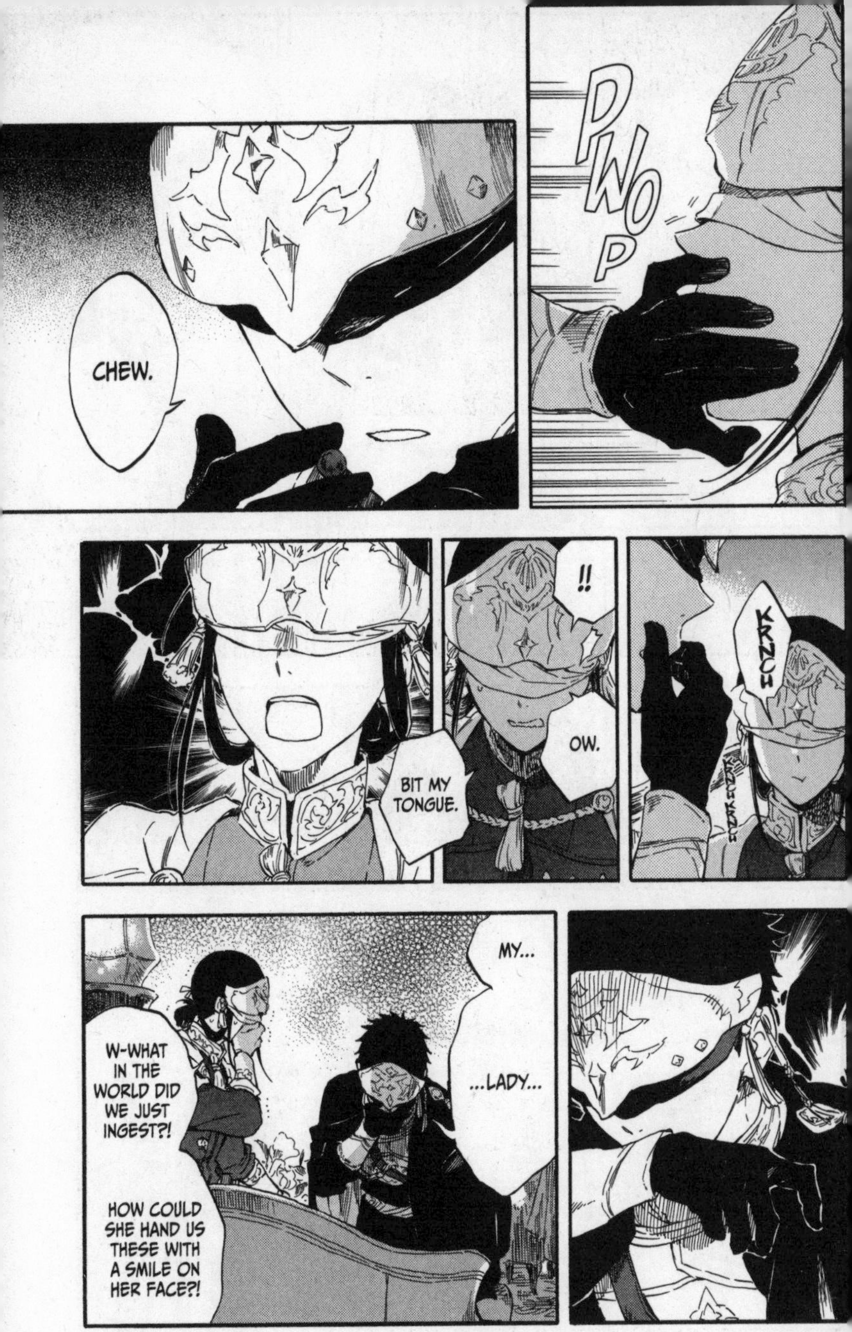
PWOP
CHEW.
KRNCH
KRNCH KRNCH
!!
OW.
BIT MY TONGUE.
MY...
...LADY...
W-WHAT IN THE WORLD DID WE JUST INGEST?!
HOW COULD SHE HAND US THESE WITH A SMILE ON HER FACE?!

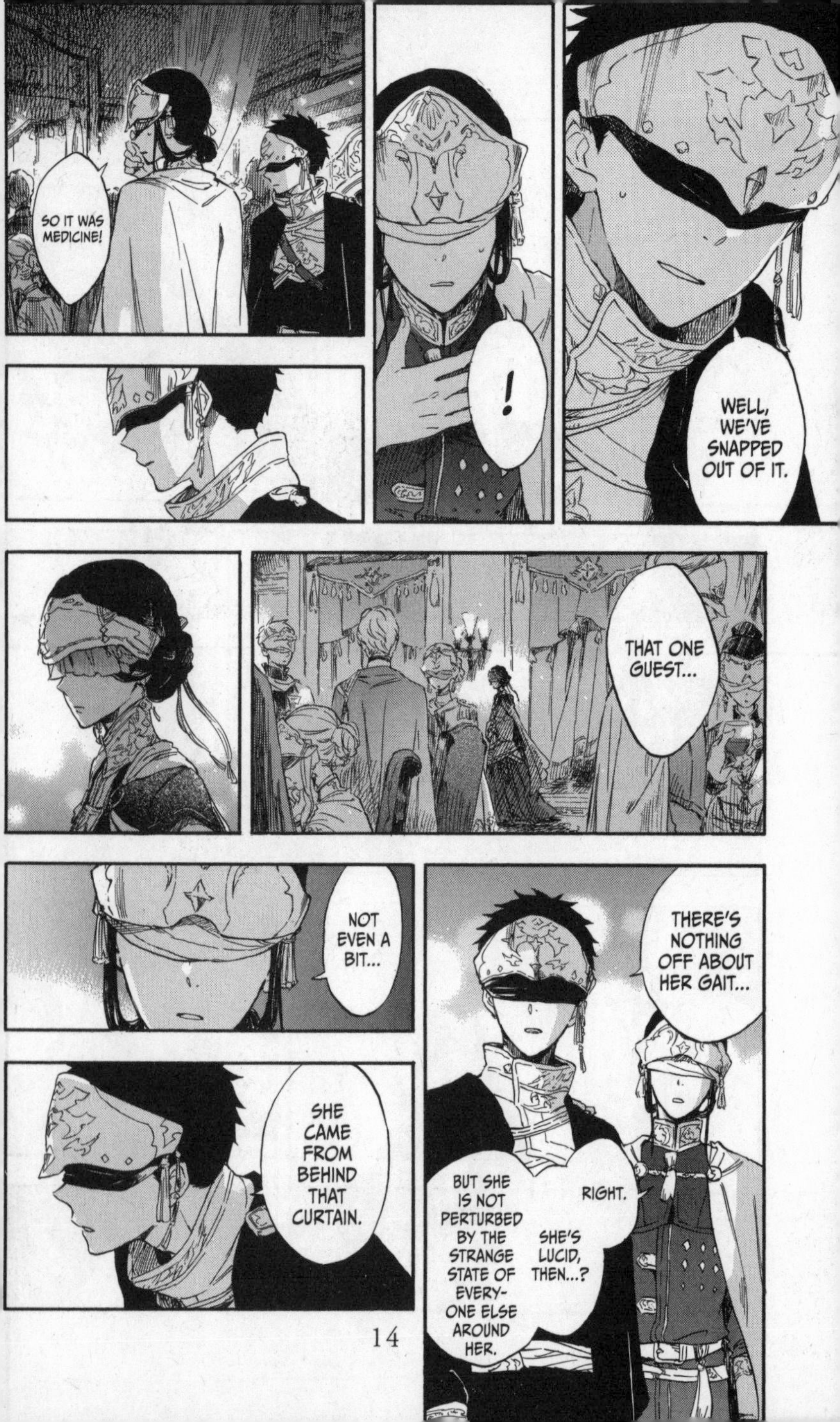
WELL, WE'VE SNAPPED OUT OF IT.
!
SO IT WAS MEDICINE!
THAT ONE GUEST...
THERE'S NOTHING OFF ABOUT HER GAIT...
RIGHT.
SHE'S LUCID, THEN...?
BUT SHE IS NOT PERTURBED BY THE STRANGE STATE OF EVERY-ONE ELSE AROUND HER.
NOT EVEN A BIT...
SHE CAME FROM BEHIND THAT CURTAIN.

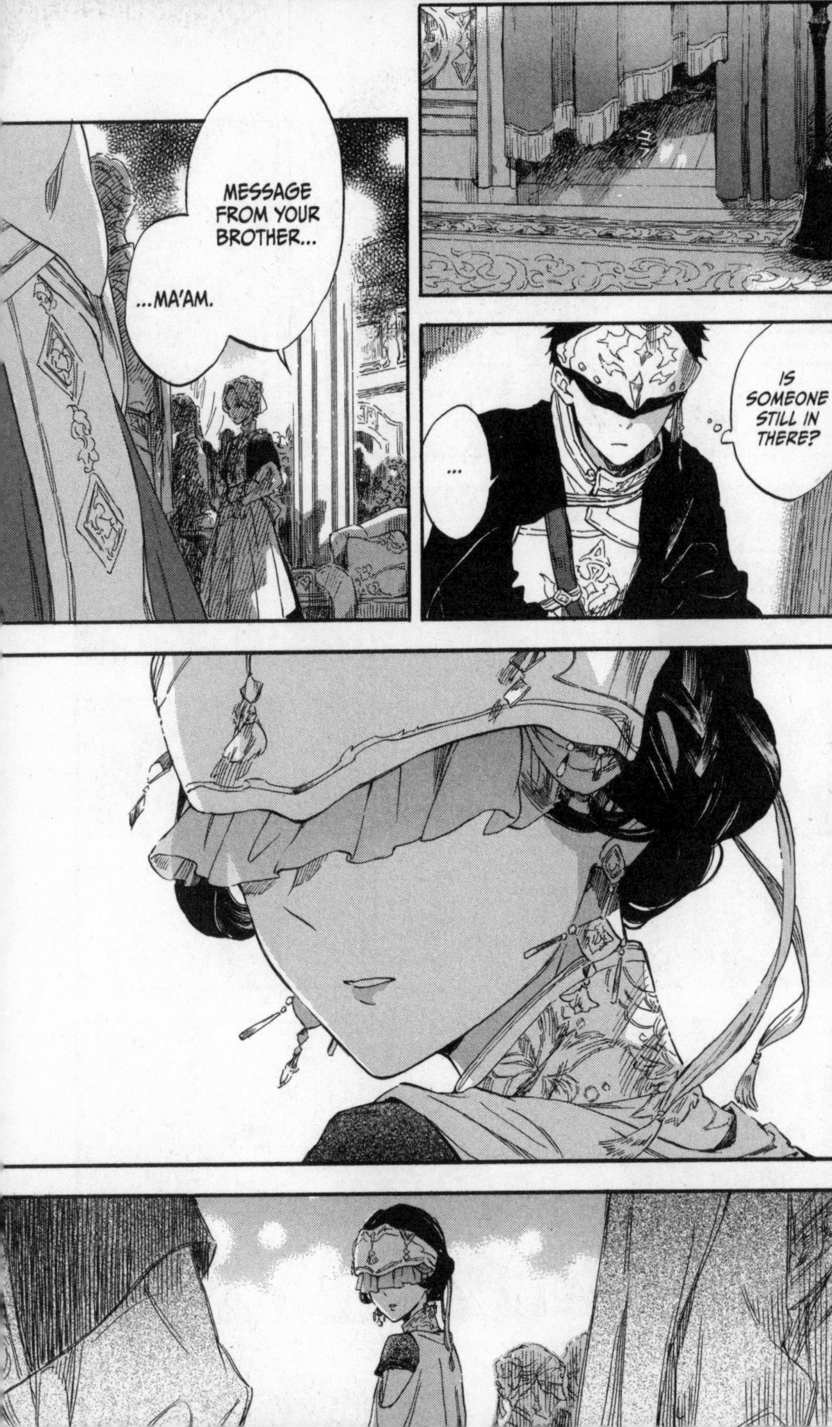
IS SOMEONE STILL IN THERE?
...
MESSAGE FROM YOUR BROTHER...
...MA'AM.

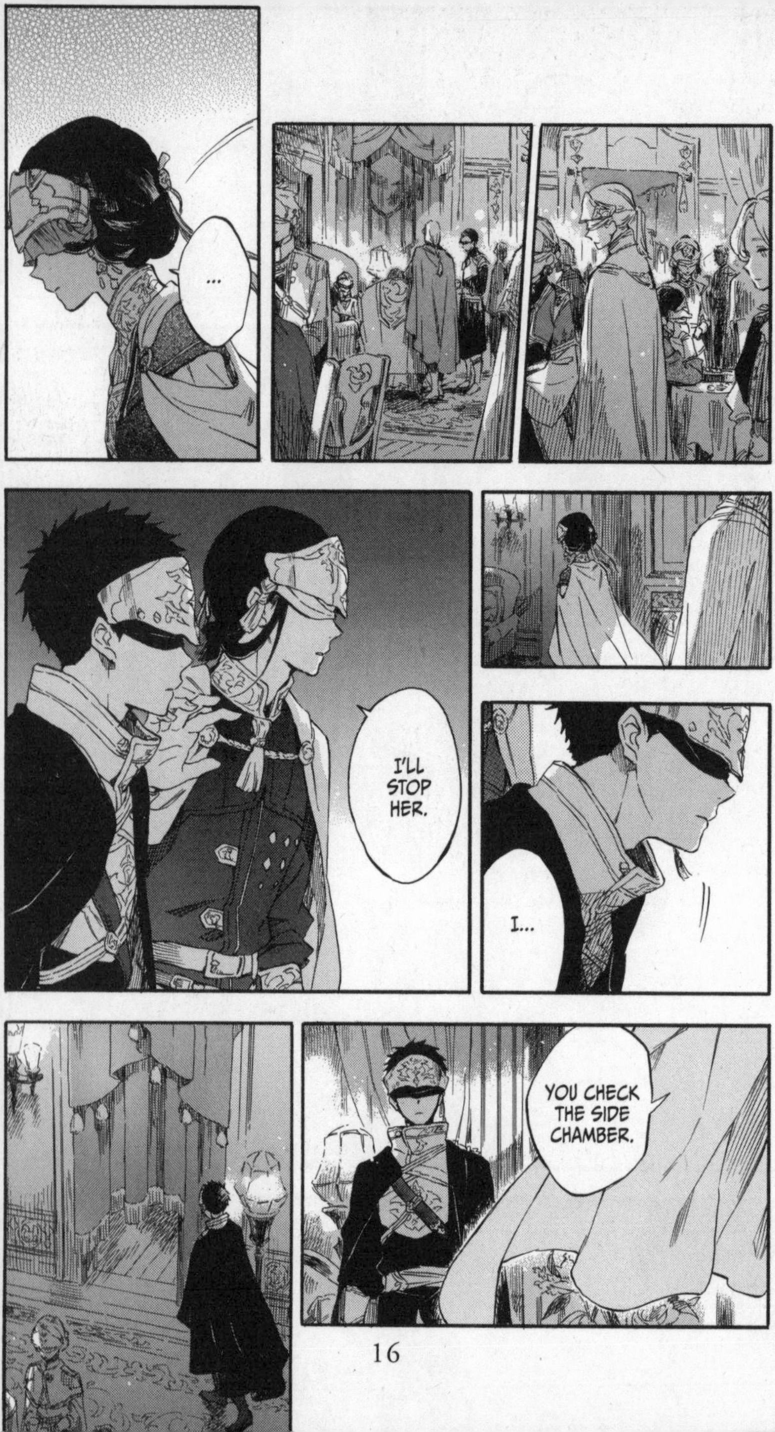
...
I...
I'LL STOP HER.
YOU CHECK THE SIDE CHAMBER.

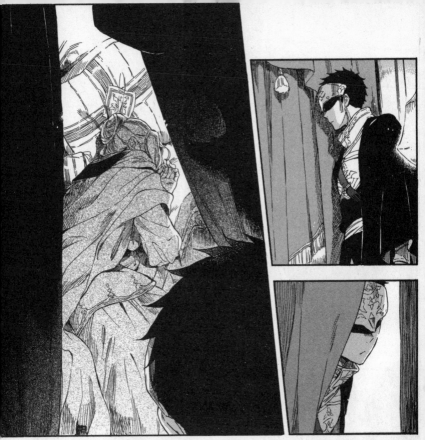

STILL BREATH-ING.

FLAP

...

WHAT THE...?

THE AIR'S THICK WITH THE SCENT, BUT ONLY IN HERE.

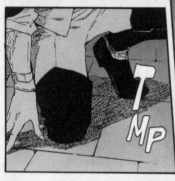

SORRY, BUT...

...COULD YOU HELP ME UP?

LORD TSURUBA.

AH.

TSURUBA?

SORRY, OF COURSE...

18

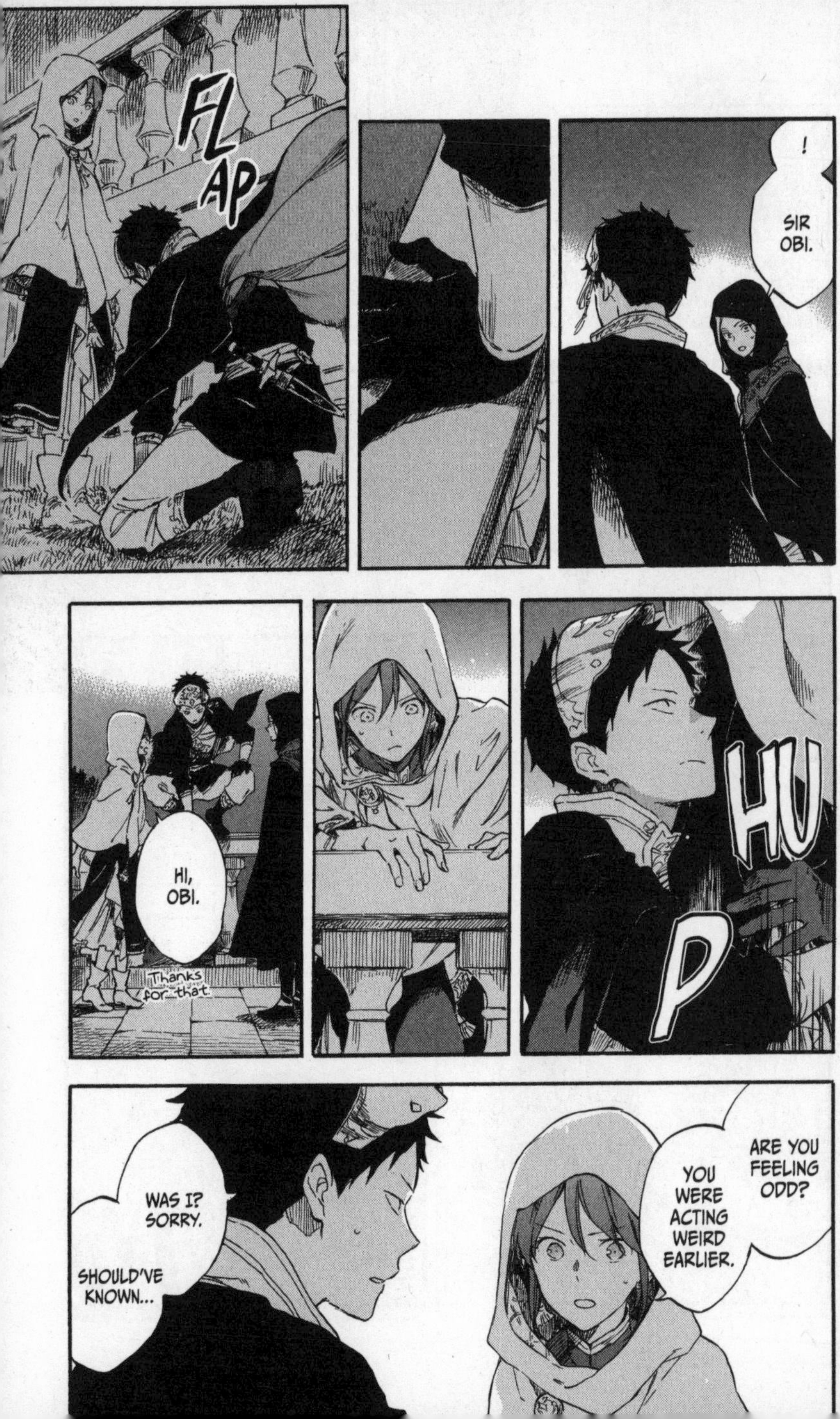
!
SIR OBI.
FLAP
HUP
HI, OBI.
Thanks for that.
ARE YOU FEELING ODD?
YOU WERE ACTING WEIRD EARLIER.
WAS I? SORRY.
SHOULD'VE KNOWN...

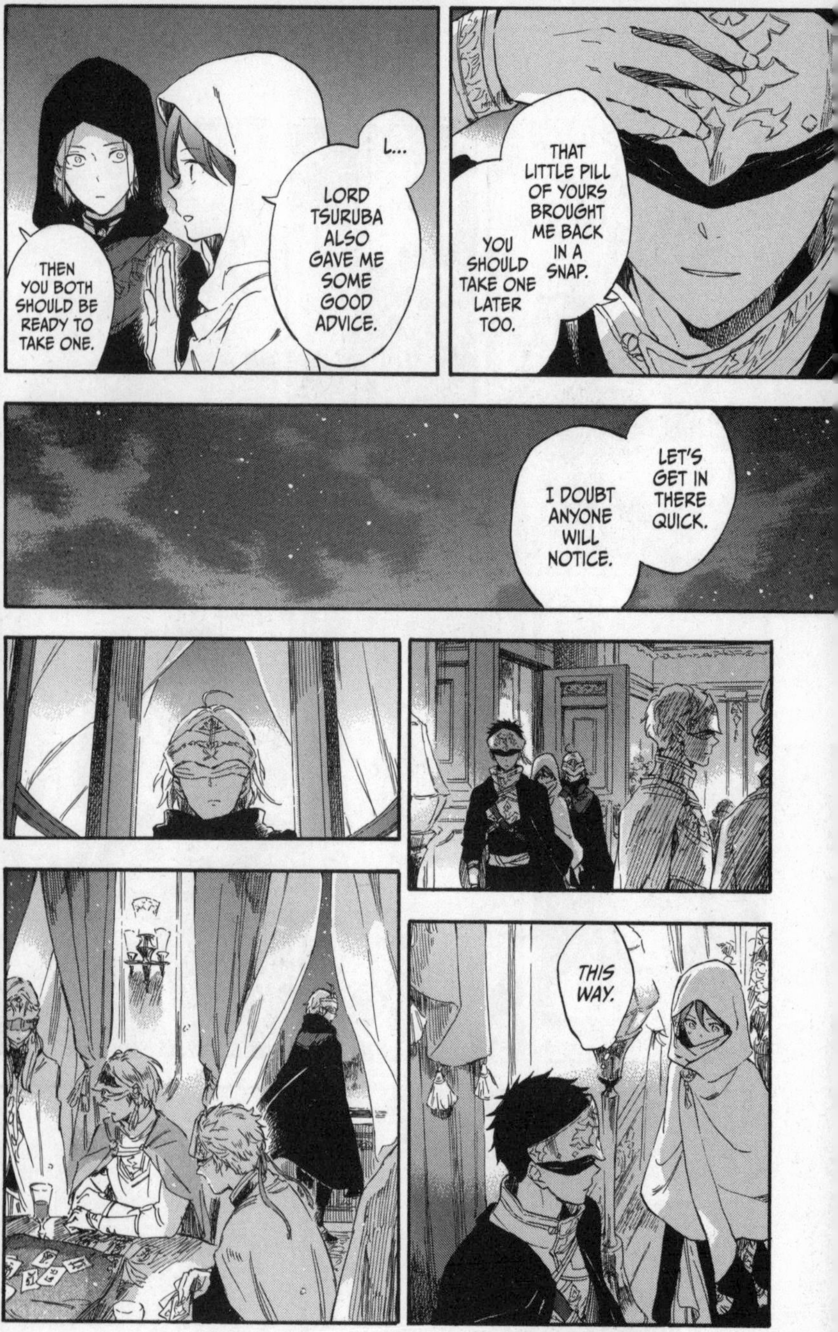
THAT LITTLE PILL OF YOURS BROUGHT ME BACK IN A SNAP.
YOU SHOULD TAKE ONE LATER TOO.
L...
LORD TSURUBA ALSO GAVE ME SOME GOOD ADVICE.
THEN YOU BOTH SHOULD BE READY TO TAKE ONE.
LET'S GET IN THERE QUICK.
I DOUBT ANYONE WILL NOTICE.
THIS WAY.

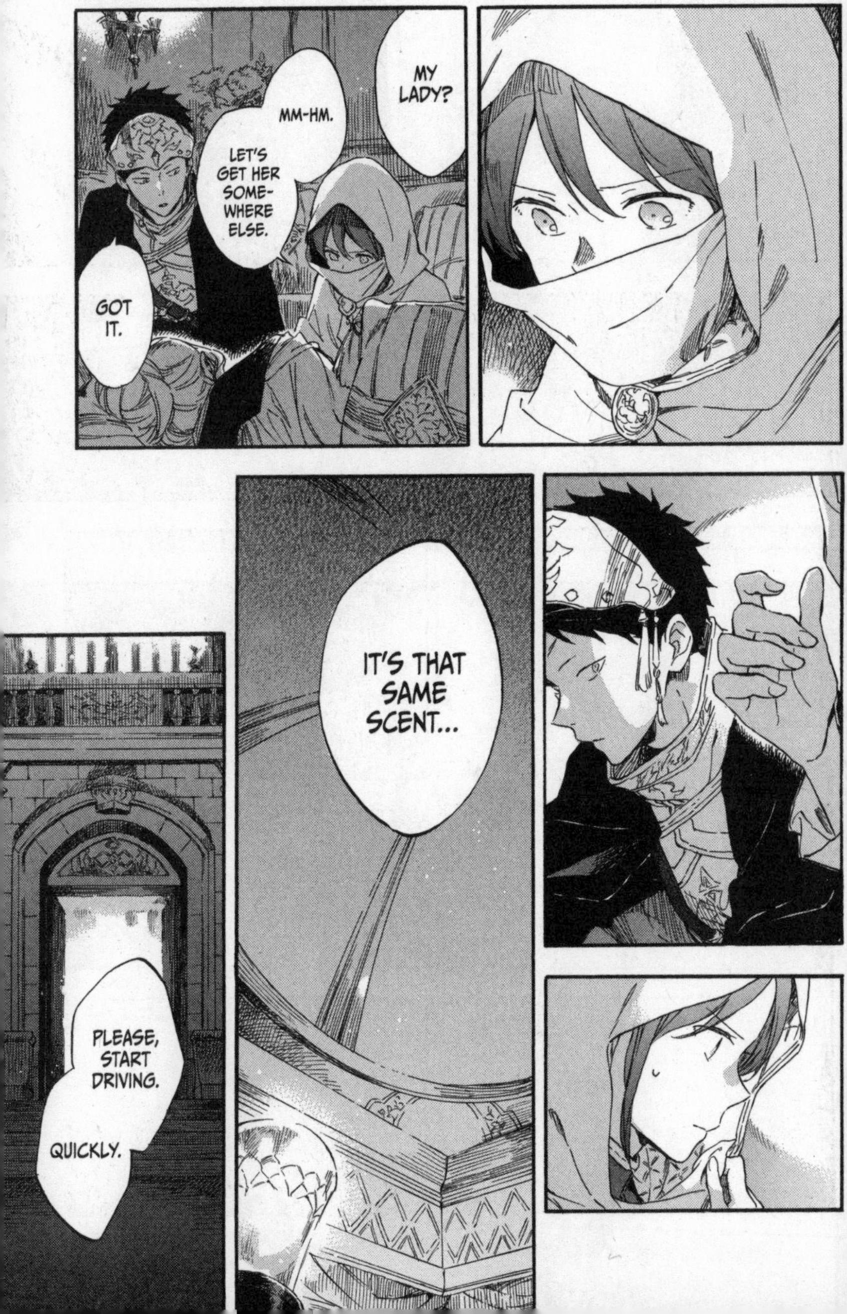
MY LADY?
MM-HM.
LET'S GET HER SOME-WHERE ELSE.
GOT IT.
IT'S THAT SAME SCENT...
PLEASE, START DRIVING.
QUICKLY.

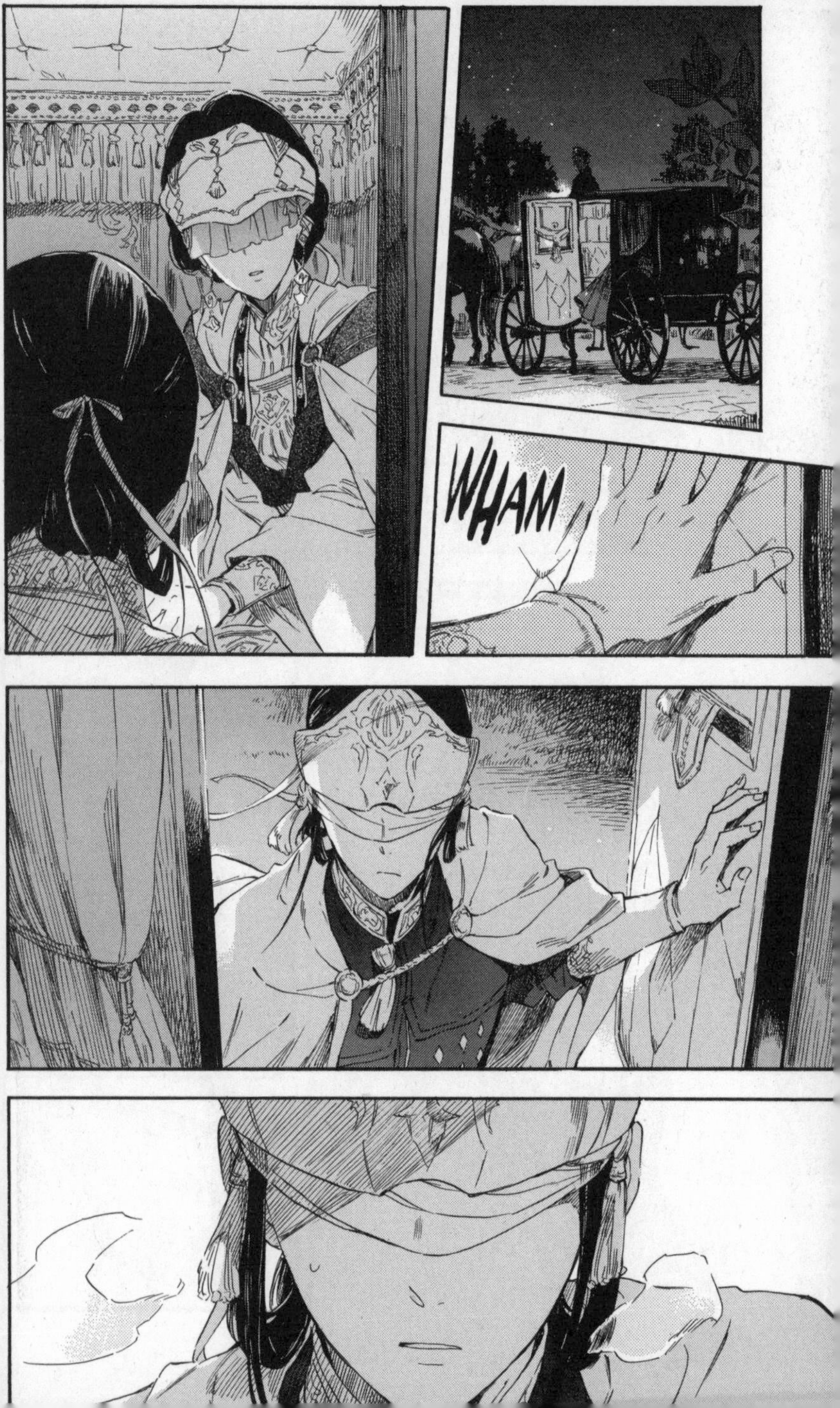
WHAM

WON'T YOU REMOVE YOUR MASK FOR ME?

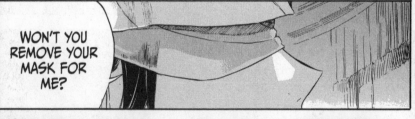

SH WP

TWITCH

SUCH A REQUEST COMING FROM A MASKED MAN?

...

NO, I'M AFRAID I WON'T.

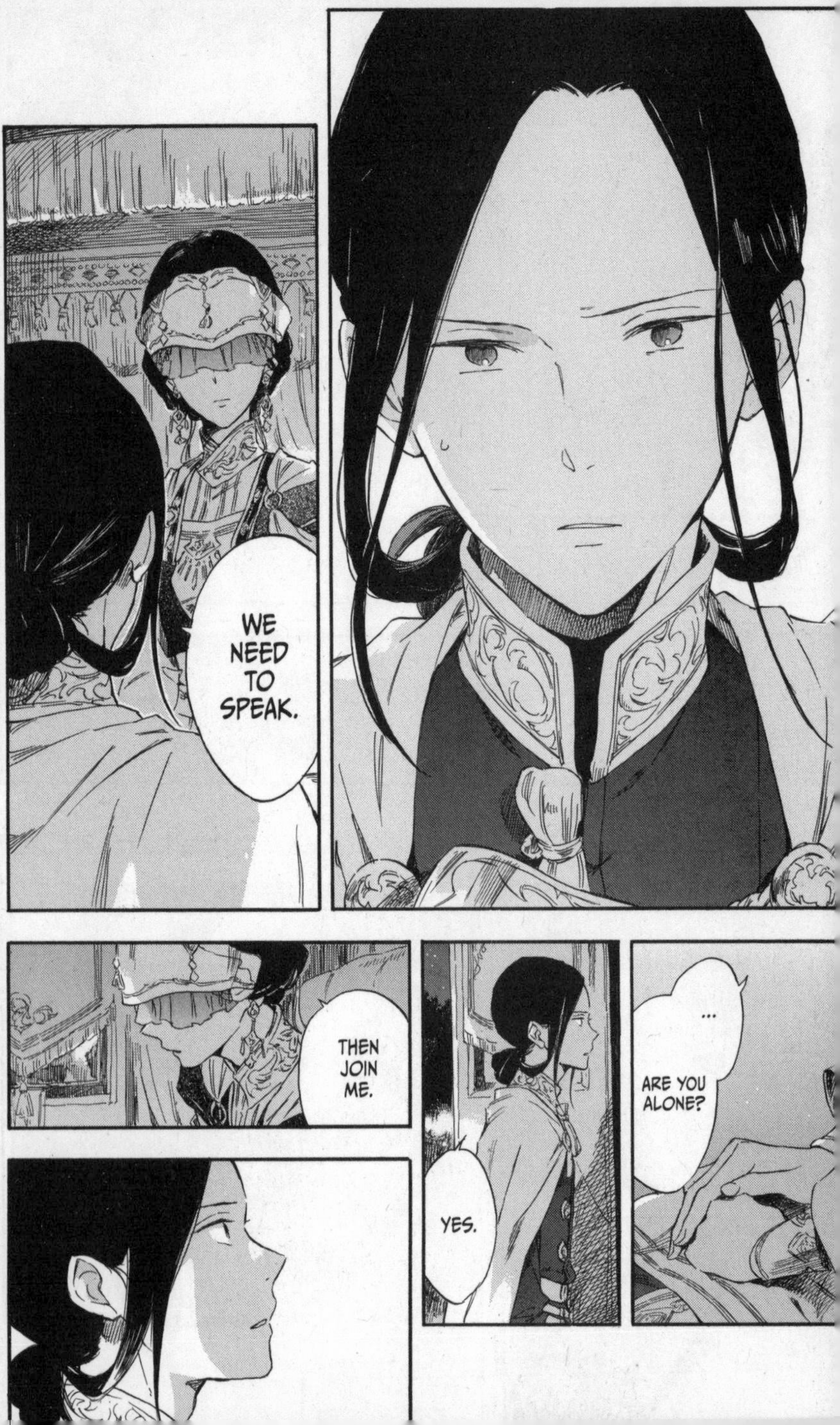
WE NEED TO SPEAK.
...
ARE YOU ALONE?
YES.
THEN JOIN ME.

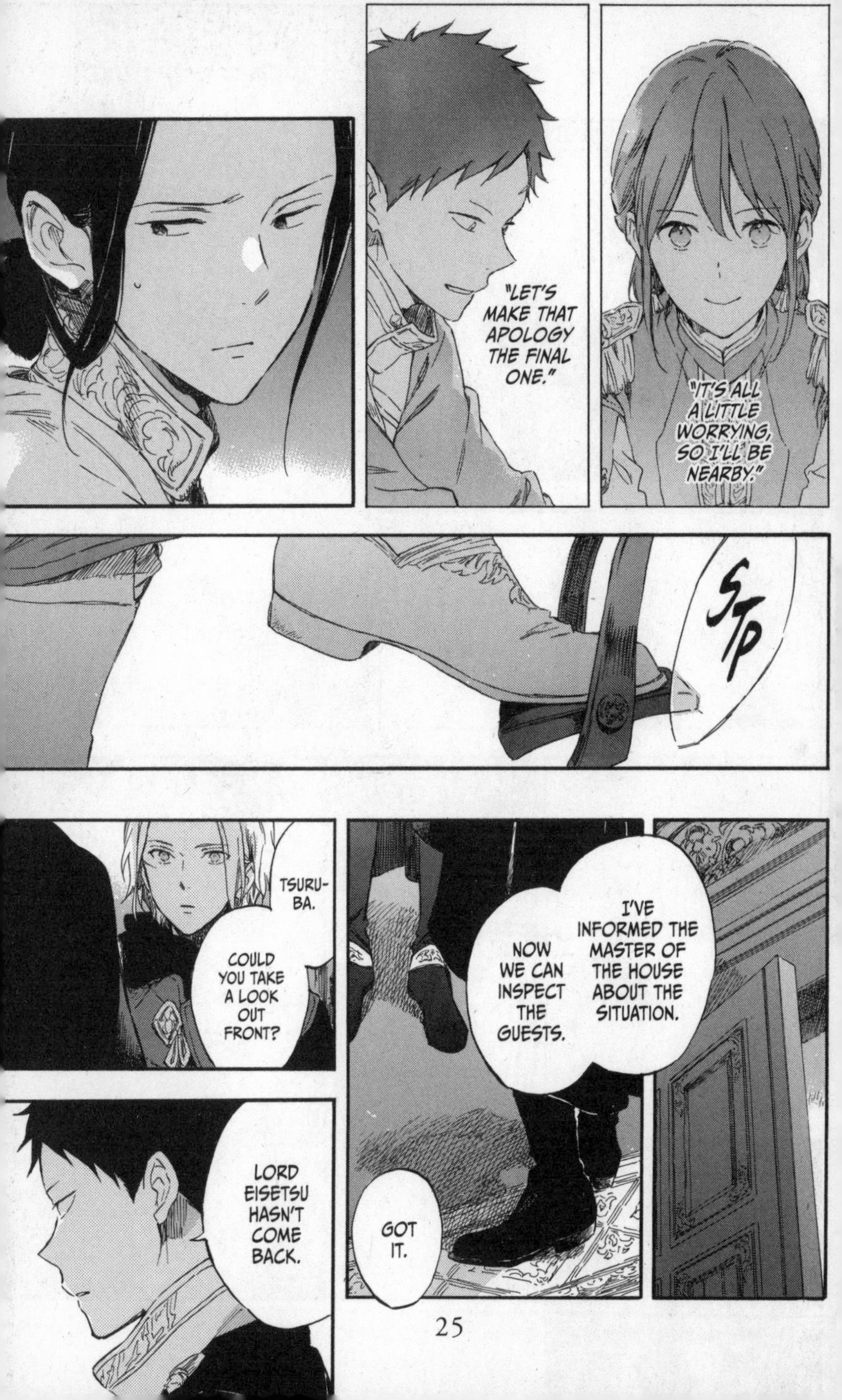
"IT'S ALL A LITTLE WORRYING, SO I'LL BE NEARBY."
"LET'S MAKE THAT APOLOGY THE FINAL ONE."
STP
I'VE INFORMED THE MASTER OF THE HOUSE ABOUT THE SITUATION.
NOW WE CAN INSPECT THE GUESTS.
GOT IT.
TSURU-BA.
COULD YOU TAKE A LOOK OUT FRONT?
LORD EISETSU HASN'T COME BACK.

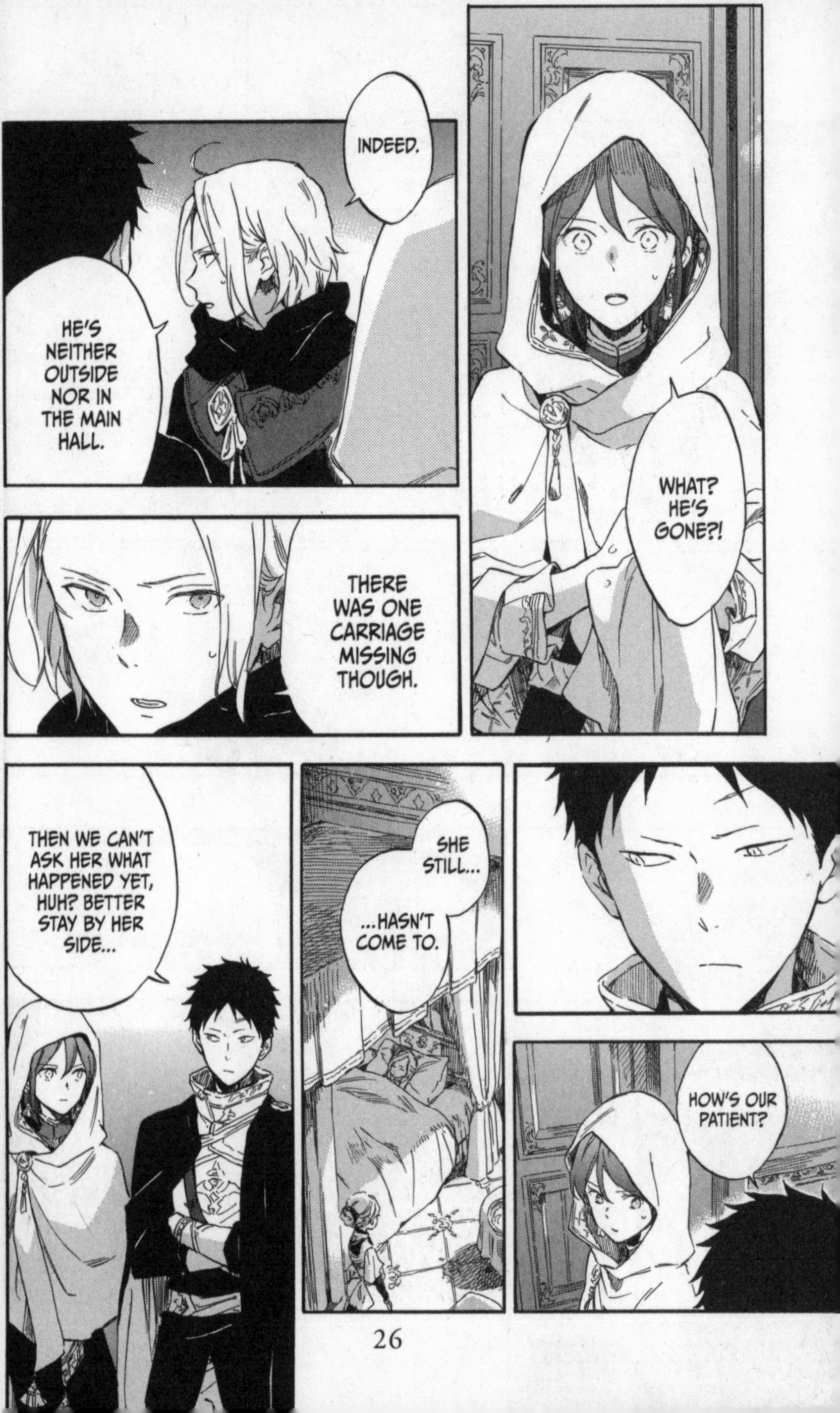
WHAT? HE'S GONE?!
INDEED.
HE'S NEITHER OUTSIDE NOR IN THE MAIN HALL.
THERE WAS ONE CARRIAGE MISSING THOUGH.
HOW'S OUR PATIENT?
SHE STILL...
...HASN'T COME TO.
THEN WE CAN'T ASK HER WHAT HAPPENED YET, HUH? BETTER STAY BY HER SIDE...

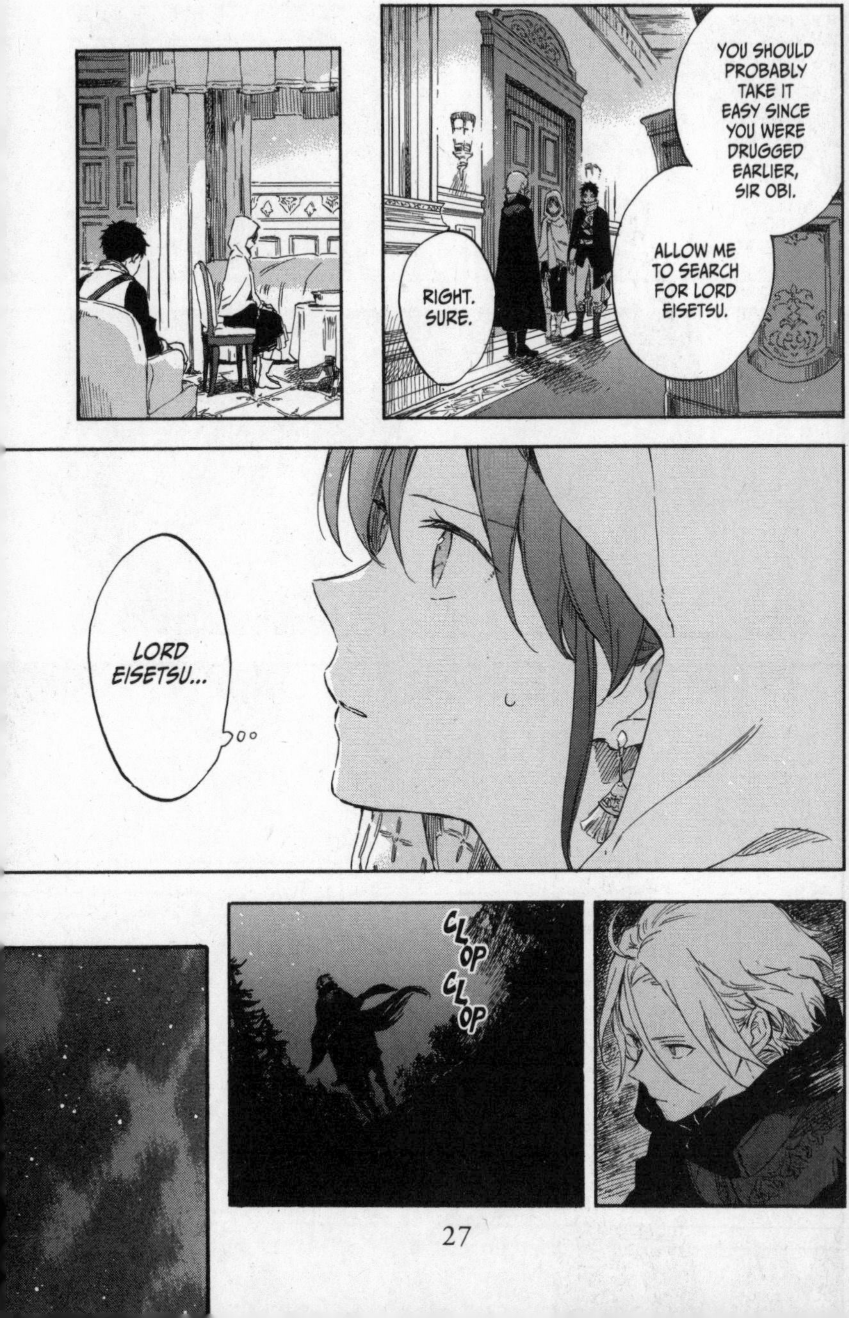
YOU SHOULD PROBABLY TAKE IT EASY SINCE YOU WERE DRUGGED EARLIER, SIR OBI.
ALLOW ME TO SEARCH FOR LORD EISETSU.
RIGHT. SURE.
LORD EISETSU...
CLOP CLOP

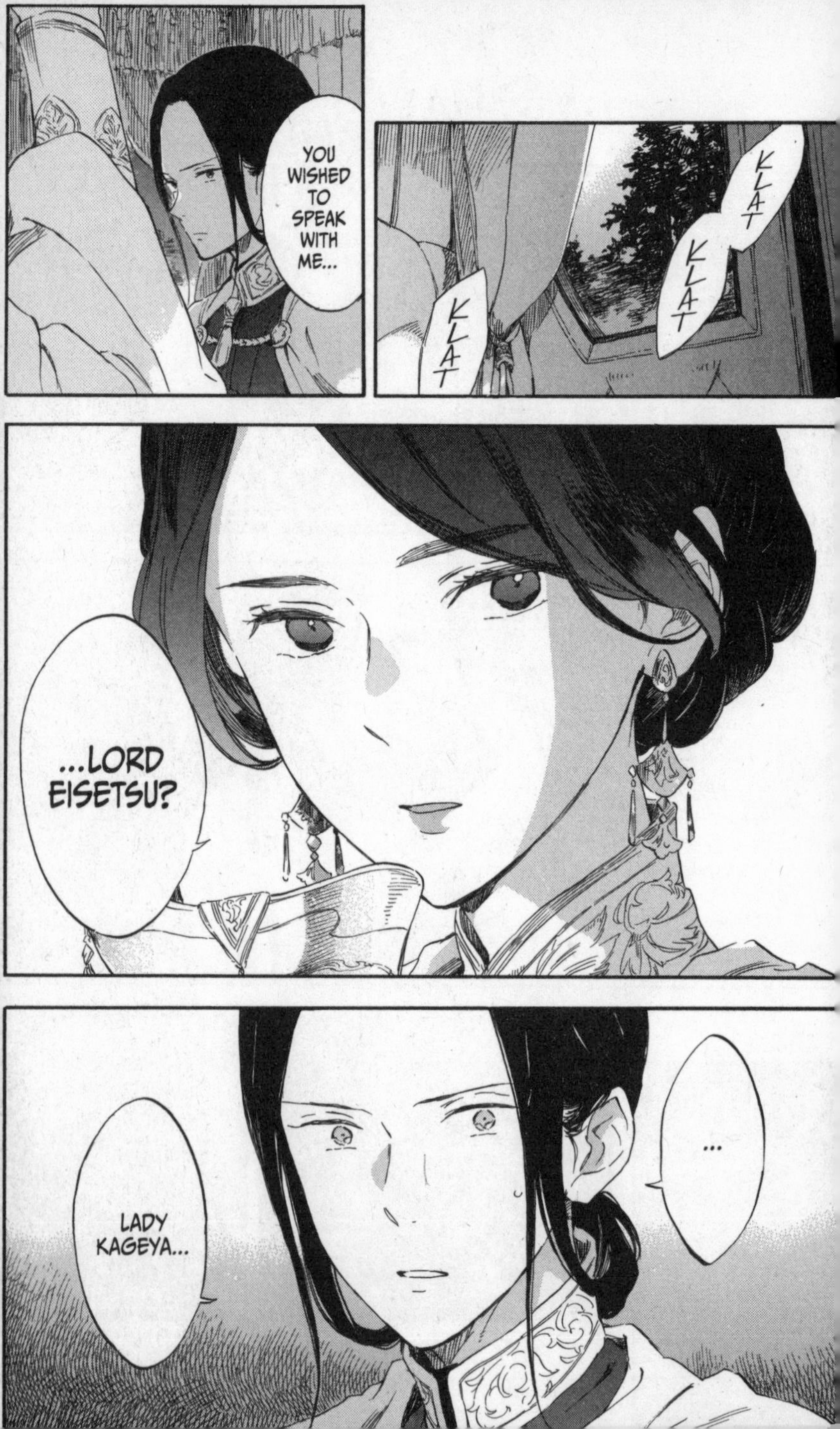
KLAT
KLAT
KLAT
YOU WISHED TO SPEAK WITH ME...
...LORD EISETSU?
...
LADY KAGEYA...

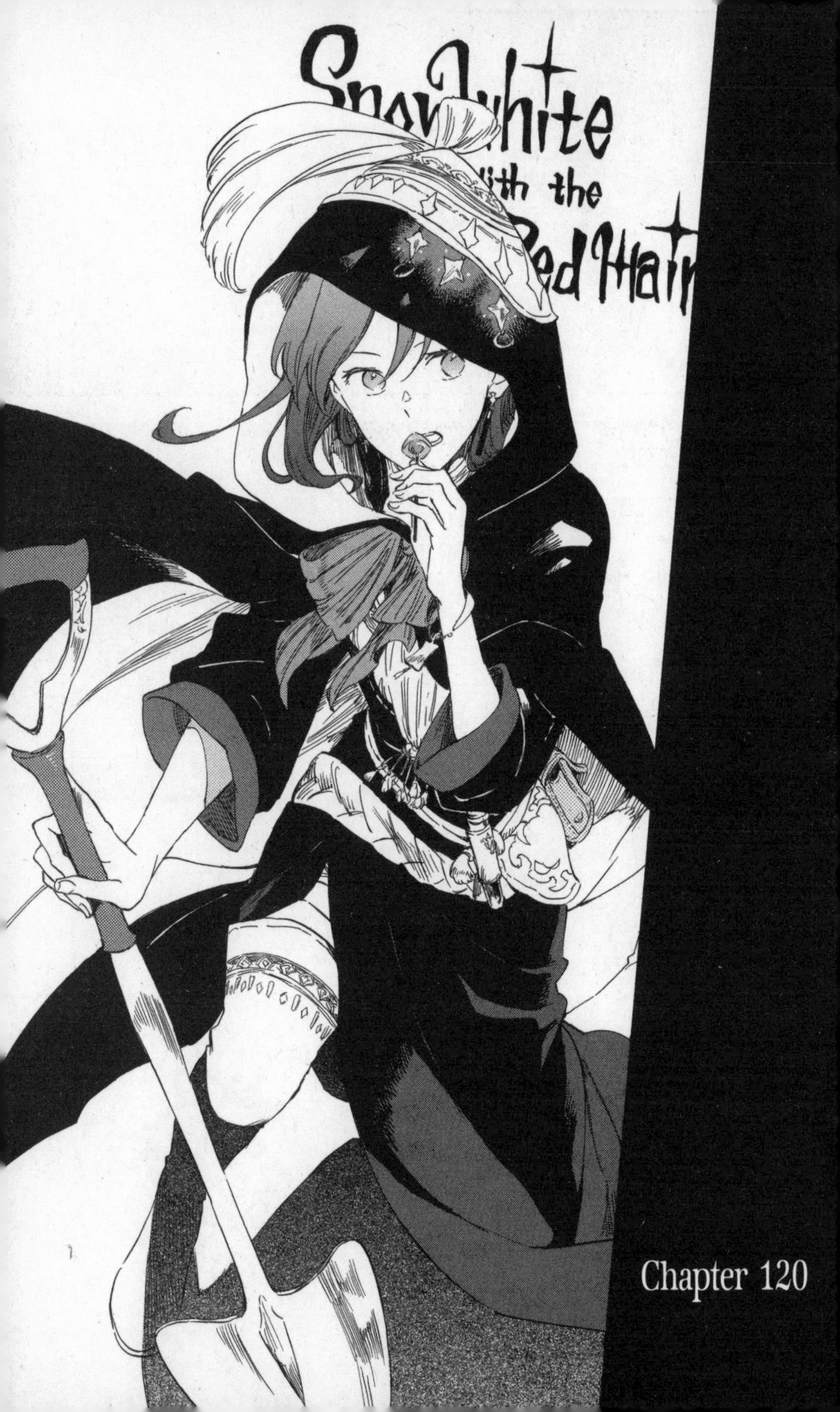
Snow White with the Red Hair
Chapter 120

WELL DONE... NOTICING ME AMIDST ALL THAT.

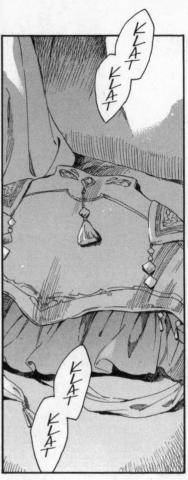

KLAT
KLAT

YES, WELL...

I COULD HARDLY BELIEVE IT MYSELF.

KLAT
KLAT

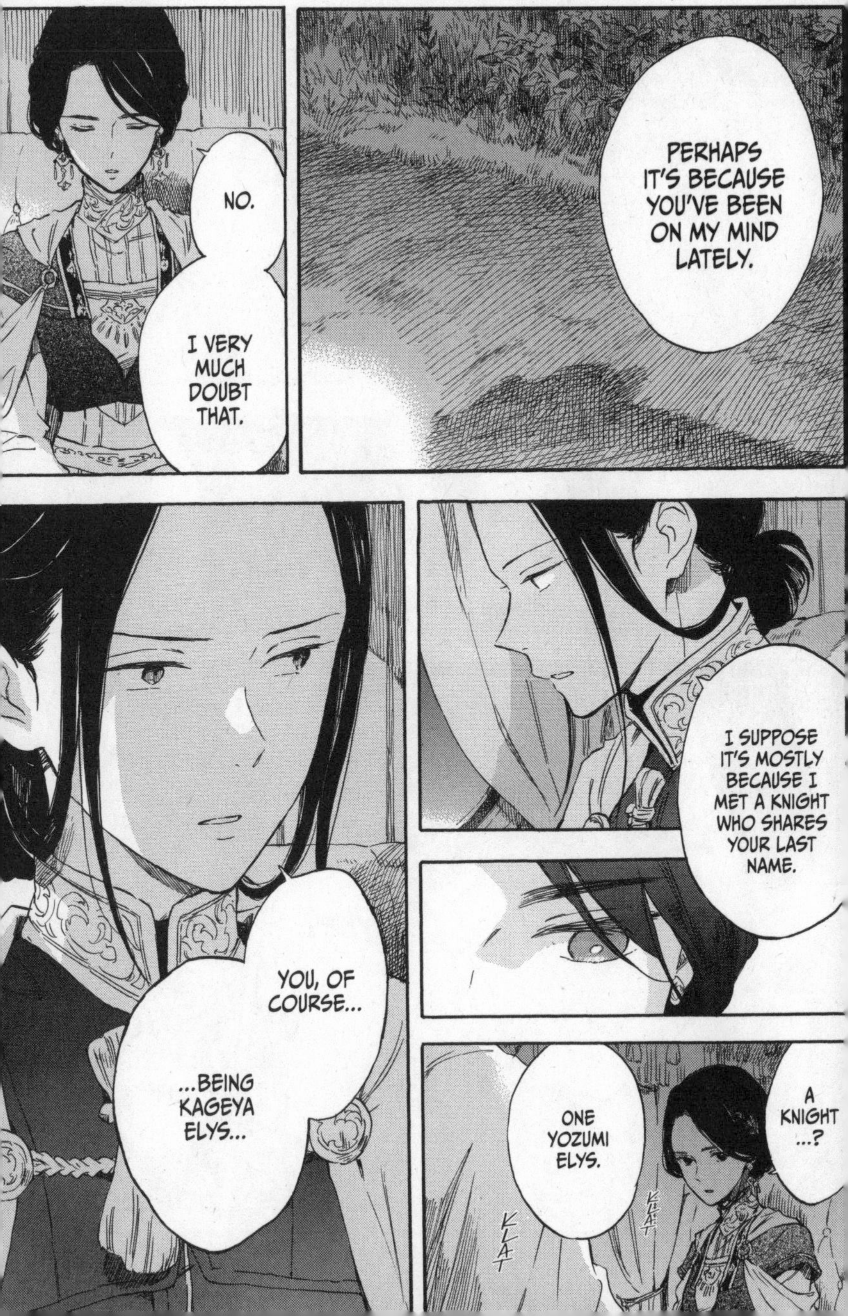
PERHAPS IT'S BECAUSE YOU'VE BEEN ON MY MIND LATELY.
NO.
I VERY MUCH DOUBT THAT.
I SUPPOSE IT'S MOSTLY BECAUSE I MET A KNIGHT WHO SHARES YOUR LAST NAME.
A KNIGHT ...?
ONE YOZUMI ELYS.
KLAT
KLAT
YOU, OF COURSE...
...BEING KAGEYA ELYS...

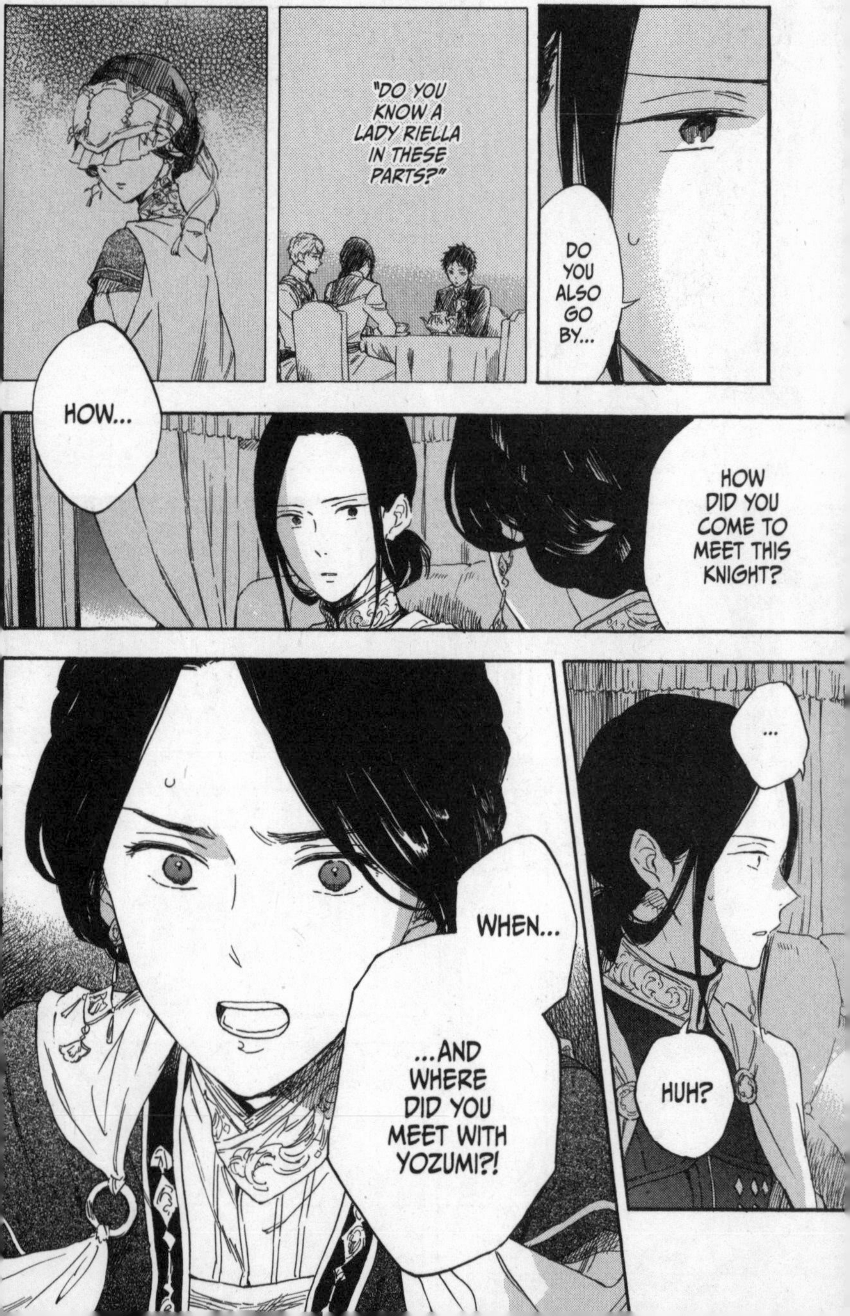
DO YOU ALSO GO BY...
"DO YOU KNOW A LADY RIELLA IN THESE PARTS?"
HOW...
HOW DID YOU COME TO MEET THIS KNIGHT?
...
HUH?
WHEN...
...AND WHERE DID YOU MEET WITH YOZUMI?!

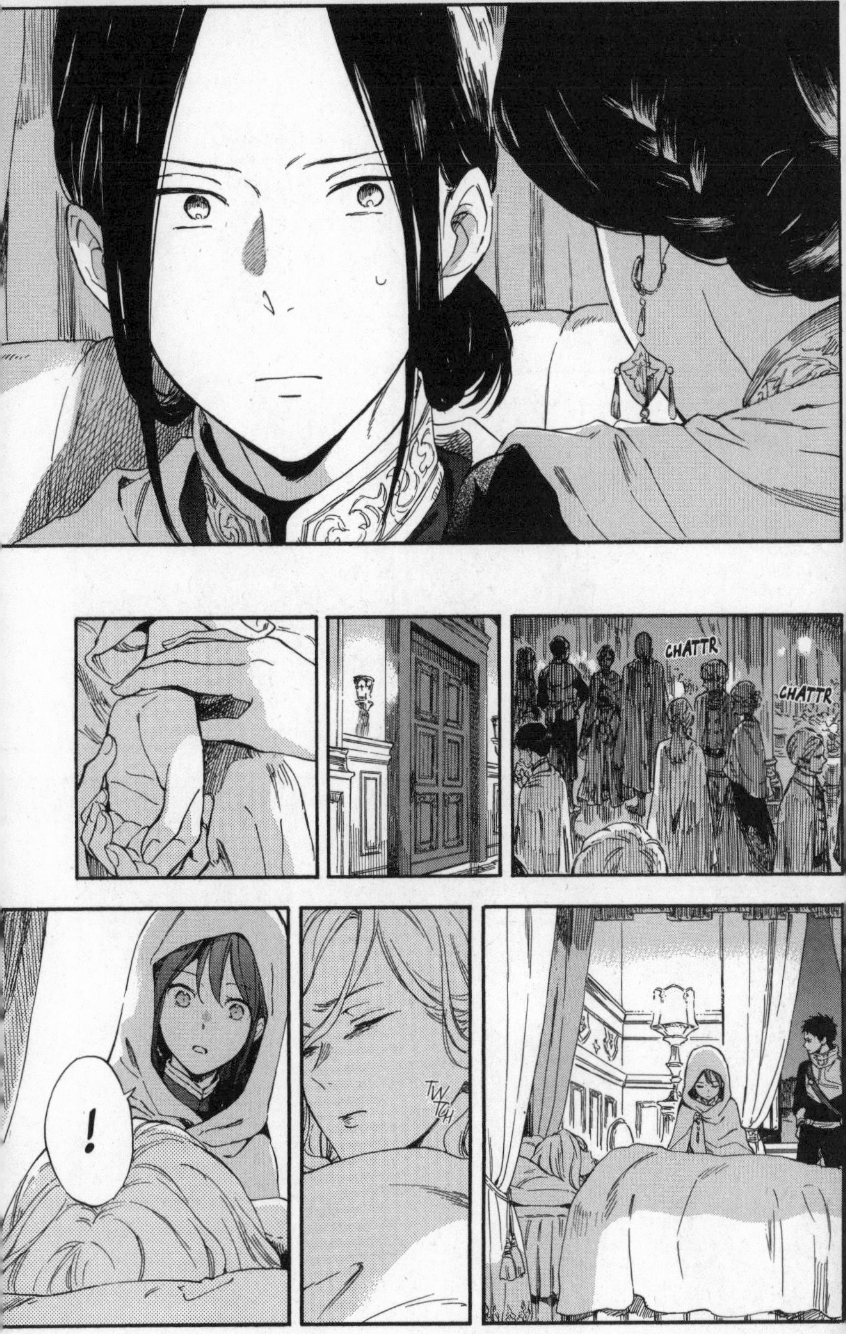
CHATTR
CHATTR
TWTCH
!

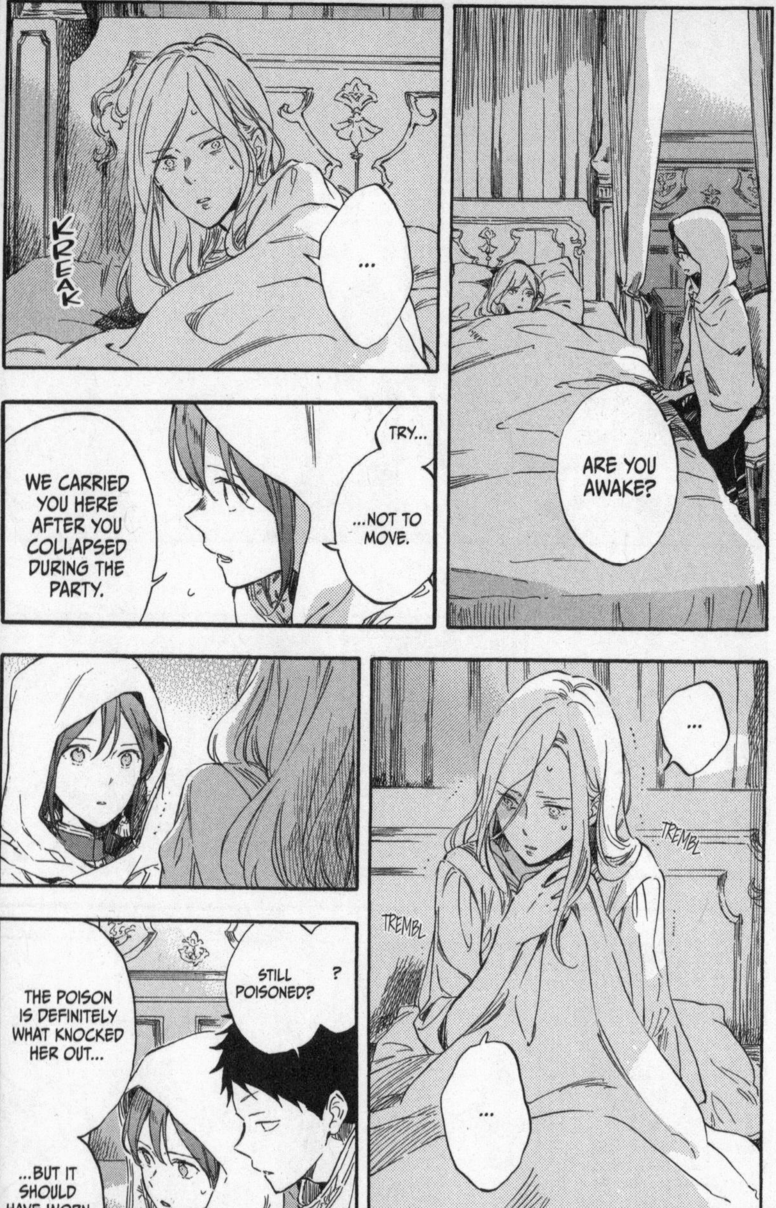
ARE YOU AWAKE?
KREAK
...
TRY...
...NOT TO MOVE.
WE CARRIED YOU HERE AFTER YOU COLLAPSED DURING THE PARTY.
...
TREMBL
TREMBL
...
STILL POISONED?
THE POISON IS DEFINITELY WHAT KNOCKED HER OUT...
...BUT IT SHOULD HAVE WORN OFF BY NOW.

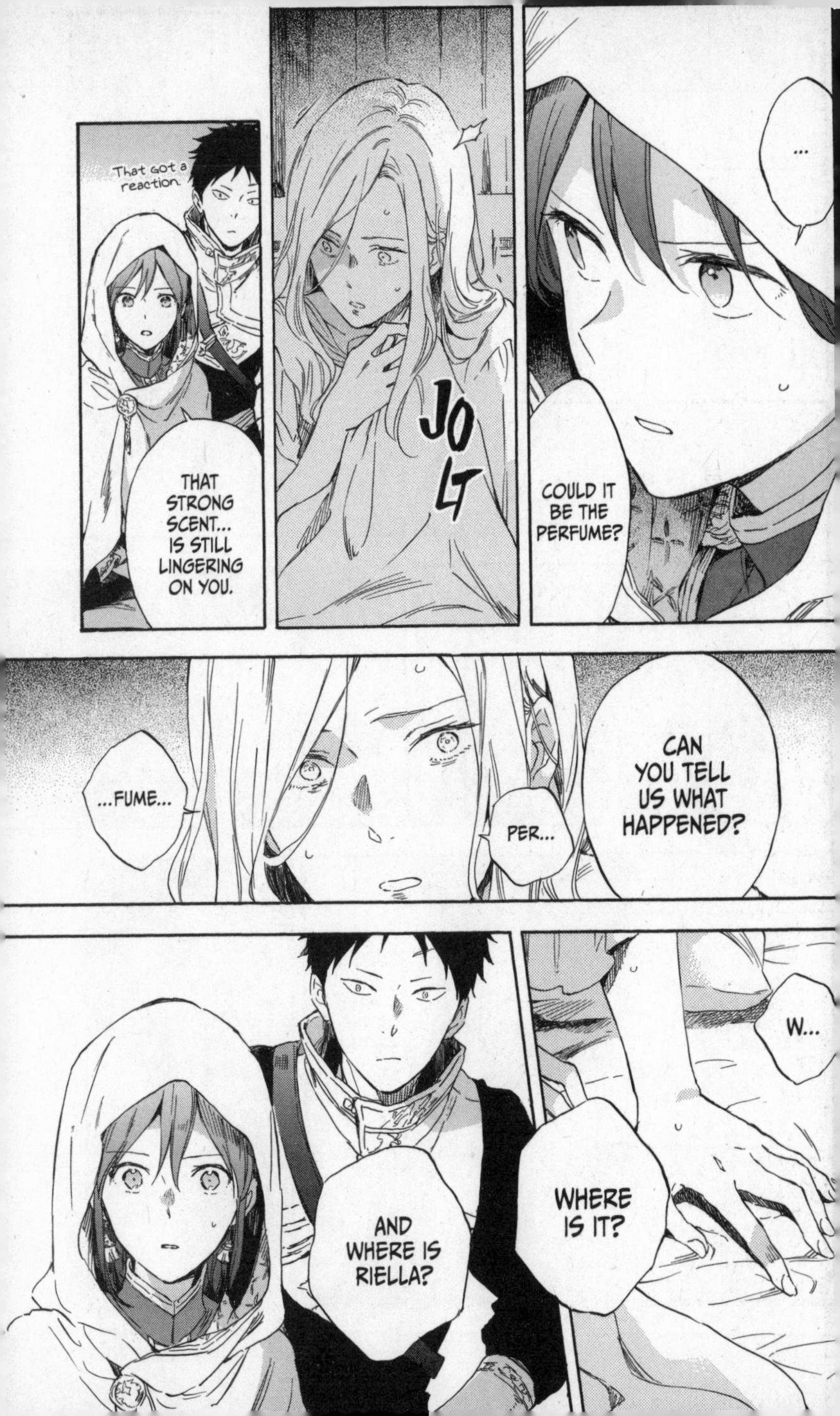
...
COULD IT BE THE PERFUME?
JOLT
That got a reaction.
THAT STRONG SCENT... IS STILL LINGERING ON YOU.
CAN YOU TELL US WHAT HAPPENED?
PER...
...FUME...
W...
WHERE IS IT?
AND WHERE IS RIELLA?

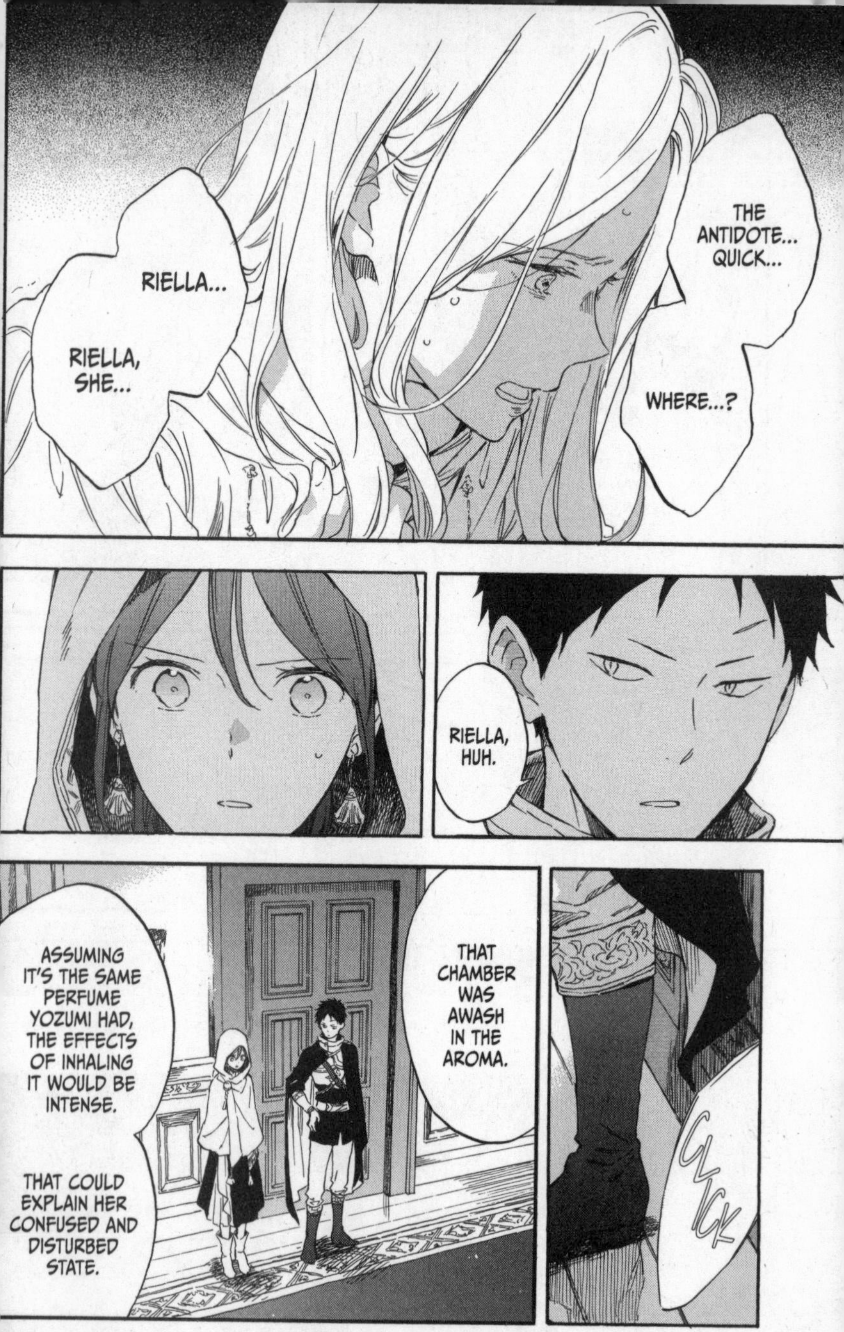
THE ANTIDOTE... QUICK...
WHERE...?
RIELLA...
RIELLA, SHE...
RIELLA, HUH.
CLICK
THAT CHAMBER WAS AWASH IN THE AROMA.
ASSUMING IT'S THE SAME PERFUME YOZUMI HAD, THE EFFECTS OF INHALING IT WOULD BE INTENSE.
THAT COULD EXPLAIN HER CONFUSED AND DISTURBED STATE.

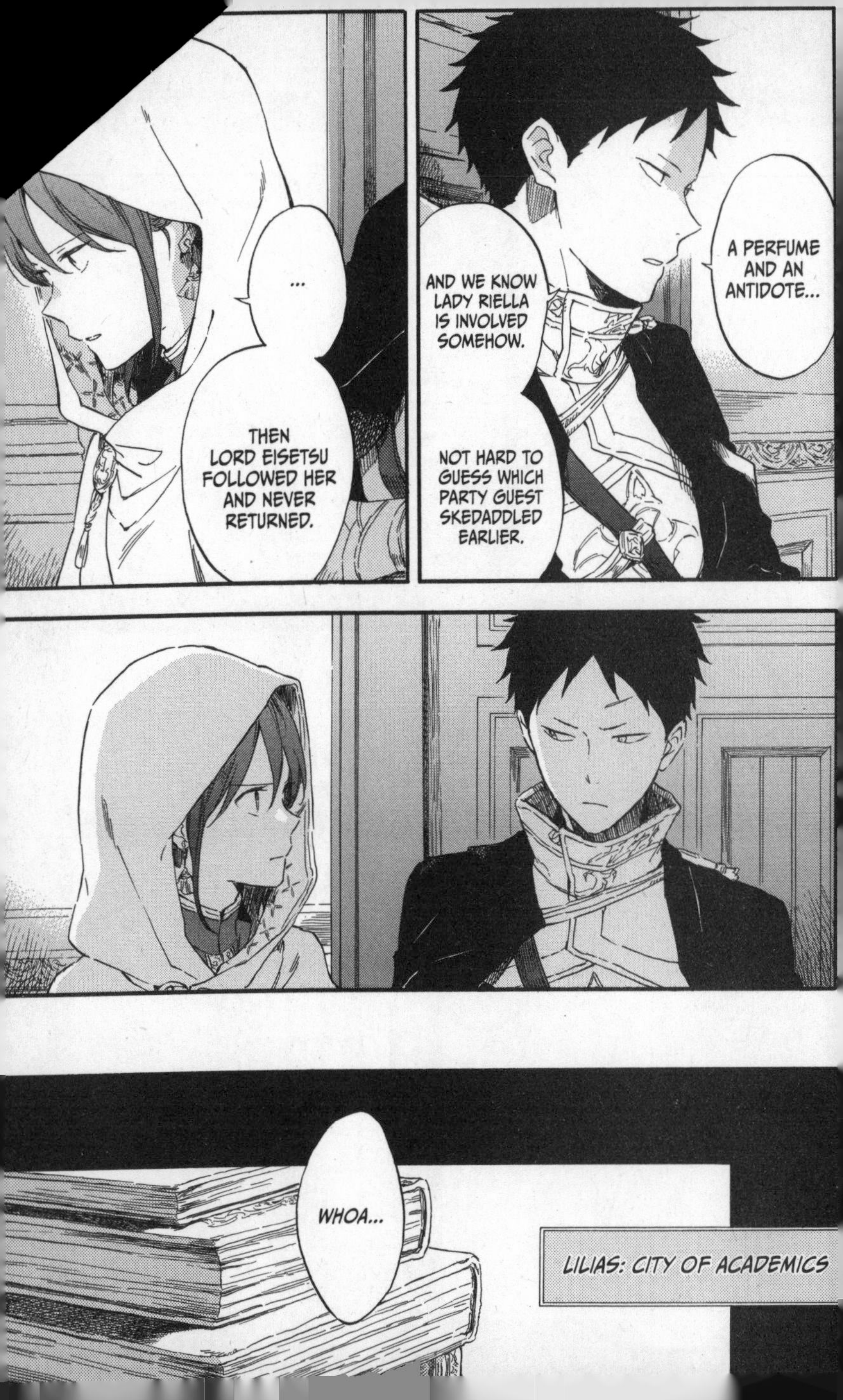
A PERFUME AND AN ANTIDOTE...
AND WE KNOW LADY RIELLA IS INVOLVED SOMEHOW.
NOT HARD TO GUESS WHICH PARTY GUEST SKEDADDLED EARLIER.
...
THEN LORD EISETSU FOLLOWED HER AND NEVER RETURNED.
LILIAS: CITY OF ACADEMICS
WHOA...

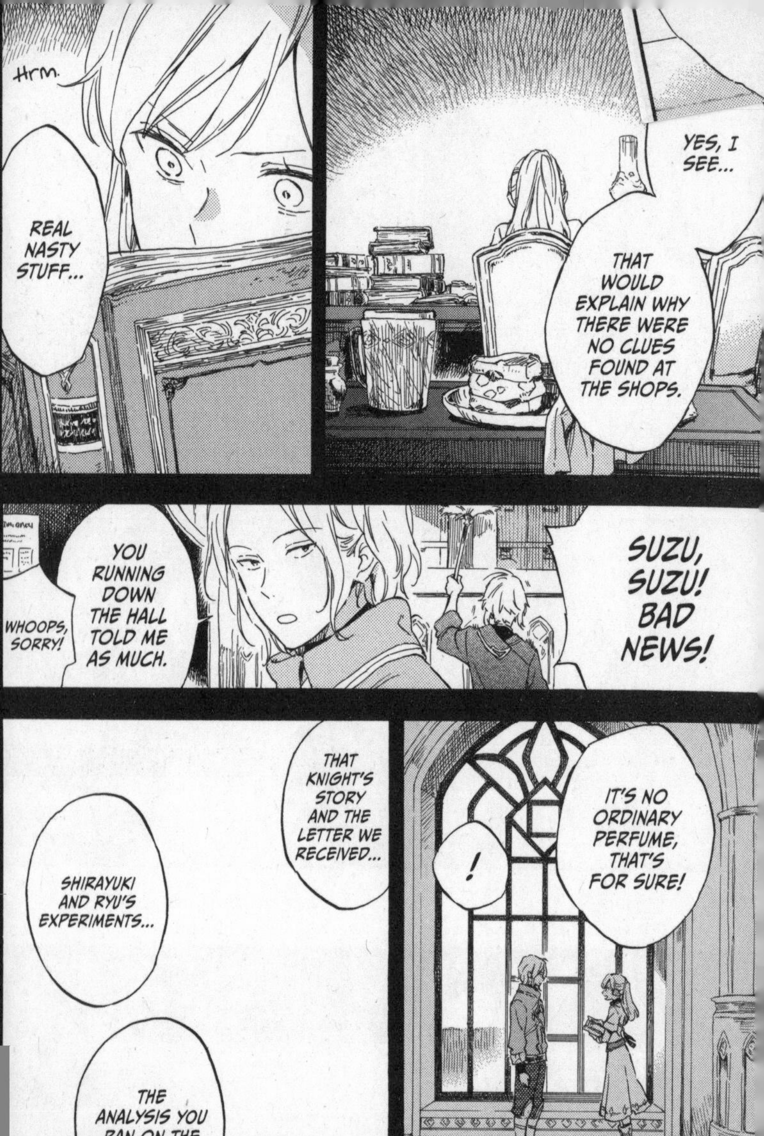
YES, I SEE...
THAT WOULD EXPLAIN WHY THERE WERE NO CLUES FOUND AT THE SHOPS.
Hrm.
REAL NASTY STUFF...
SUZU, SUZU! BAD NEWS!
YOU RUNNING DOWN THE HALL TOLD ME AS MUCH.
WHOOPS, SORRY!
IT'S NO ORDINARY PERFUME, THAT'S FOR SURE!
!
THAT KNIGHT'S STORY AND THE LETTER WE RECEIVED...
SHIRAYUKI AND RYU'S EXPERIMENTS...
THE ANALYSIS YOU RAN ON THE PERFUME...

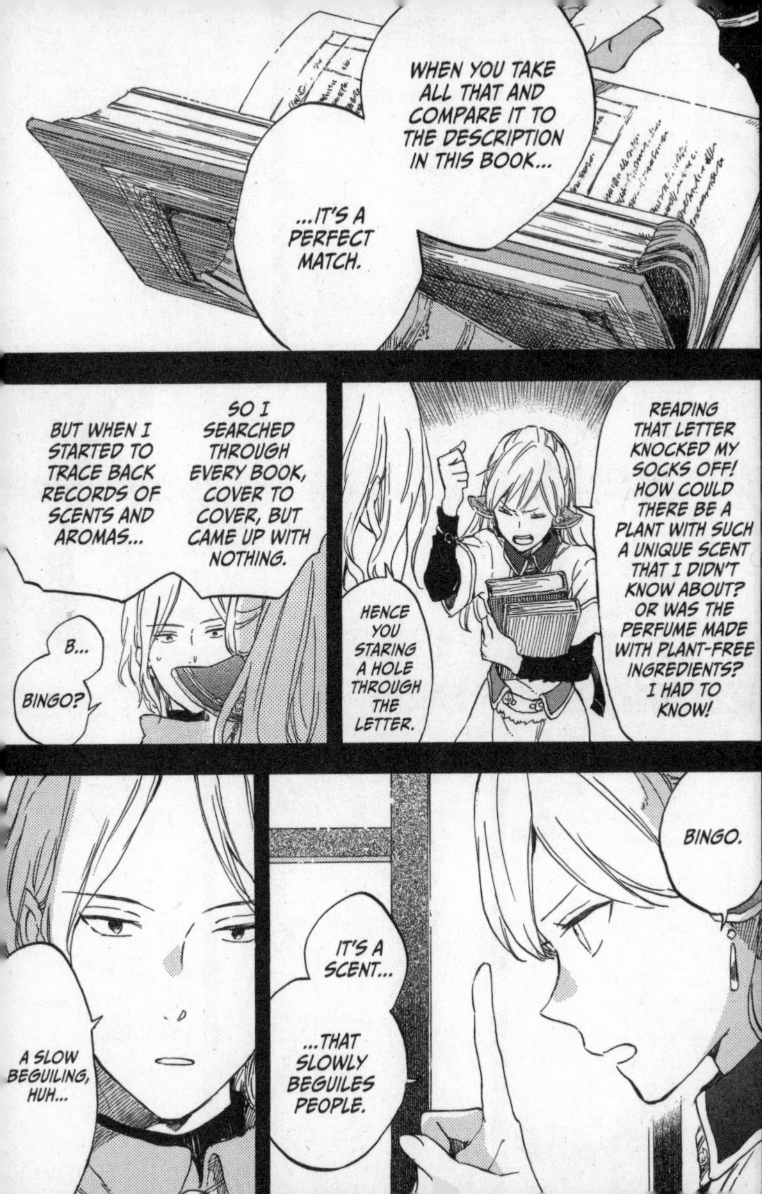
WHEN YOU TAKE ALL THAT AND COMPARE IT TO THE DESCRIPTION IN THIS BOOK...
...IT'S A PERFECT MATCH.
READING THAT LETTER KNOCKED MY SOCKS OFF! HOW COULD THERE BE A PLANT WITH SUCH A UNIQUE SCENT THAT I DIDN'T KNOW ABOUT? OR WAS THE PERFUME MADE WITH PLANT-FREE INGREDIENTS? I HAD TO KNOW!
HENCE YOU STARING A HOLE THROUGH THE LETTER.
SO I SEARCHED THROUGH EVERY BOOK, COVER TO COVER, BUT CAME UP WITH NOTHING.
BUT WHEN I STARTED TO TRACE BACK RECORDS OF SCENTS AND AROMAS...
B...
BINGO?
BINGO.
IT'S A SCENT...
...THAT SLOWLY BEGUILES PEOPLE.
A SLOW BEGUILING, HUH...

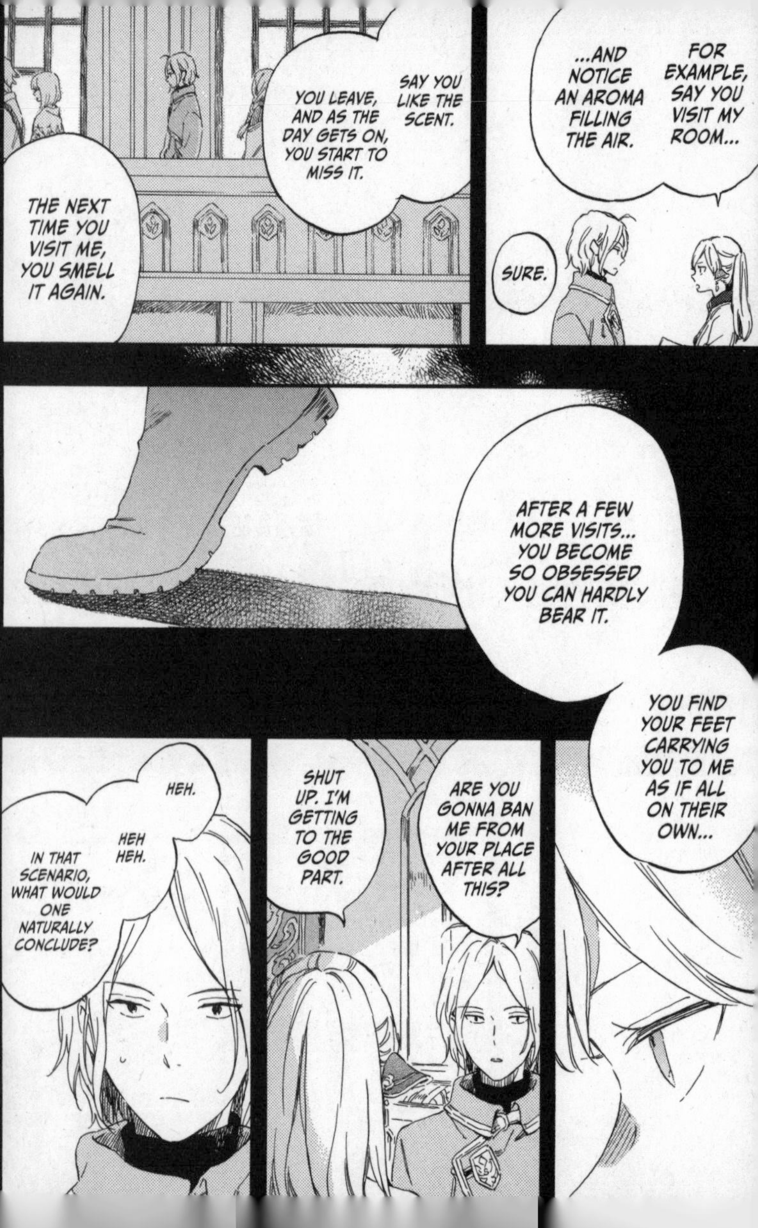
FOR EXAMPLE, SAY YOU VISIT MY ROOM...
...AND NOTICE AN AROMA FILLING THE AIR.
SURE.
SAY YOU LIKE THE SCENT.
YOU LEAVE, AND AS THE DAY GETS ON, YOU START TO MISS IT.
THE NEXT TIME YOU VISIT ME, YOU SMELL IT AGAIN.
AFTER A FEW MORE VISITS... YOU BECOME SO OBSESSED YOU CAN HARDLY BEAR IT.
YOU FIND YOUR FEET CARRYING YOU TO ME AS IF ALL ON THEIR OWN...
ARE YOU GONNA BAN ME FROM YOUR PLACE AFTER ALL THIS?
SHUT UP. I'M GETTING TO THE GOOD PART.
HEH.
HEH HEH.
IN THAT SCENARIO, WHAT WOULD ONE NATURALLY CONCLUDE?

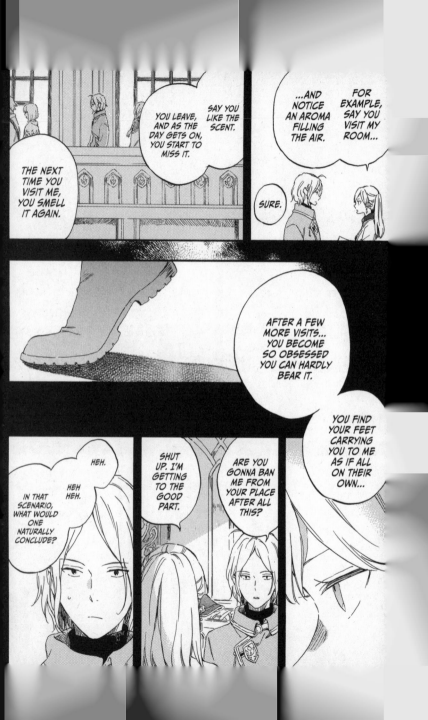

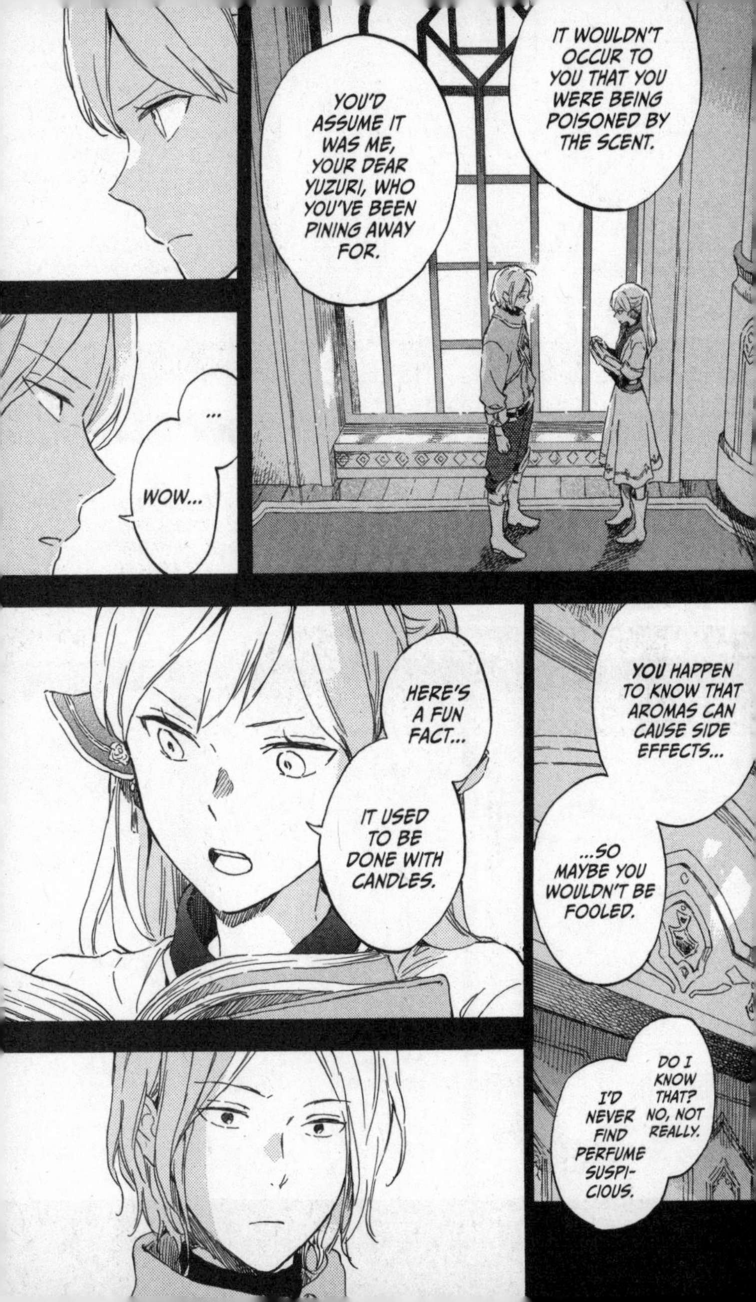
IT WOULDN'T OCCUR TO YOU THAT YOU WERE BEING POISONED BY THE SCENT.
YOU'D ASSUME IT WAS ME, YOUR DEAR YUZURI, WHO YOU'VE BEEN PINING AWAY FOR.
...
WOW...
YOU HAPPEN TO KNOW THAT AROMAS CAN CAUSE SIDE EFFECTS...
...SO MAYBE YOU WOULDN'T BE FOOLED.
DO I KNOW THAT? NO, NOT REALLY.
I'D NEVER FIND PERFUME SUSPICIOUS.
HERE'S A FUN FACT...
IT USED TO BE DONE WITH CANDLES.

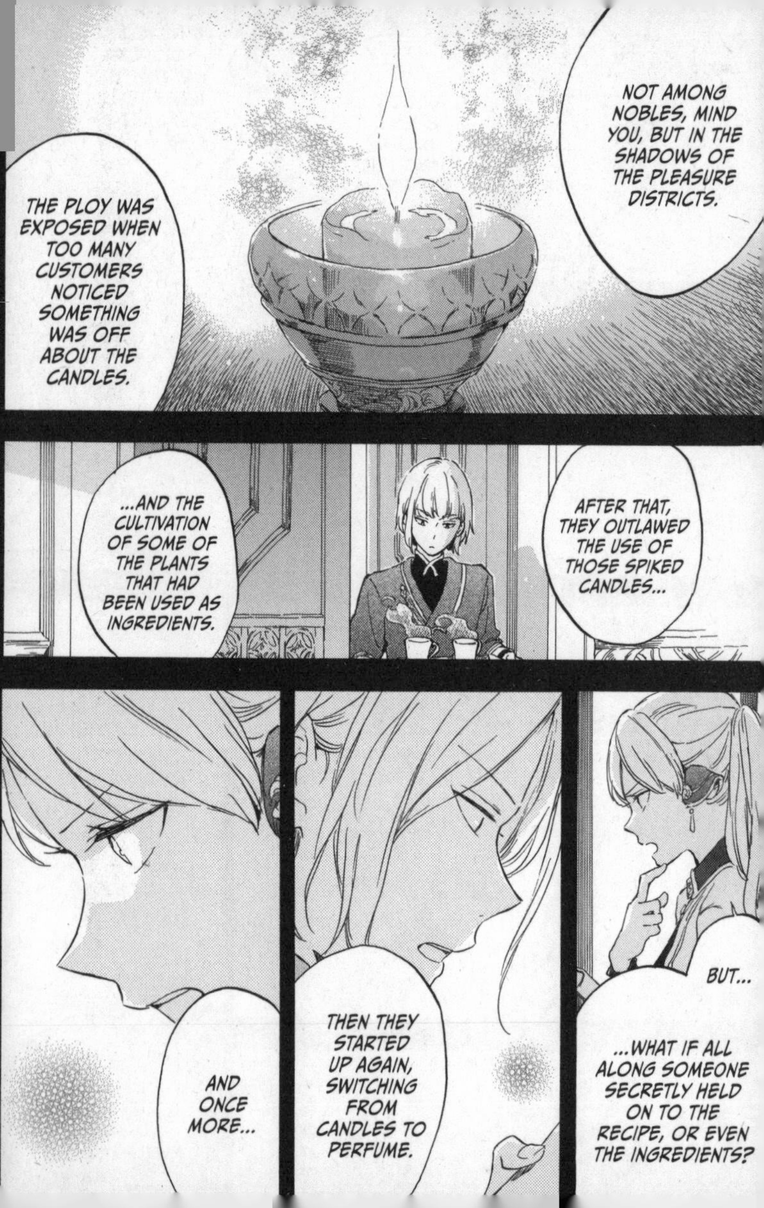
NOT AMONG NOBLES, MIND YOU, BUT IN THE SHADOWS OF THE PLEASURE DISTRICTS.
THE PLOY WAS EXPOSED WHEN TOO MANY CUSTOMERS NOTICED SOMETHING WAS OFF ABOUT THE CANDLES.
AFTER THAT, THEY OUTLAWED THE USE OF THOSE SPIKED CANDLES...
...AND THE CULTIVATION OF SOME OF THE PLANTS THAT HAD BEEN USED AS INGREDIENTS.
BUT...
...WHAT IF ALL ALONG SOMEONE SECRETLY HELD ON TO THE RECIPE, OR EVEN THE INGREDIENTS?
THEN THEY STARTED UP AGAIN, SWITCHING FROM CANDLES TO PERFUME.
AND ONCE MORE...

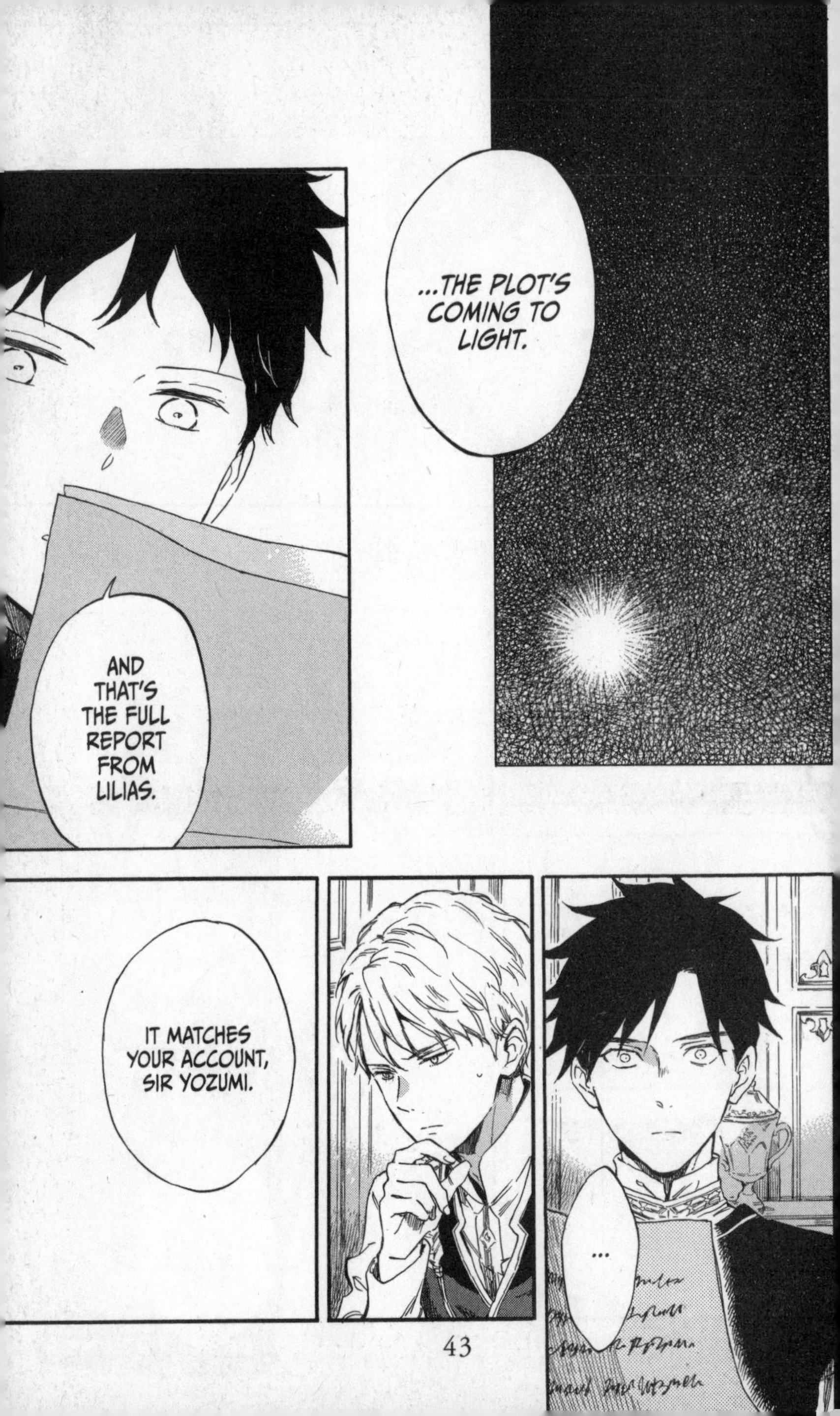
...THE PLOT'S COMING TO LIGHT.
AND THAT'S THE FULL REPORT FROM LILIAS.
...
IT MATCHES YOUR ACCOUNT, SIR YOZUMI.

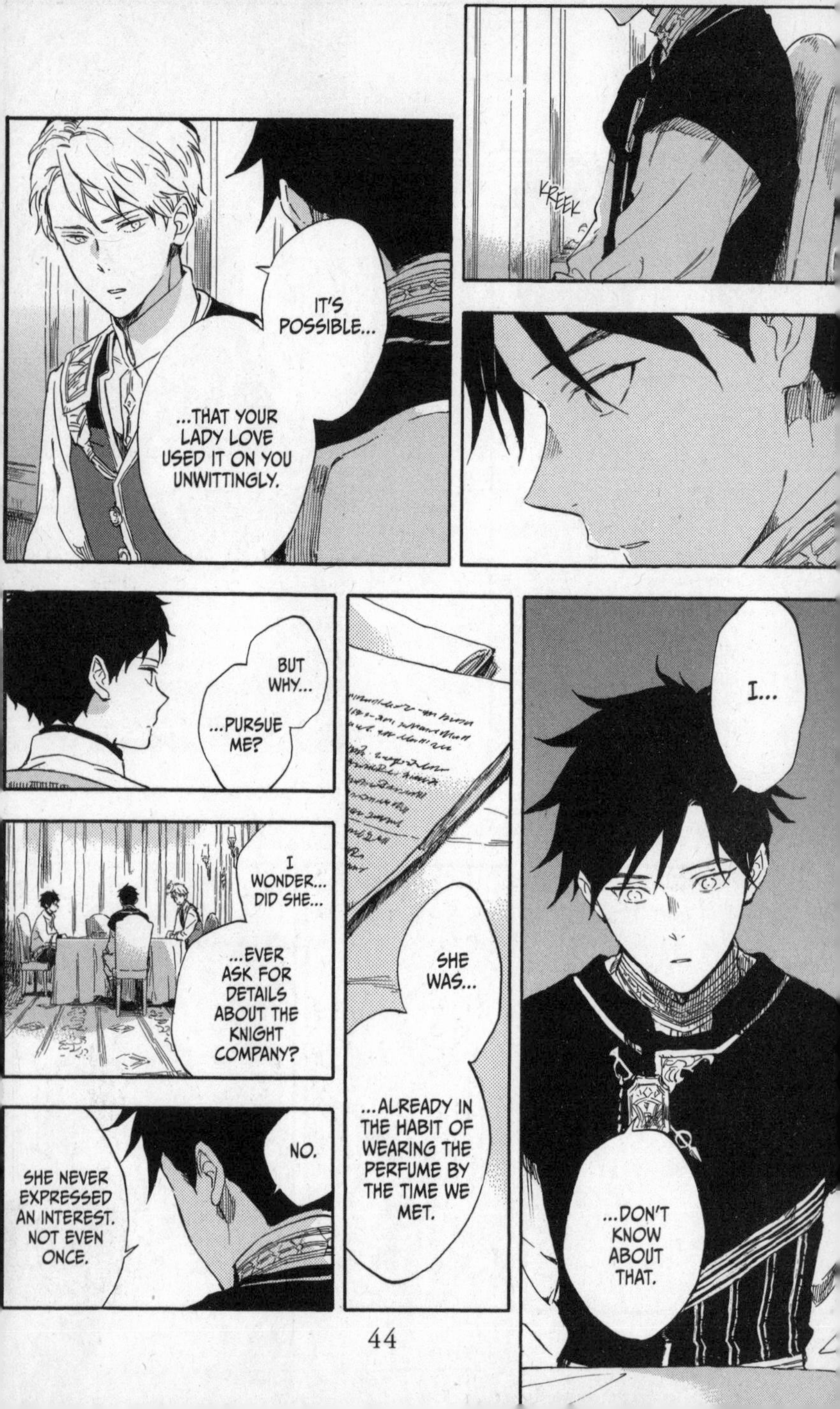
KREEK
IT'S POSSIBLE...
...THAT YOUR LADY LOVE USED IT ON YOU UNWITTINGLY.
I...
...DON'T KNOW ABOUT THAT.
SHE WAS...
...ALREADY IN THE HABIT OF WEARING THE PERFUME BY THE TIME WE MET.
BUT WHY...
...PURSUE ME?
I WONDER... DID SHE...
...EVER ASK FOR DETAILS ABOUT THE KNIGHT COMPANY?
NO.
SHE NEVER EXPRESSED AN INTEREST. NOT EVEN ONCE.

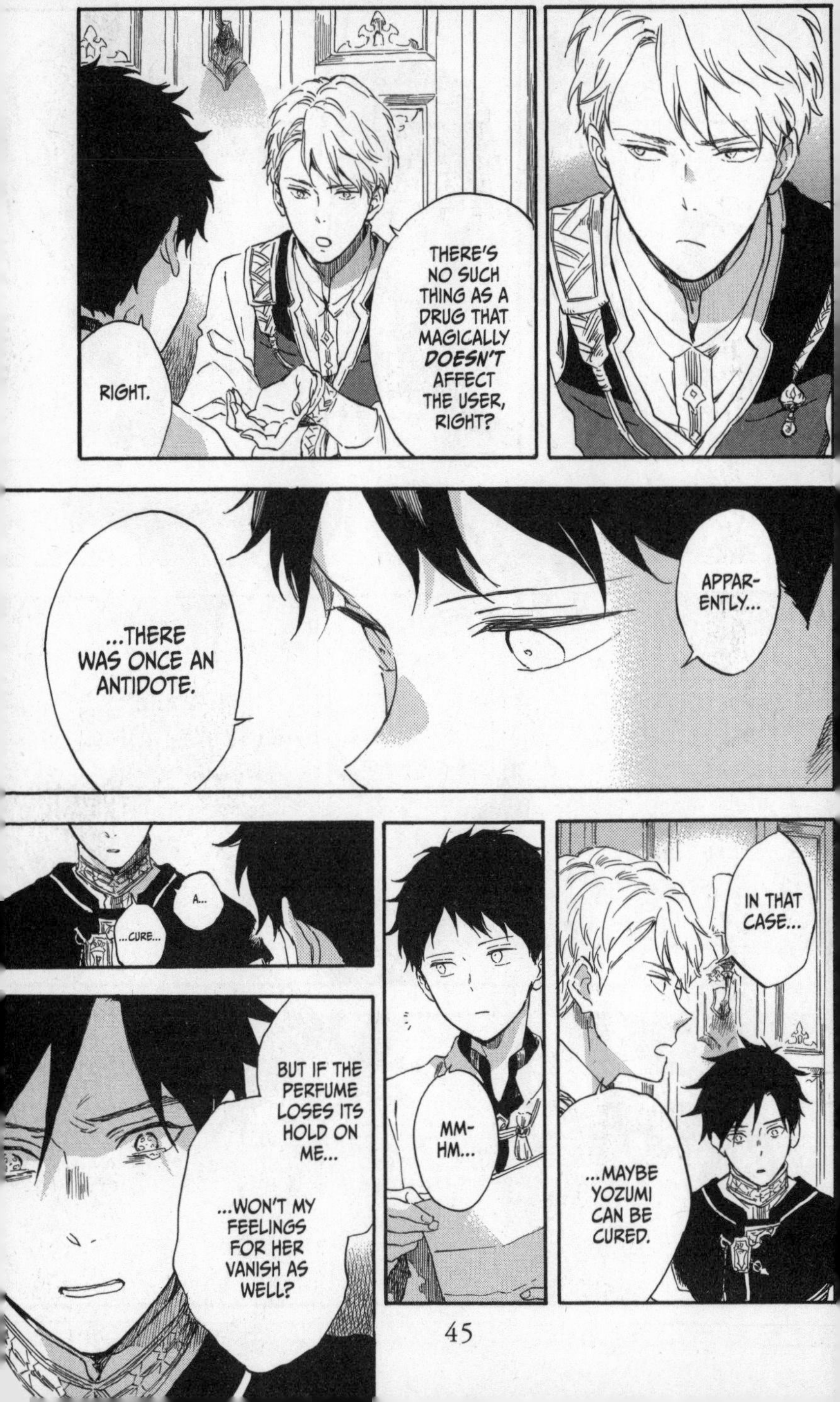
THERE'S NO SUCH THING AS A DRUG THAT MAGICALLY *DOESN'T* AFFECT THE USER, RIGHT?
RIGHT.
APPARENTLY...
...THERE WAS ONCE AN ANTIDOTE.
IN THAT CASE...
...MAYBE YOZUMI CAN BE CURED.
MM-HM...
A...
...CURE...
BUT IF THE PERFUME LOSES ITS HOLD ON ME...
...WON'T MY FEELINGS FOR HER VANISH AS WELL?

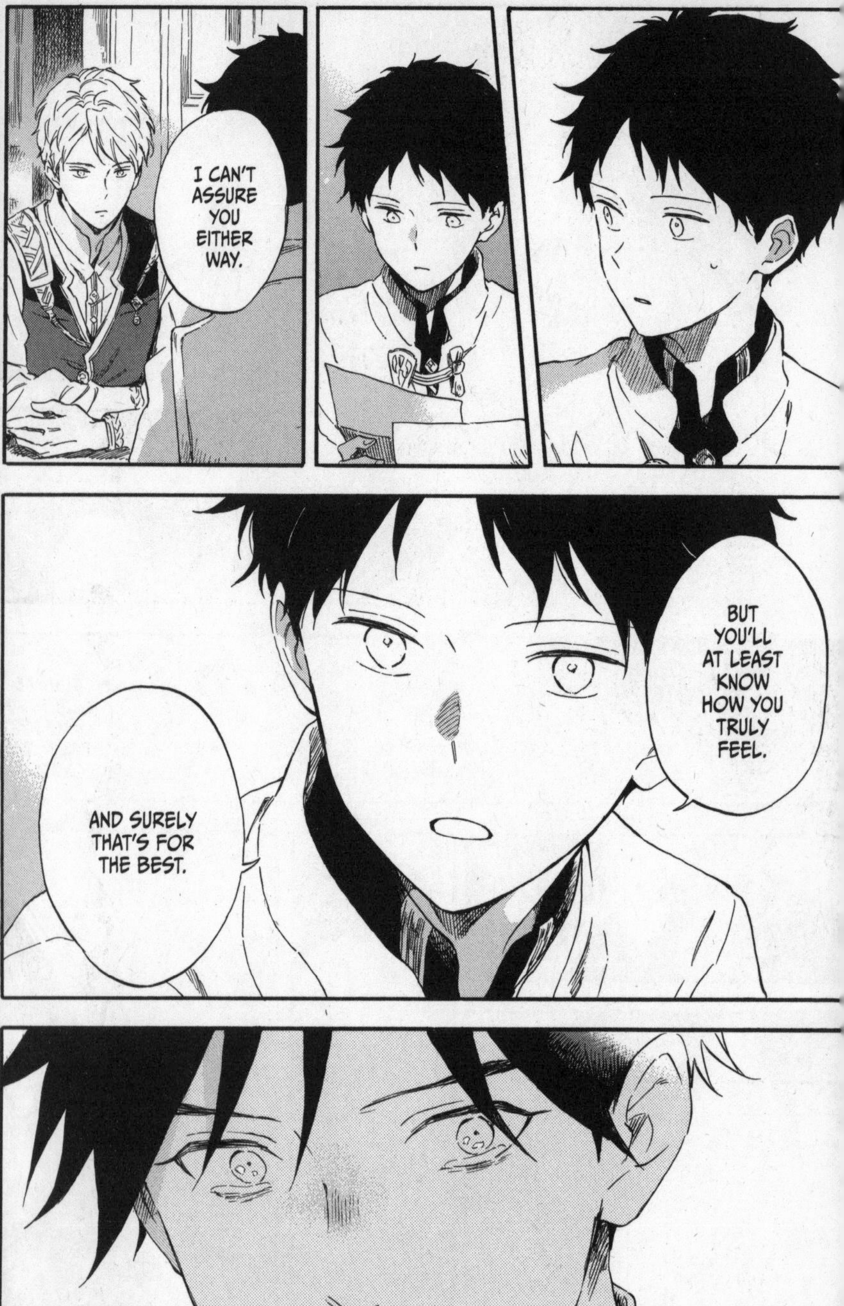
I CAN'T ASSURE YOU EITHER WAY.
BUT YOU'LL AT LEAST KNOW HOW YOU TRULY FEEL.
AND SURELY THAT'S FOR THE BEST.

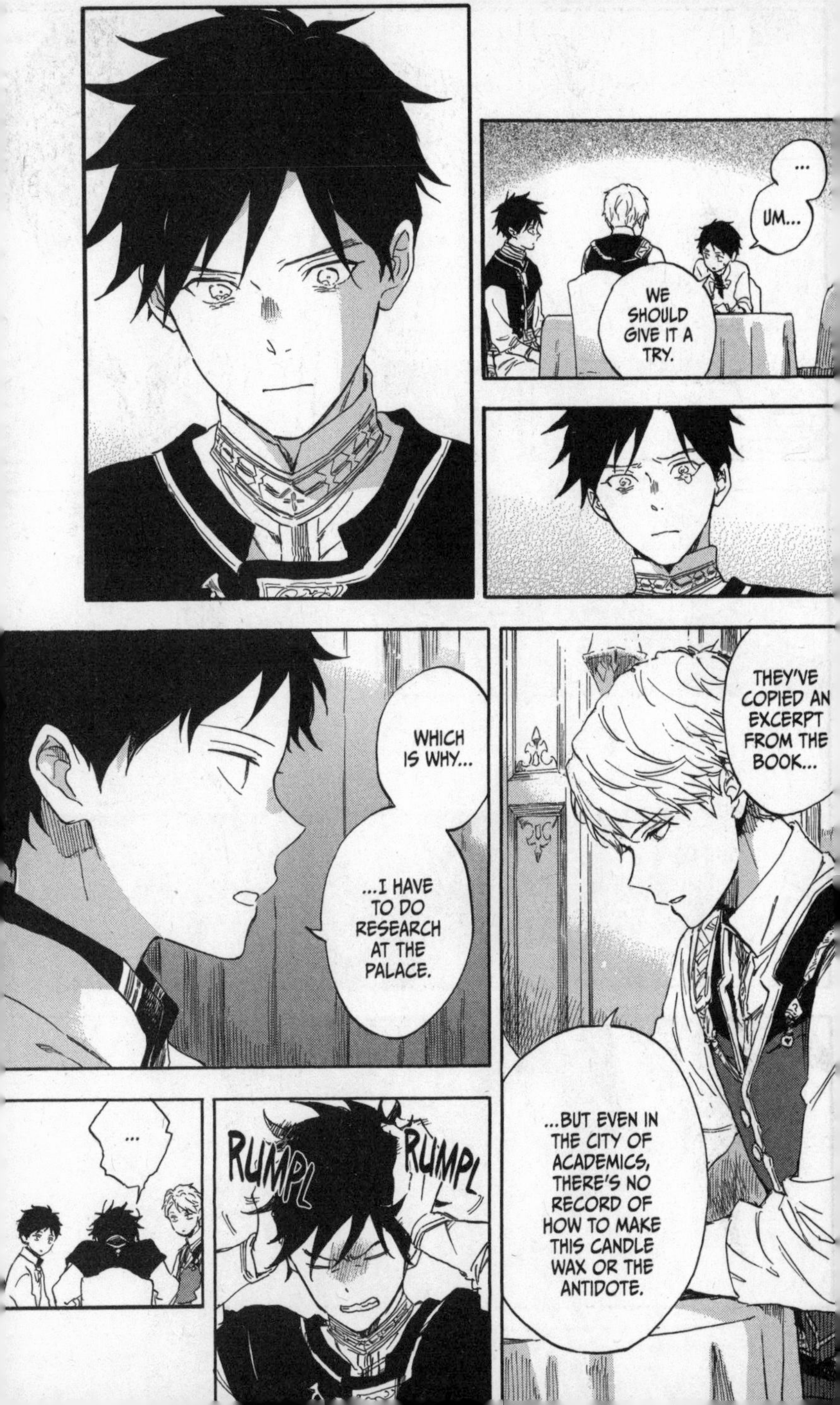
...
UM...
WE SHOULD GIVE IT A TRY.
THEY'VE COPIED AN EXCERPT FROM THE BOOK...
...BUT EVEN IN THE CITY OF ACADEMICS, THERE'S NO RECORD OF HOW TO MAKE THIS CANDLE WAX OR THE ANTIDOTE.
WHICH IS WHY...
...I HAVE TO DO RESEARCH AT THE PALACE.
RUMPL
RUMPL
...

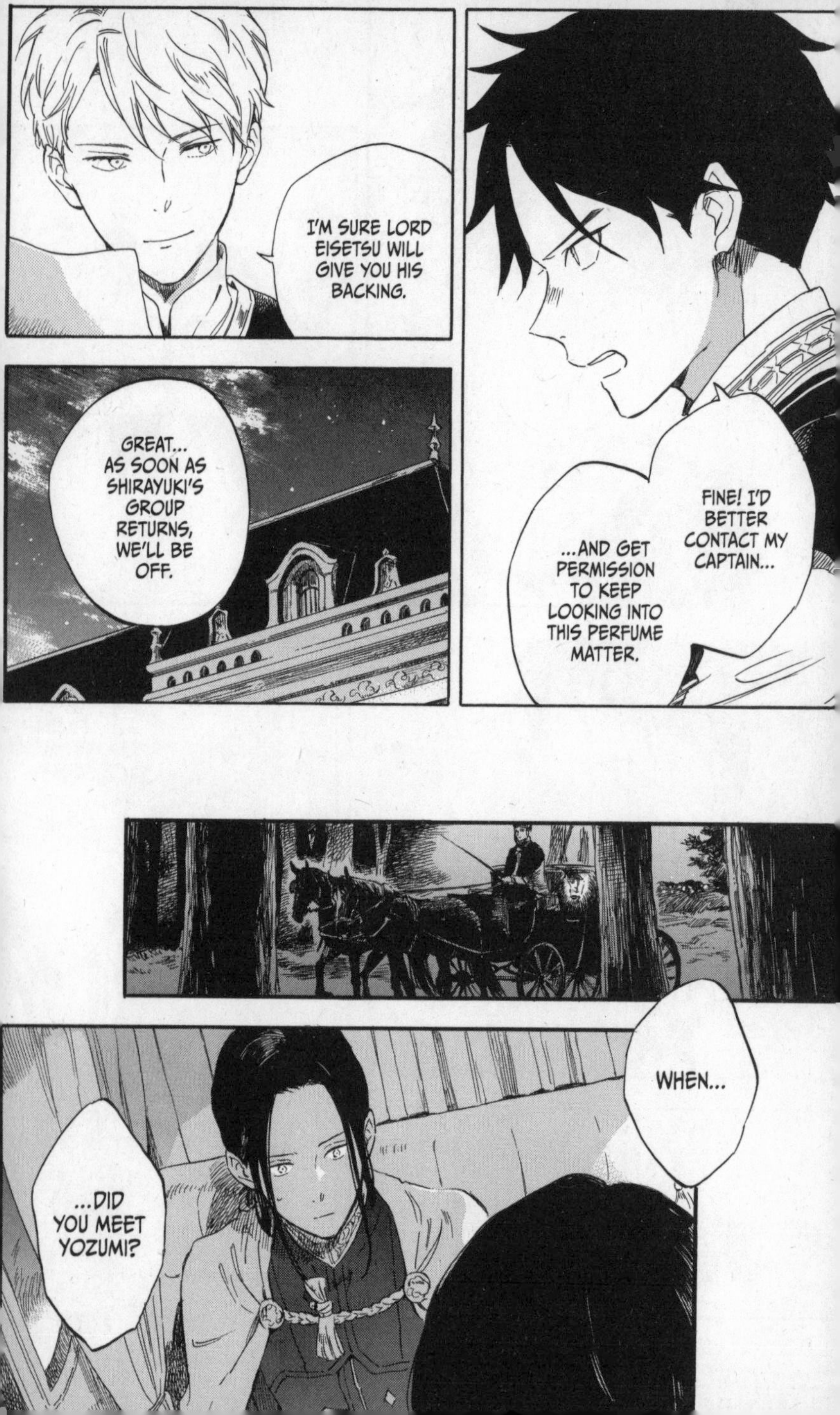
FINE! I'D BETTER CONTACT MY CAPTAIN...
...AND GET PERMISSION TO KEEP LOOKING INTO THIS PERFUME MATTER.
I'M SURE LORD EISETSU WILL GIVE YOU HIS BACKING.
GREAT... AS SOON AS SHIRAYUKI'S GROUP RETURNS, WE'LL BE OFF.
WHEN...
...DID YOU MEET YOZUMI?

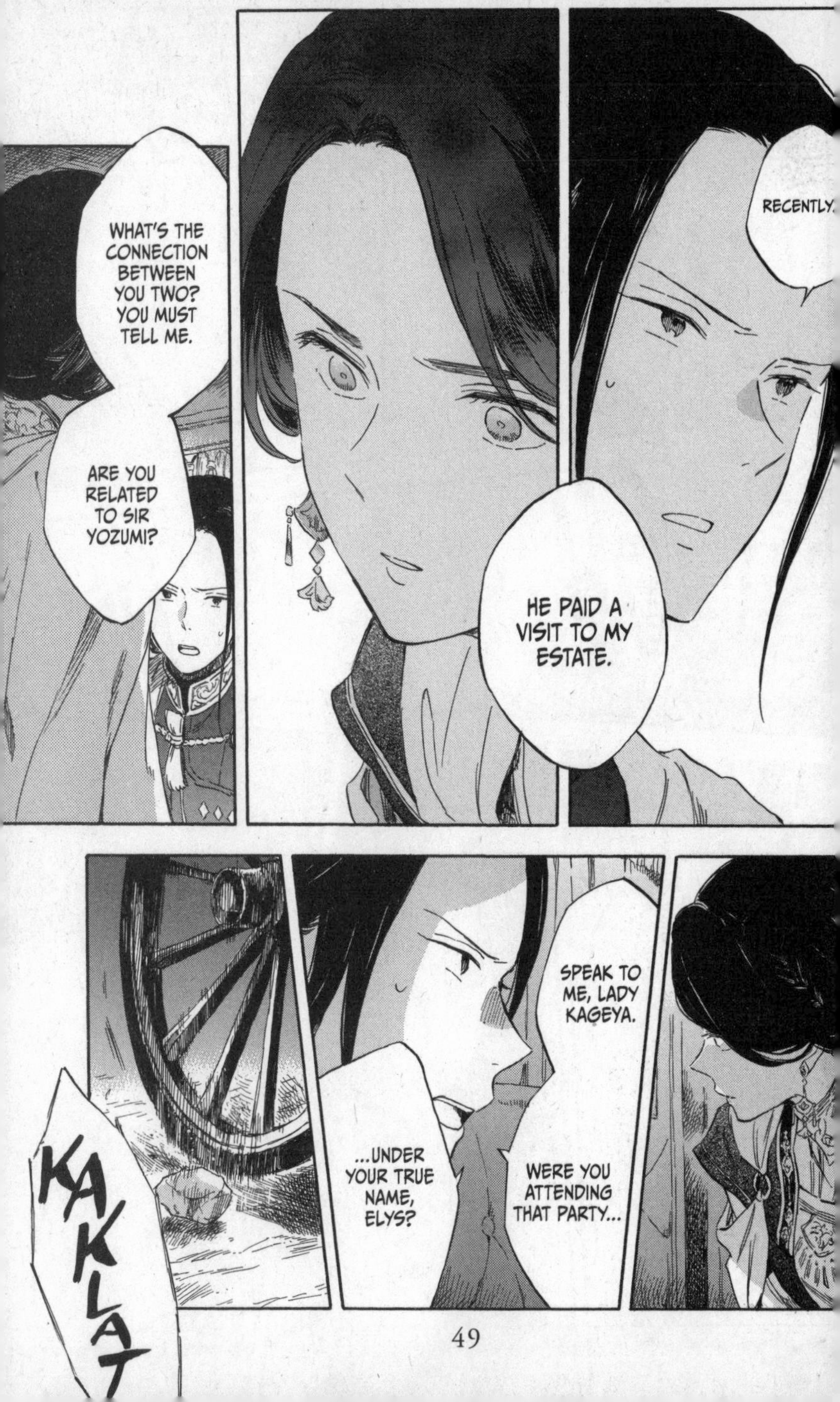
RECENTLY.
HE PAID A VISIT TO MY ESTATE.
WHAT'S THE CONNECTION BETWEEN YOU TWO? YOU MUST TELL ME.
ARE YOU RELATED TO SIR YOZUMI?
SPEAK TO ME, LADY KAGEYA.
WERE YOU ATTENDING THAT PARTY...
...UNDER YOUR TRUE NAME, ELYS?
KAKLAT

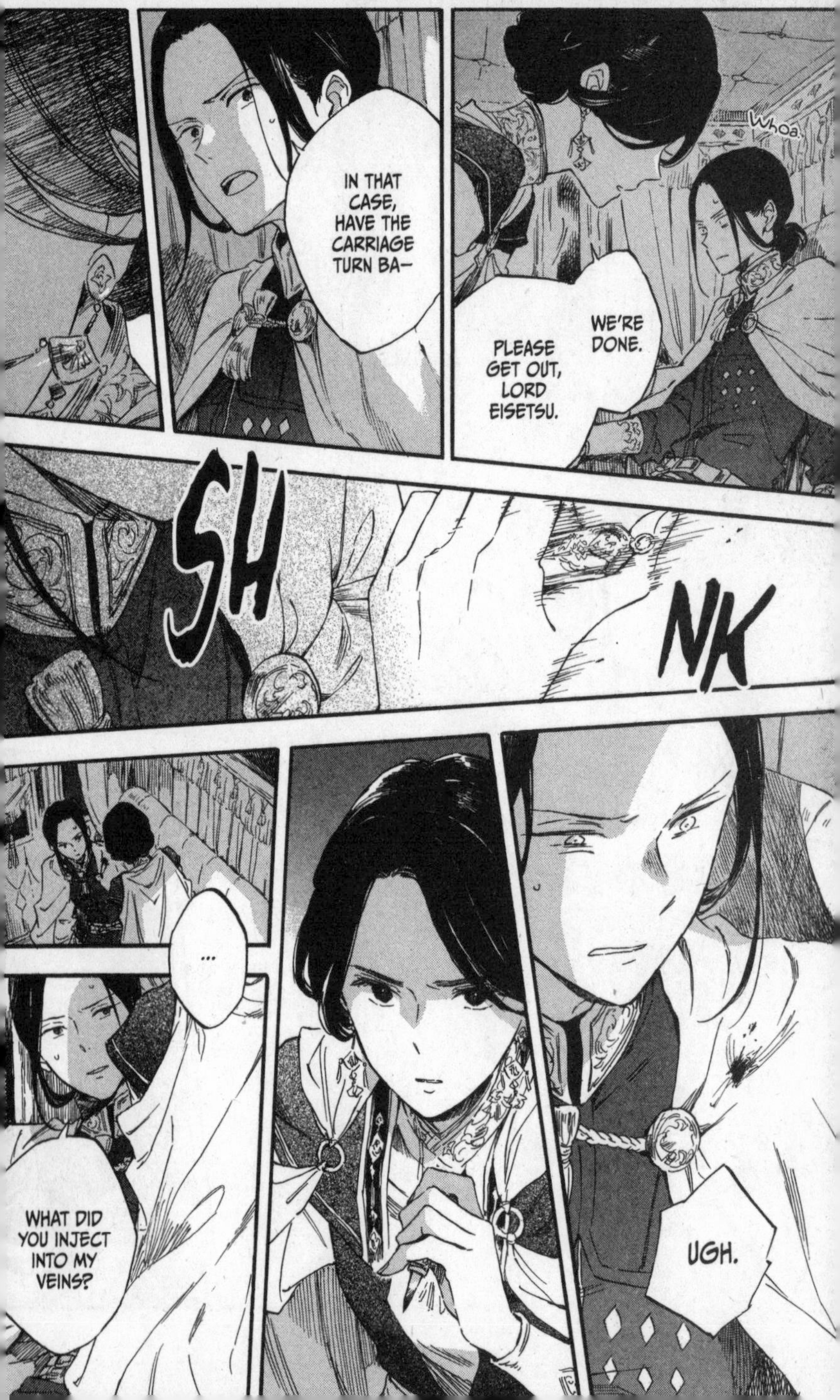
Whoa.
WE'RE DONE.
PLEASE GET OUT, LORD EISETSU.
IN THAT CASE, HAVE THE CARRIAGE TURN BA—
SH NK
UGH.
...
WHAT DID YOU INJECT INTO MY VEINS?

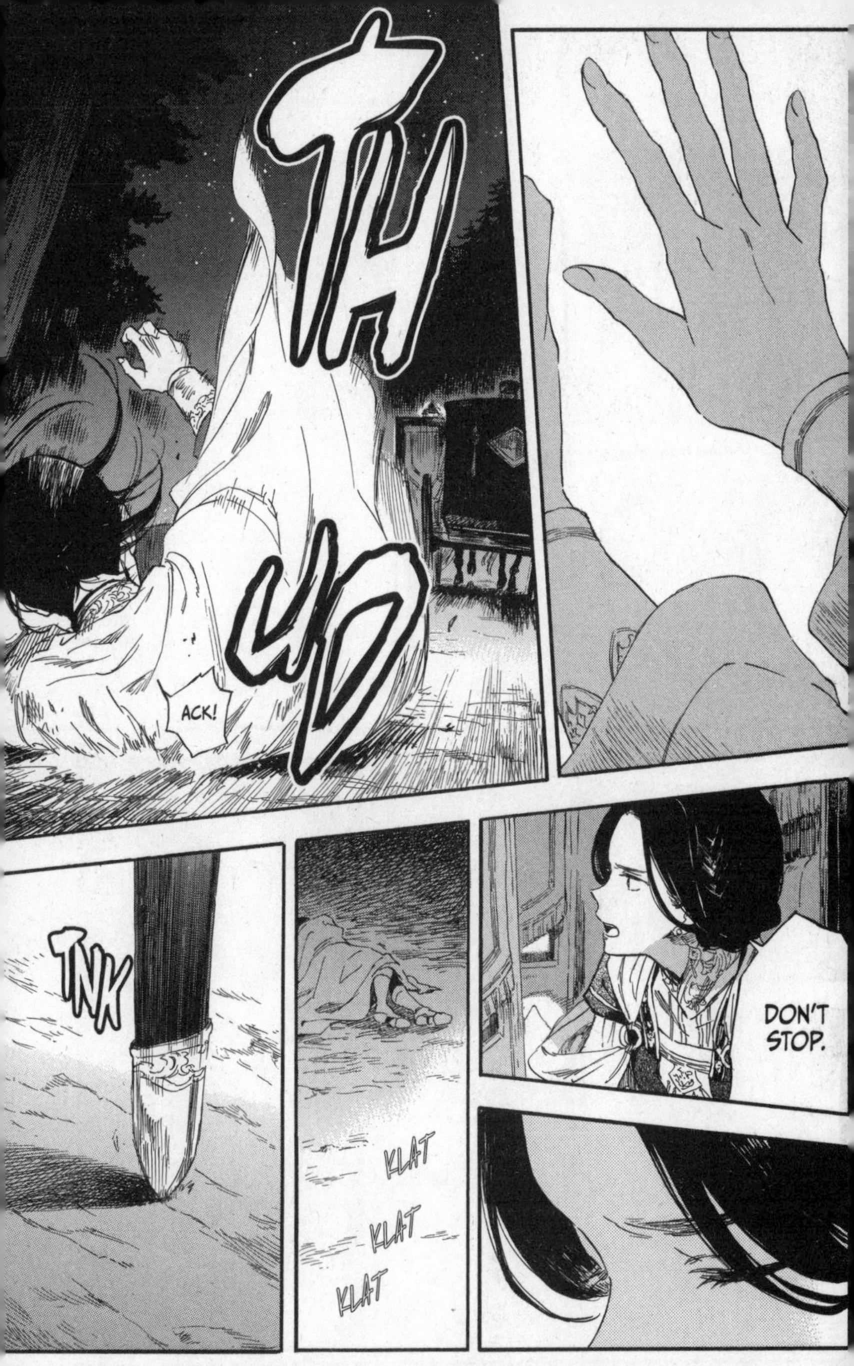
THUD
ACK!
DON'T STOP.
KLAT
KLAT
KLAT
TNK

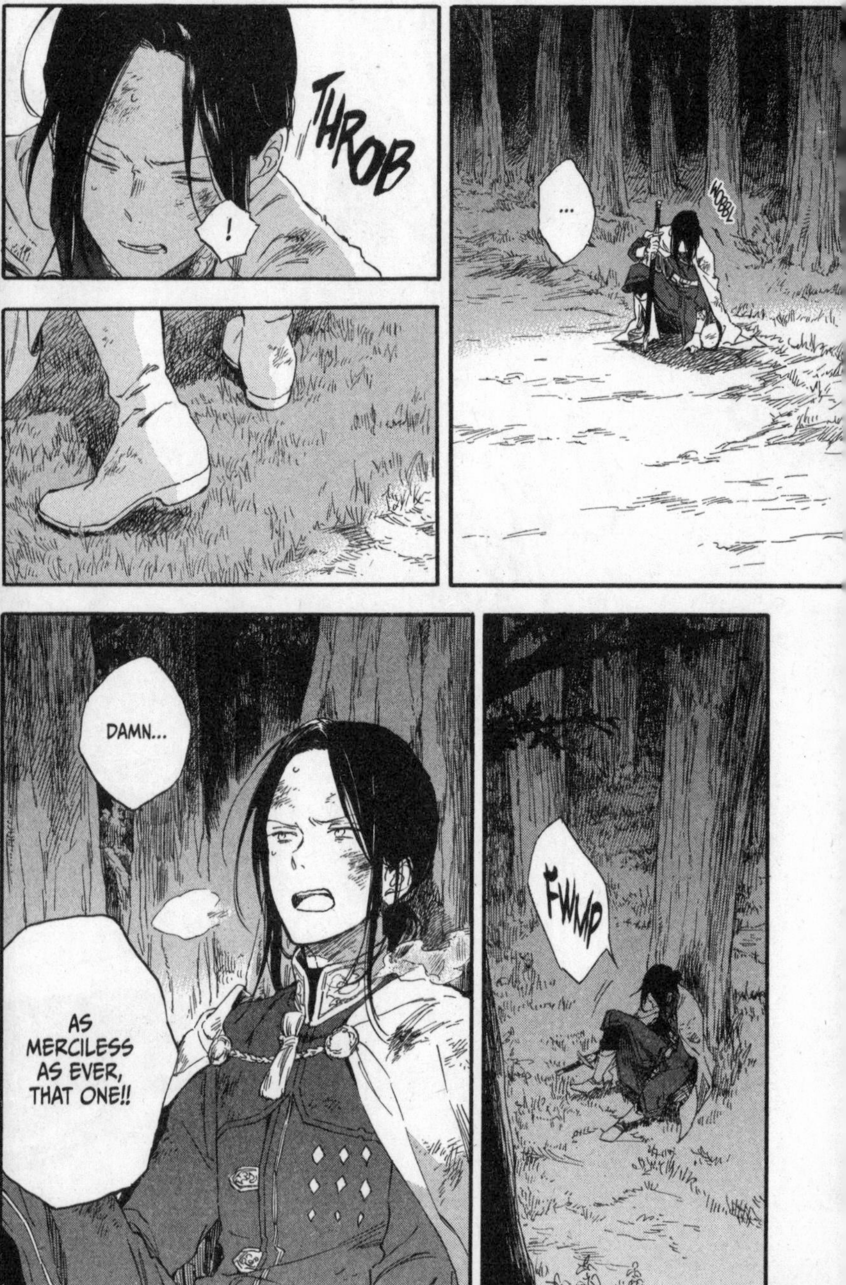
WOBBL
...
THROB
!
FWMP
DAMN...
AS MERCILESS AS EVER, THAT ONE!!

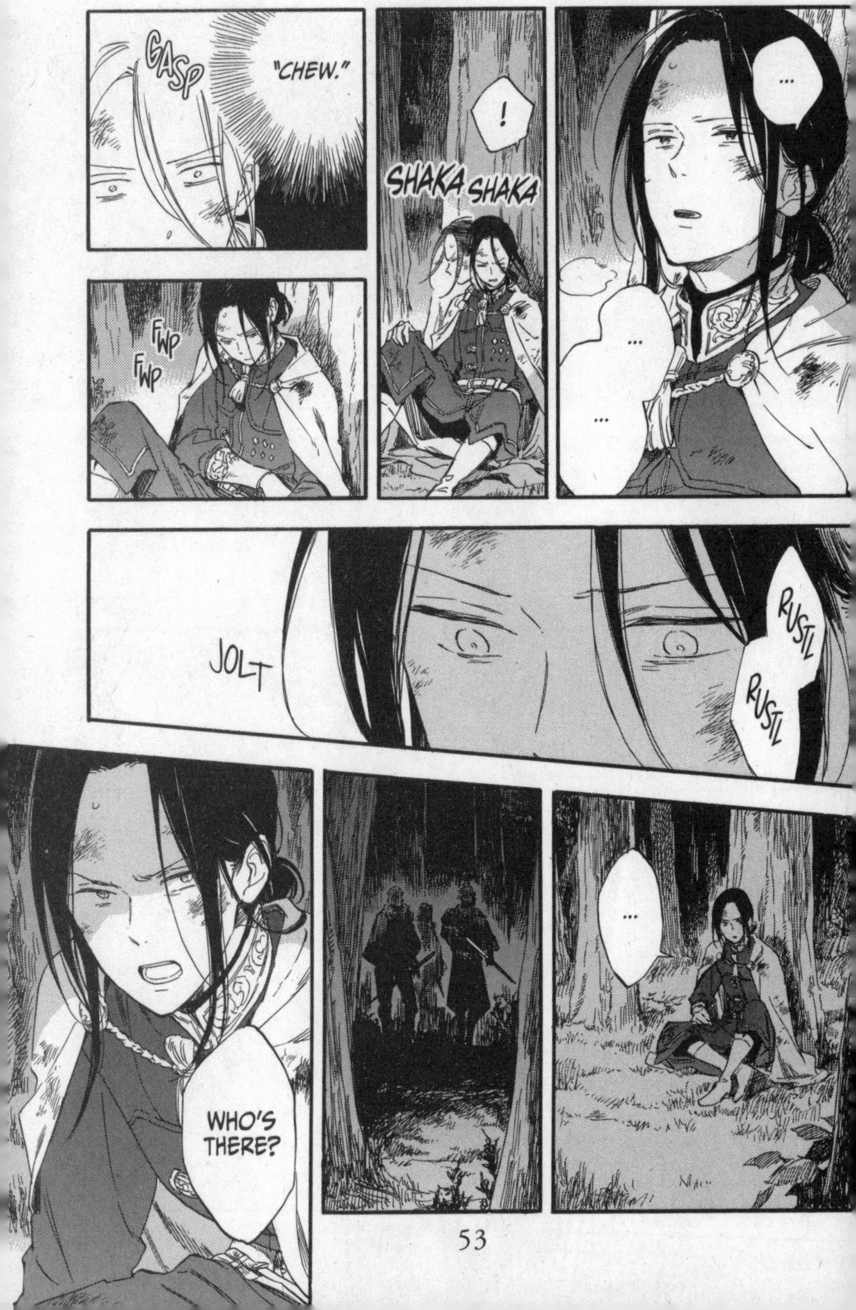
...
...
...
!
SHAKA SHAKA
GASP
"CHEW."
FWP FWP
RUSTIL RUSTIL
JOLT
...
WHO'S THERE?

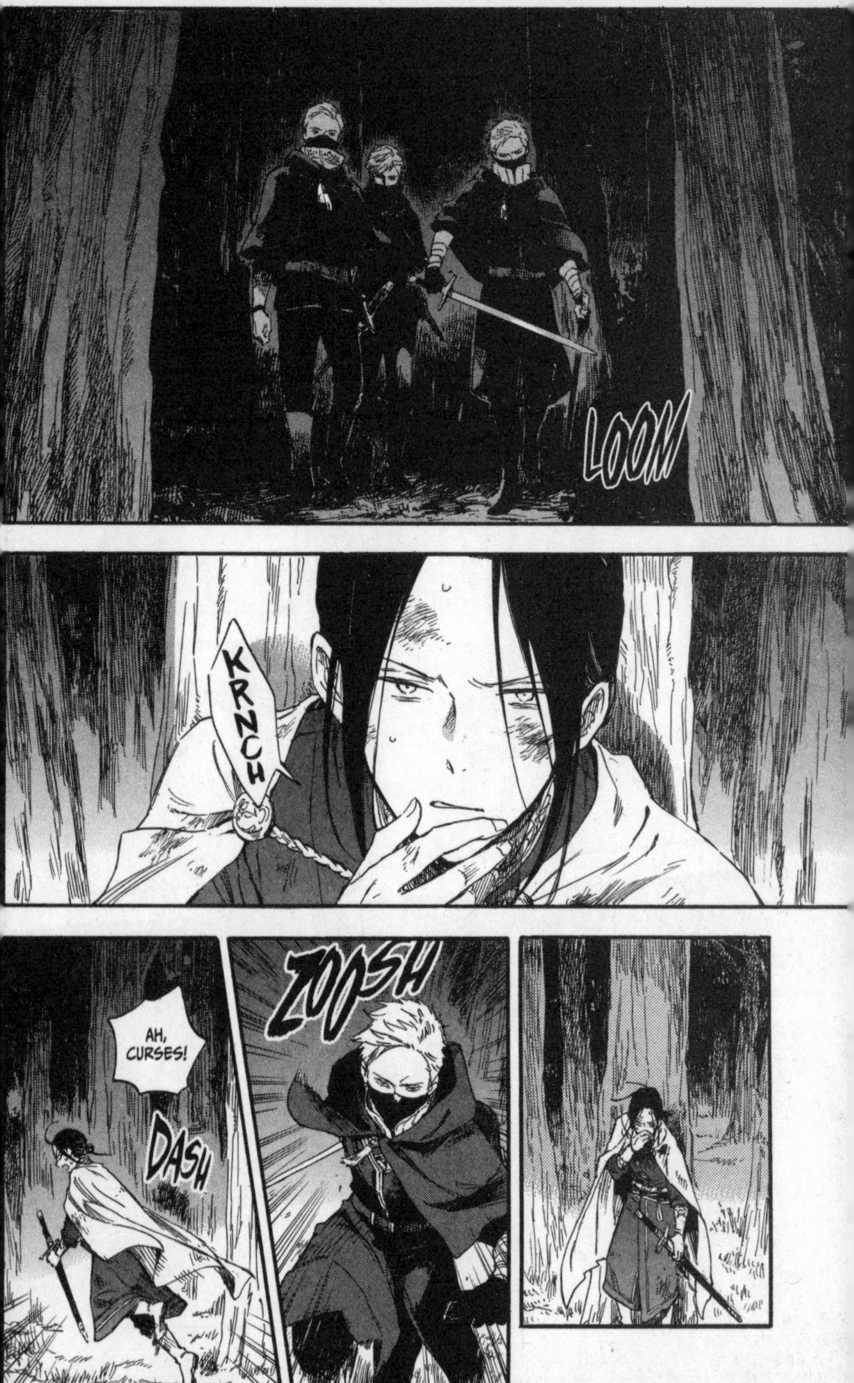
LOOM
KRNCH
ZOOSH
AH, CURSES!
DASH

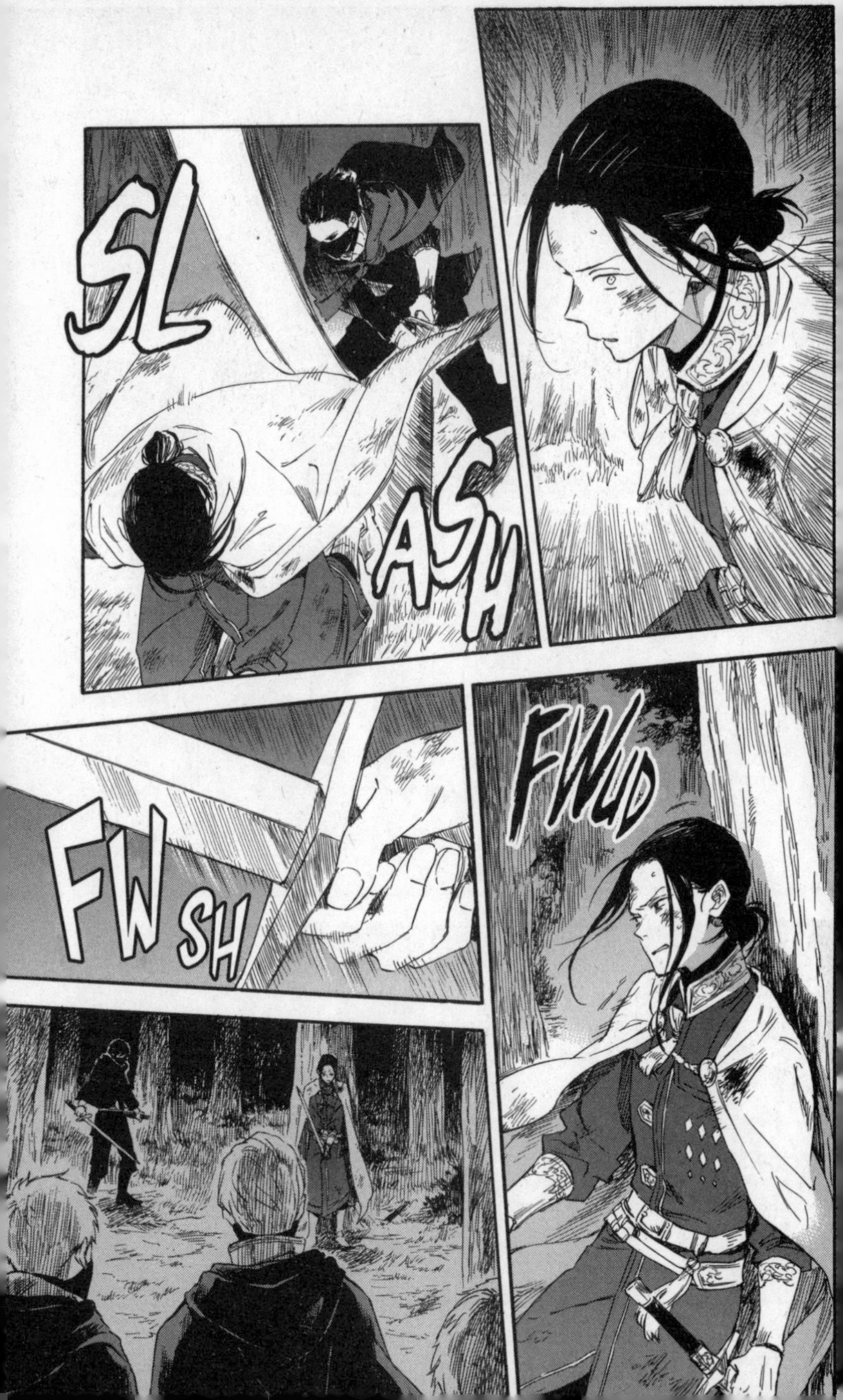
SLASH
FWUD
FWSH

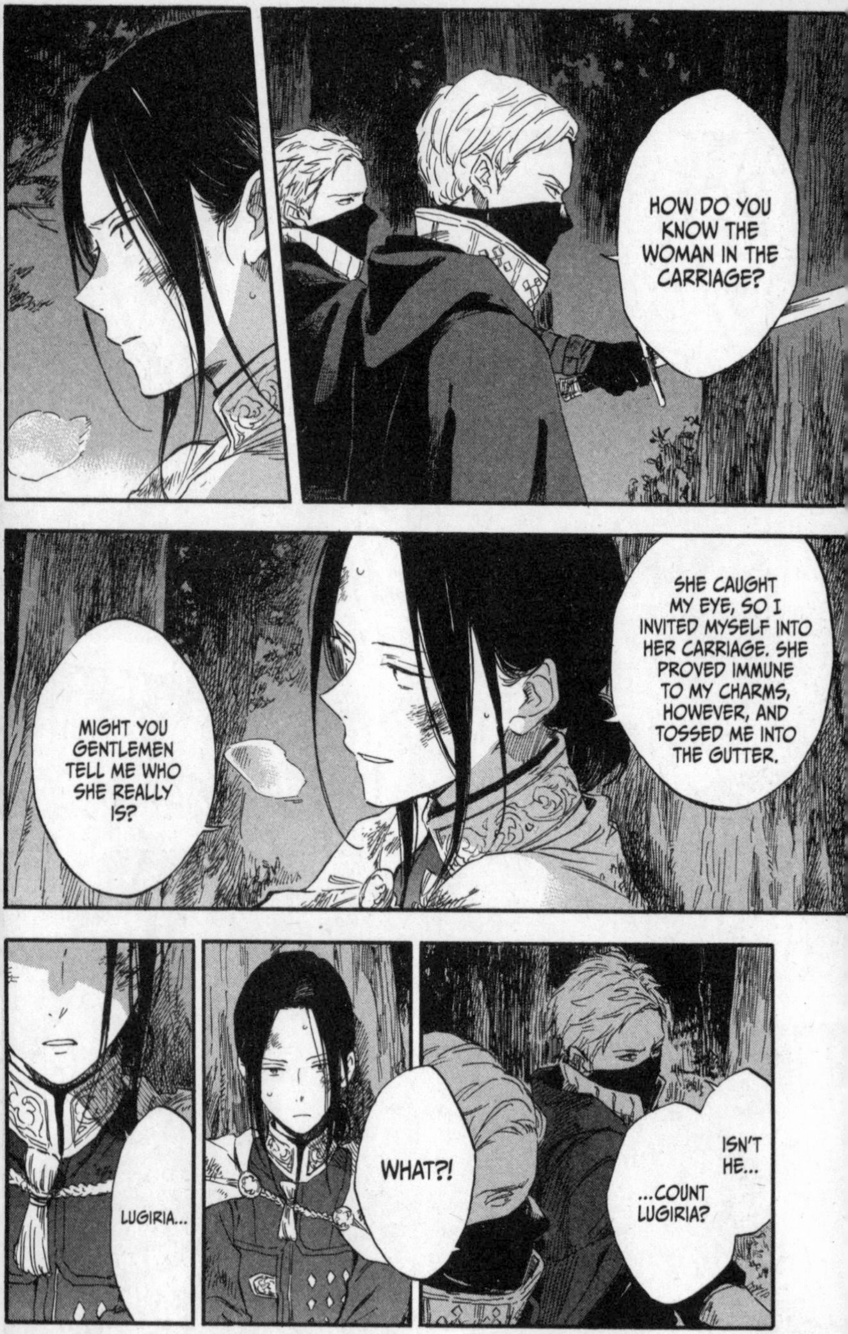
HOW DO YOU KNOW THE WOMAN IN THE CARRIAGE?
SHE CAUGHT MY EYE, SO I INVITED MYSELF INTO HER CARRIAGE. SHE PROVED IMMUNE TO MY CHARMS, HOWEVER, AND TOSSED ME INTO THE GUTTER.
MIGHT YOU GENTLEMEN TELL ME WHO SHE REALLY IS?
ISN'T HE...
...COUNT LUGIRIA?
WHAT?!
LUGIRIA...

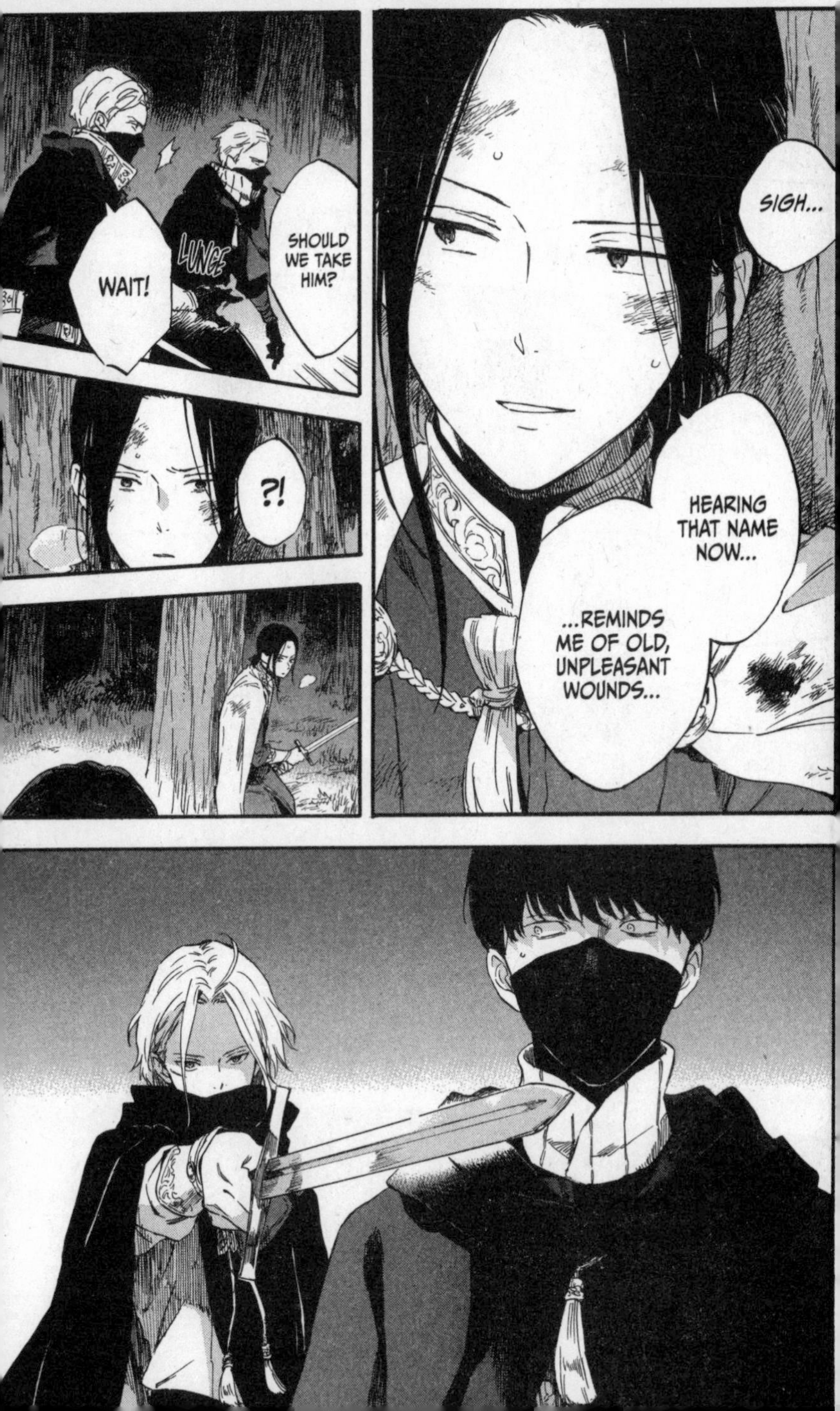
SIGH...
HEARING THAT NAME NOW...
...REMINDS ME OF OLD, UNPLEASANT WOUNDS...
SHOULD WE TAKE HIM?
LUNGE
WAIT!
?!

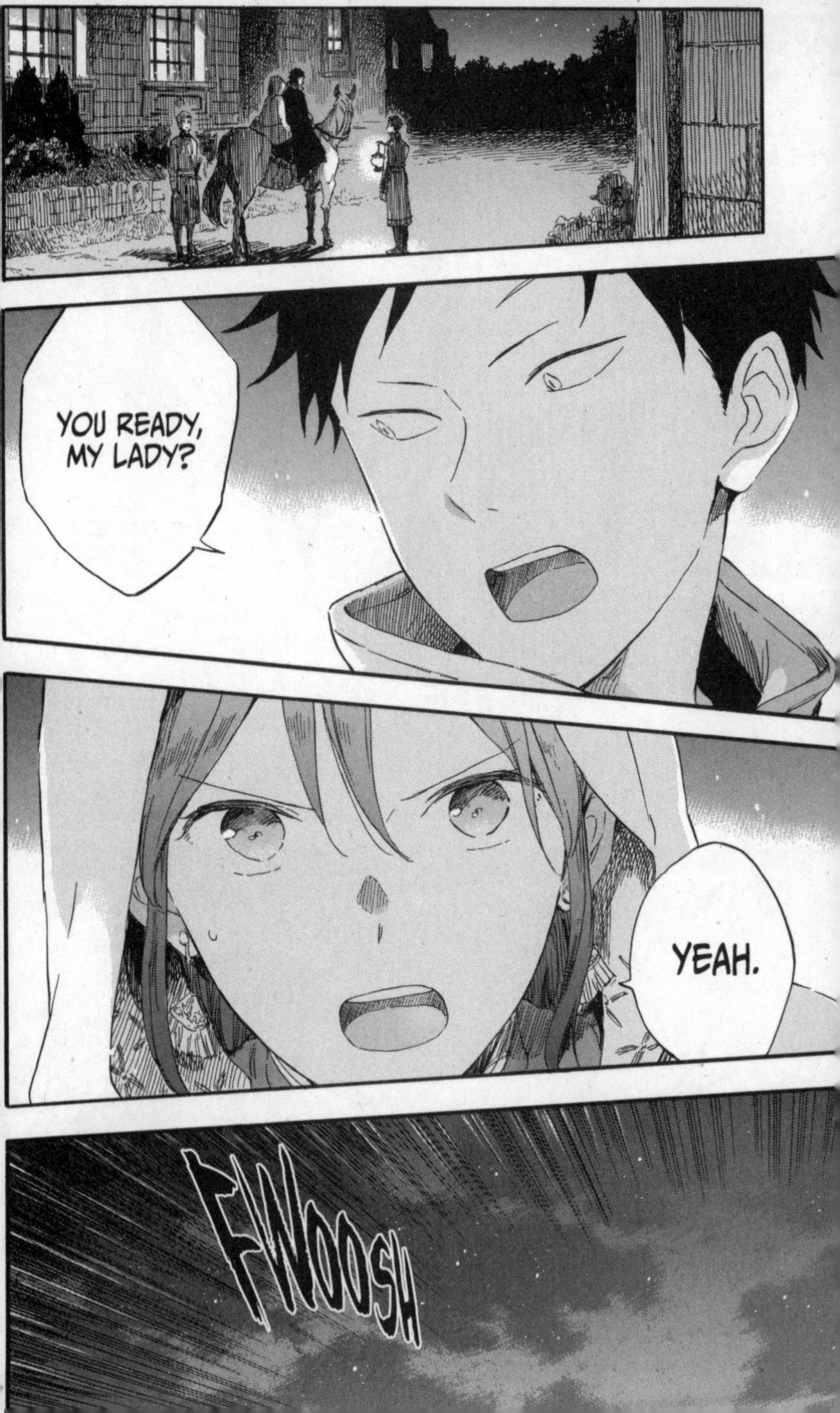
YOU READY, MY LADY?
YEAH.
FWOOSH

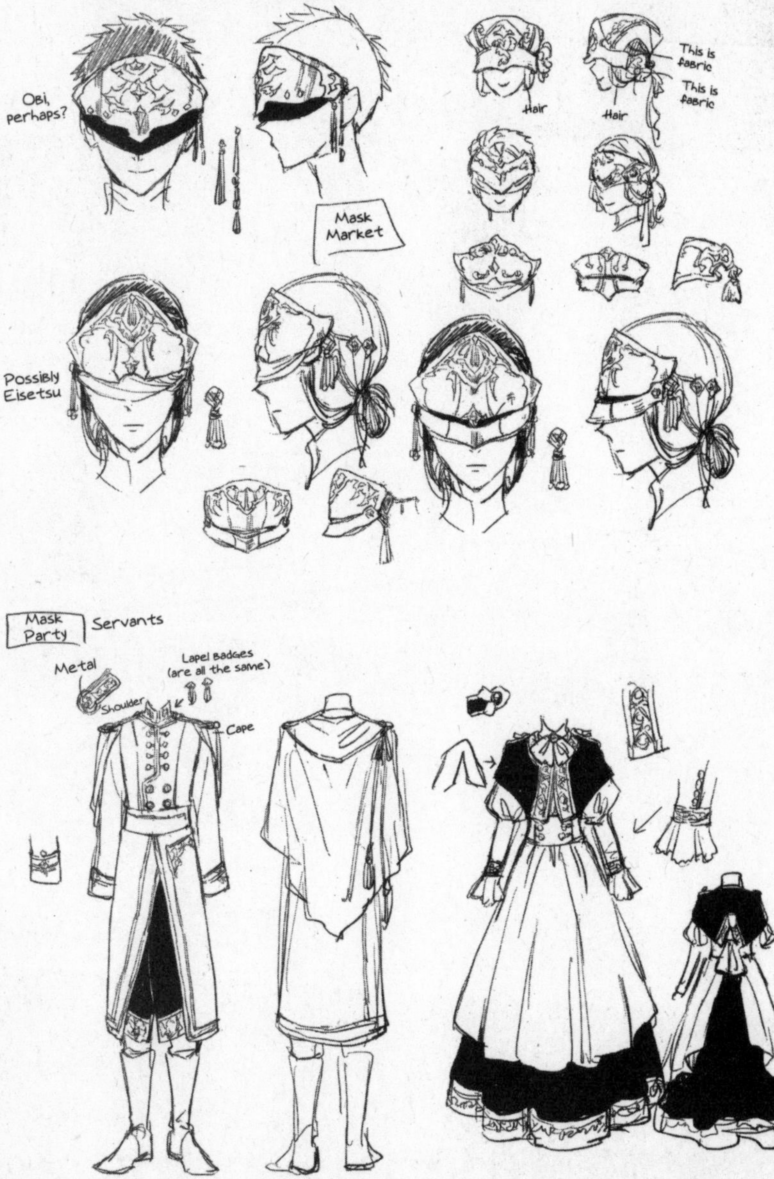
This is fabric
This is fabric
Hair
Hair
Obi, perhaps?
Mask Market
Possibly Eisetsu
Mask Party
Servants
Metal
Shoulder
Lapel badges (are all the same)
Cape

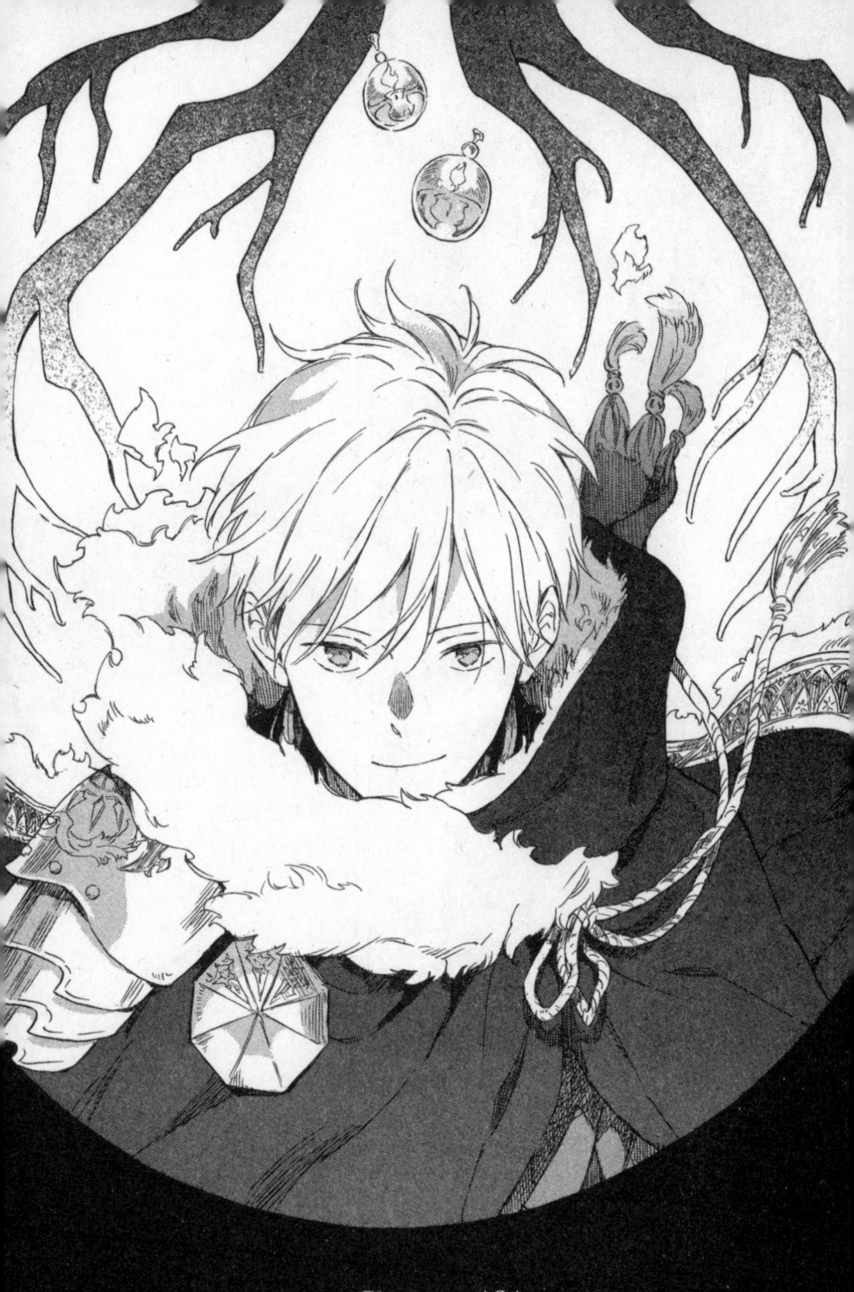

Chapter 121

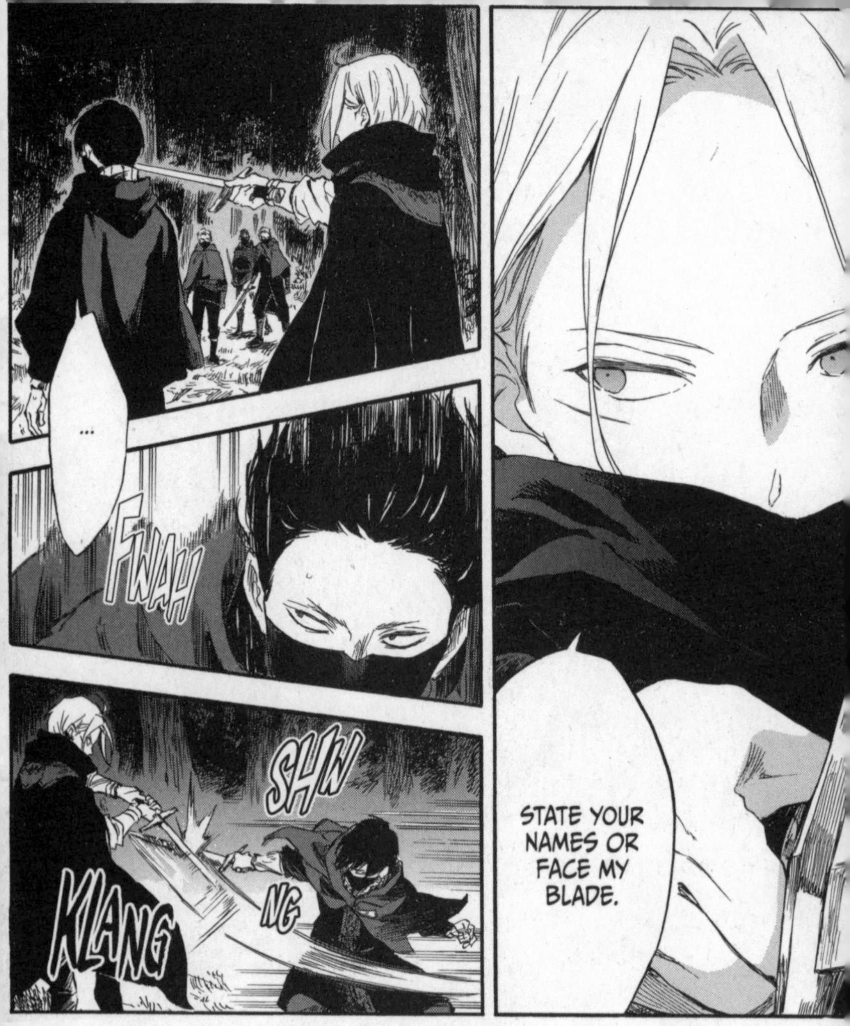
STATE YOUR NAMES OR FACE MY BLADE.
...
FWAH
SHWING
KLANG

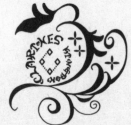

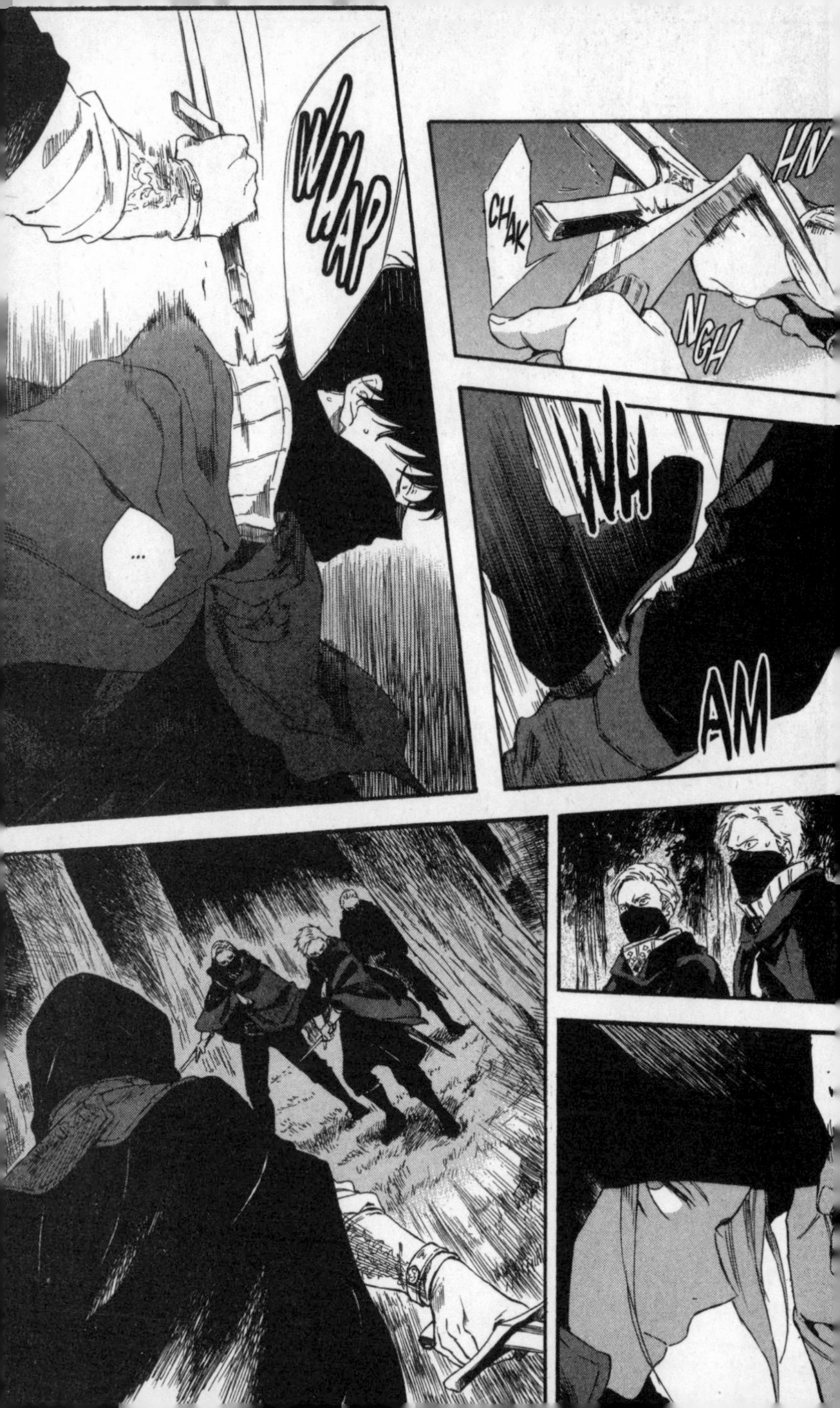
HN
CHAK
NGH
WH
AM
WHAP
...

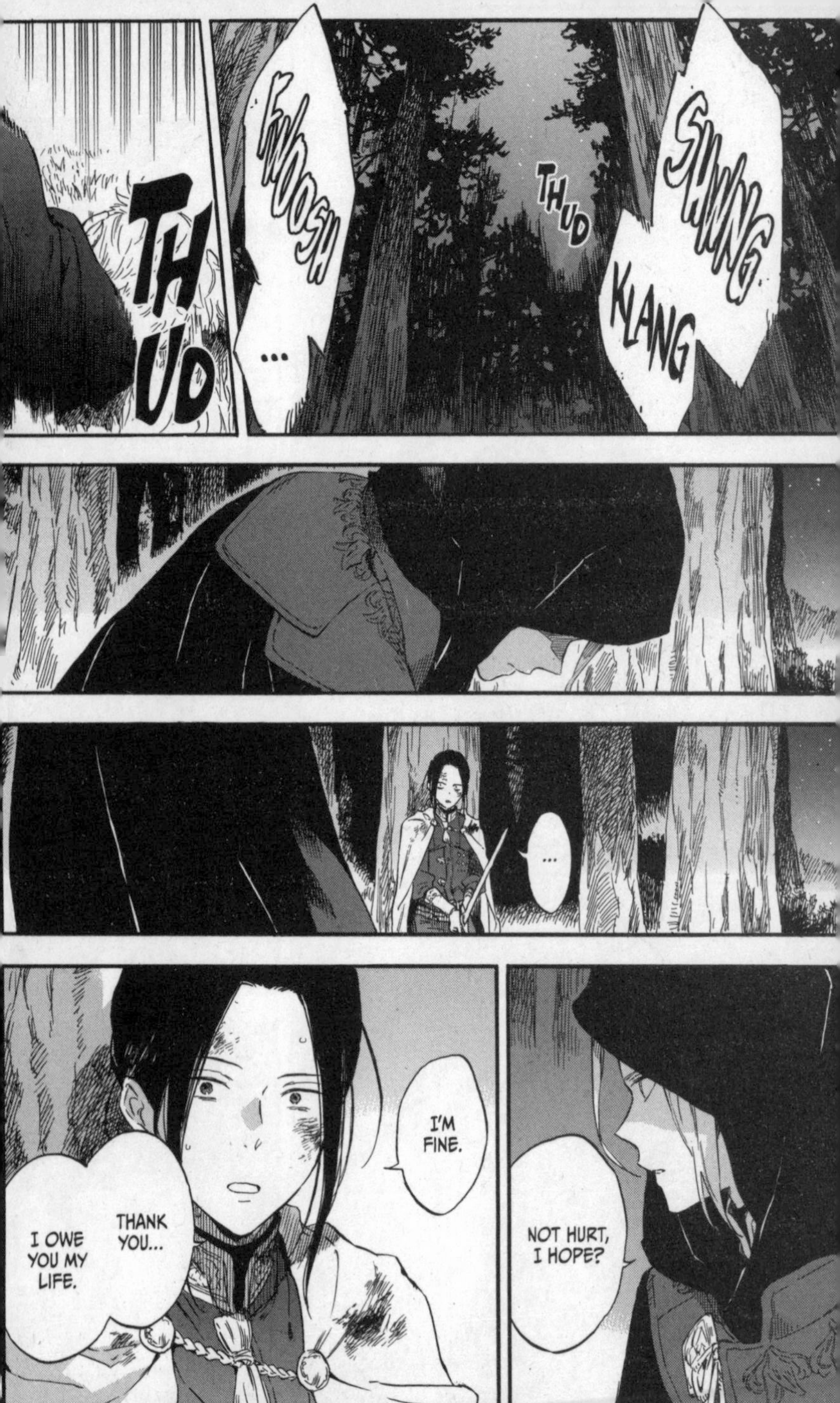
SWING
KLANG
THUD
WHOOSH
...
THUD
...
NOT HURT, I HOPE?
I'M FINE.
THANK YOU...
I OWE YOU MY LIFE.

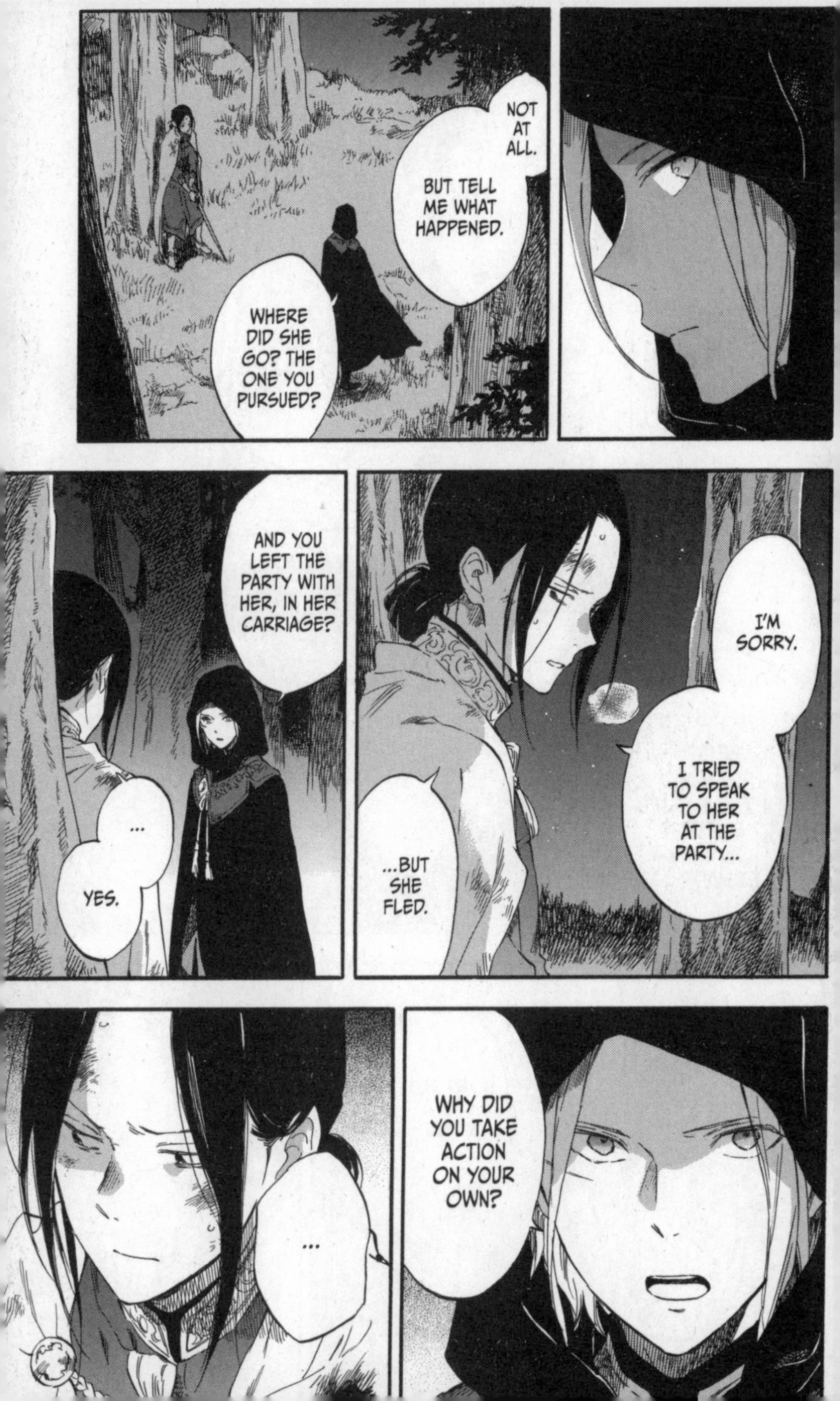
NOT AT ALL.
BUT TELL ME WHAT HAPPENED.
WHERE DID SHE GO? THE ONE YOU PURSUED?
I'M SORRY.
I TRIED TO SPEAK TO HER AT THE PARTY...
...BUT SHE FLED.
AND YOU LEFT THE PARTY WITH HER, IN HER CARRIAGE?
...
YES.
WHY DID YOU TAKE ACTION ON YOUR OWN?
...

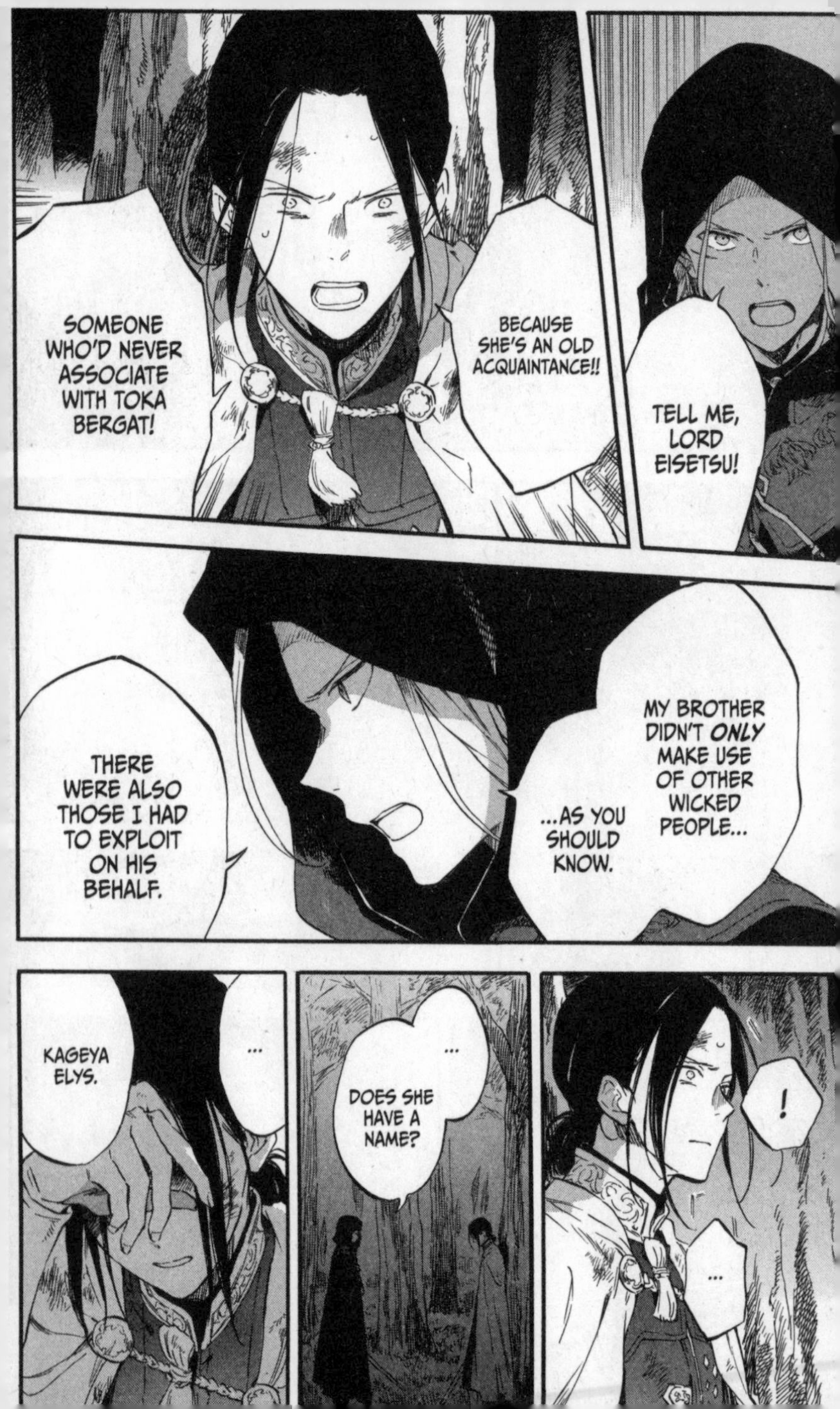
TELL ME, LORD EISETSU!
BECAUSE SHE'S AN OLD ACQUAINTANCE!!
SOMEONE WHO'D NEVER ASSOCIATE WITH TOKA BERGAT!
MY BROTHER DIDN'T *ONLY* MAKE USE OF OTHER WICKED PEOPLE...
...AS YOU SHOULD KNOW.
THERE WERE ALSO THOSE I HAD TO EXPLOIT ON HIS BEHALF.
!
...
...
DOES SHE HAVE A NAME?
...
KAGEYA ELYS.

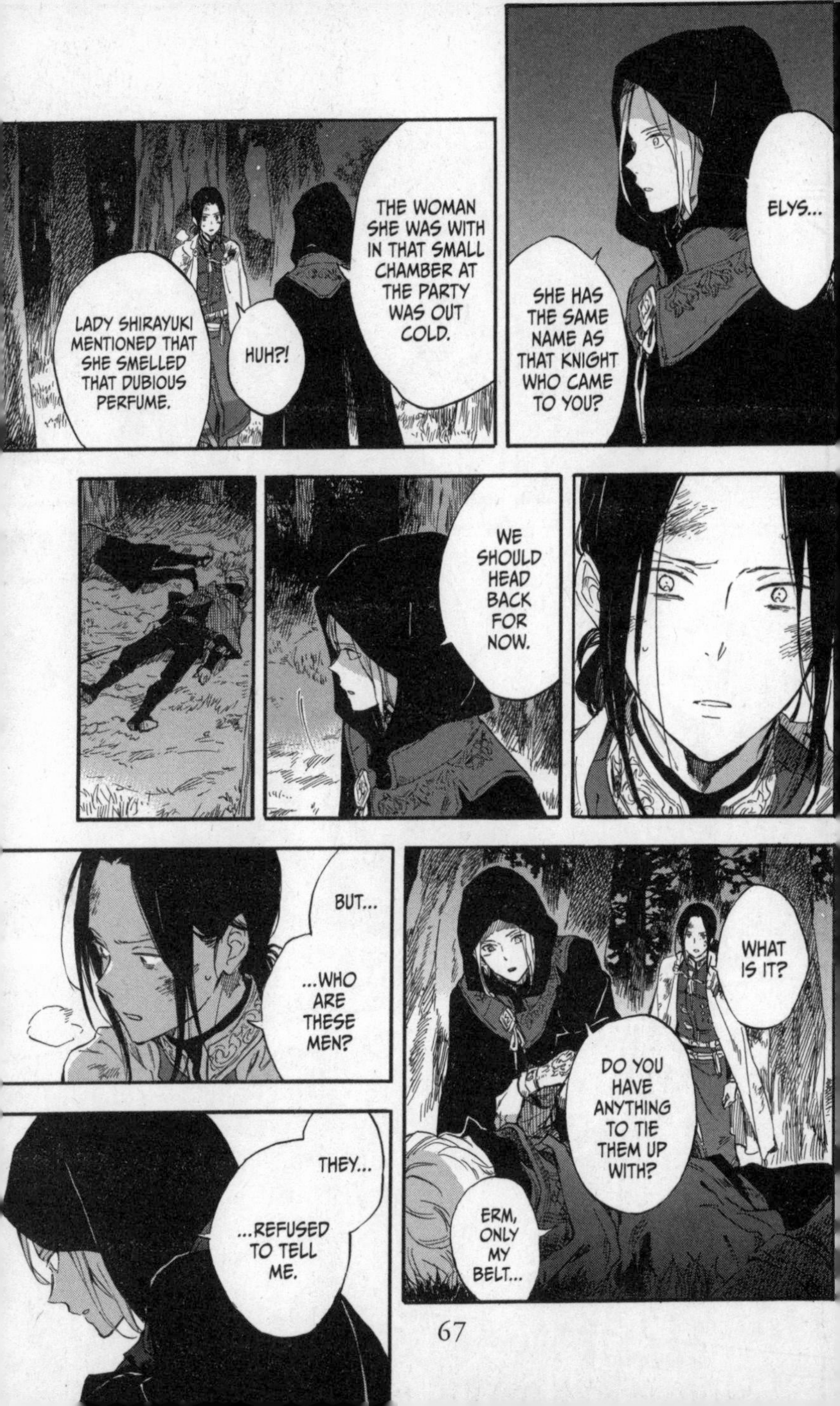
ELYS...
SHE HAS THE SAME NAME AS THAT KNIGHT WHO CAME TO YOU?
THE WOMAN SHE WAS WITH IN THAT SMALL CHAMBER AT THE PARTY WAS OUT COLD.
HUH?!
LADY SHIRAYUKI MENTIONED THAT SHE SMELLED THAT DUBIOUS PERFUME.
WE SHOULD HEAD BACK FOR NOW.
WHAT IS IT?
DO YOU HAVE ANYTHING TO TIE THEM UP WITH?
ERM, ONLY MY BELT...
BUT...
...WHO ARE THESE MEN?
THEY...
...REFUSED TO TELL ME.

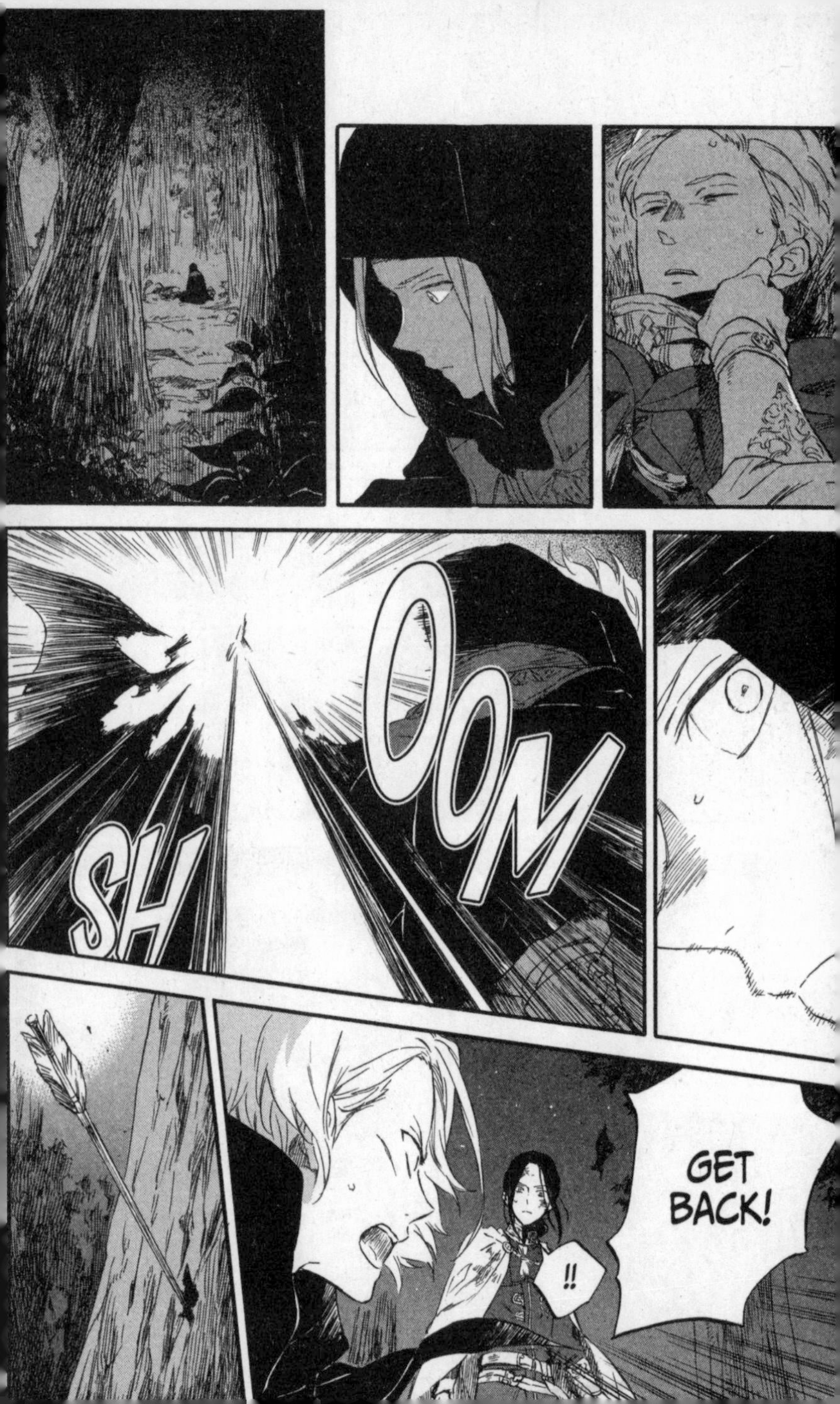
SHOOM
GET BACK!
!!

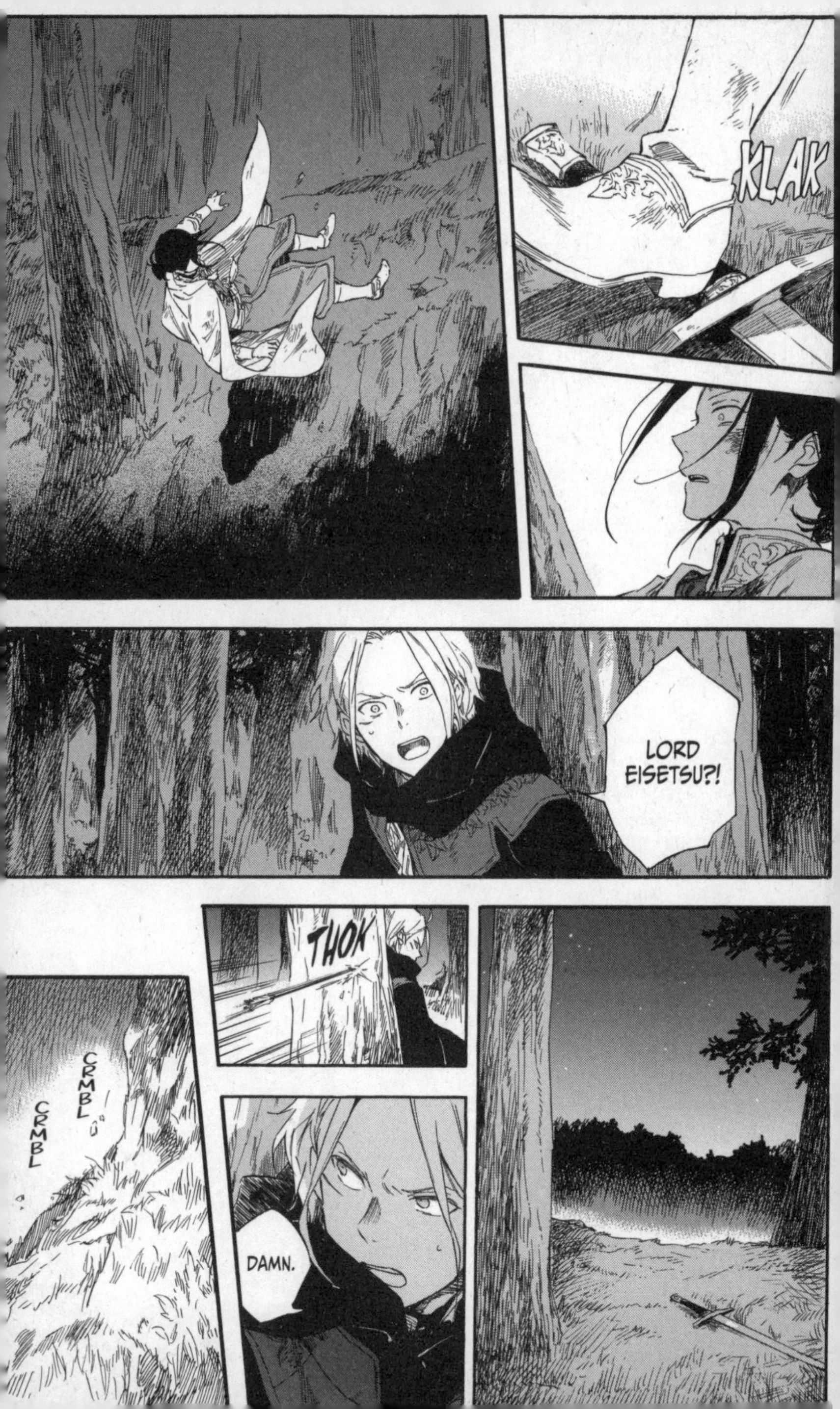
KLAK
LORD EISETSU?!
THOK
DAMN.
CRMBL
CRMBL

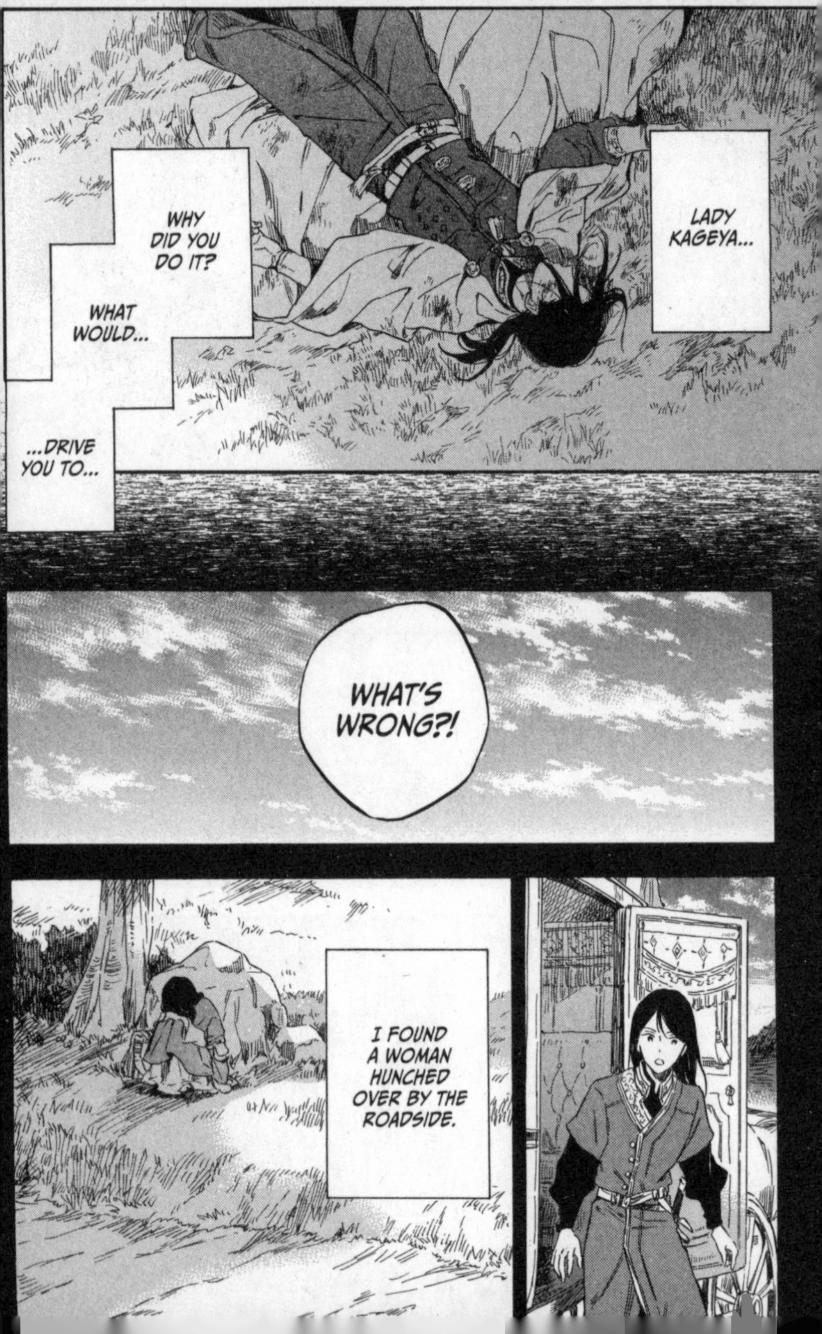
LADY KAGEYA...
WHY DID YOU DO IT?
WHAT WOULD...
...DRIVE YOU TO...
WHAT'S WRONG?!
I FOUND A WOMAN HUNCHED OVER BY THE ROADSIDE.

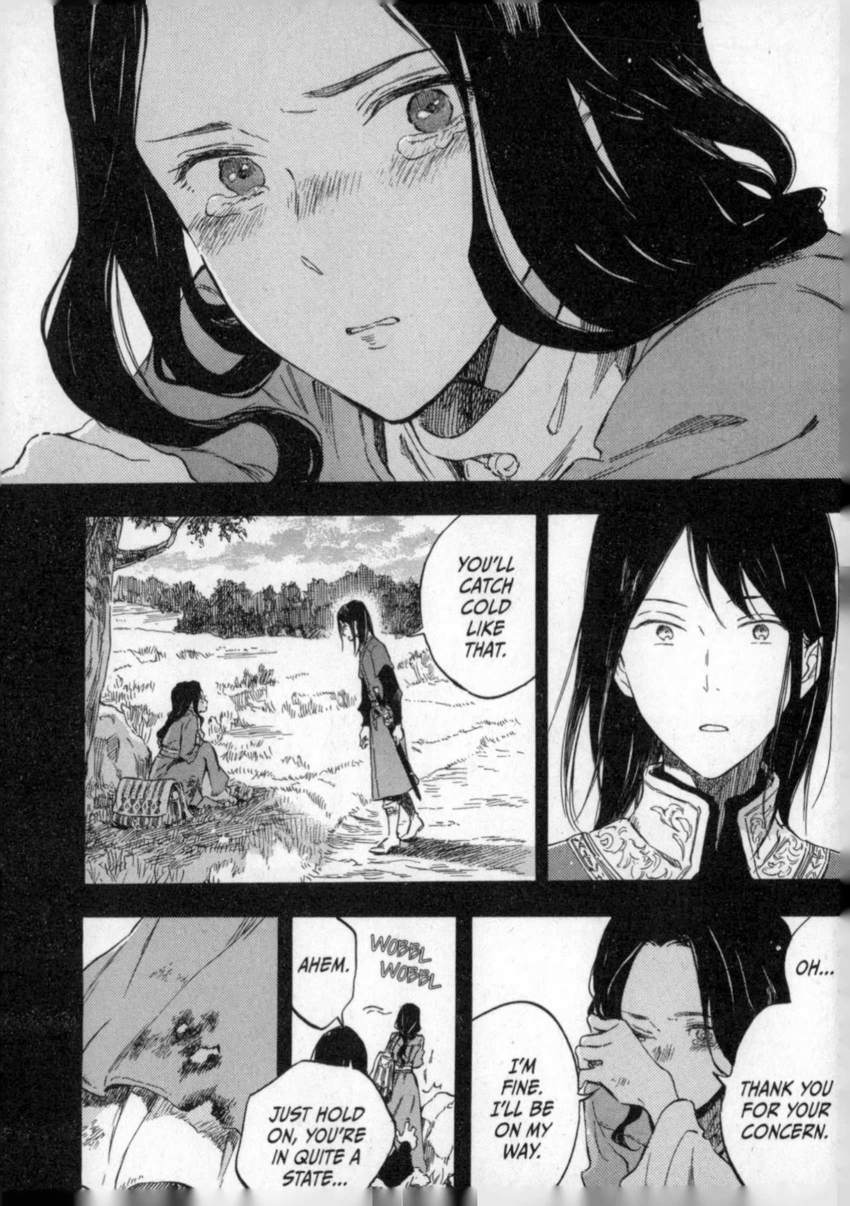
YOU'LL CATCH COLD LIKE THAT.
OH...
THANK YOU FOR YOUR CONCERN.
I'M FINE. I'LL BE ON MY WAY.
WOBBL WOBBL
AHEM.
JUST HOLD ON, YOU'RE IN QUITE A STATE...

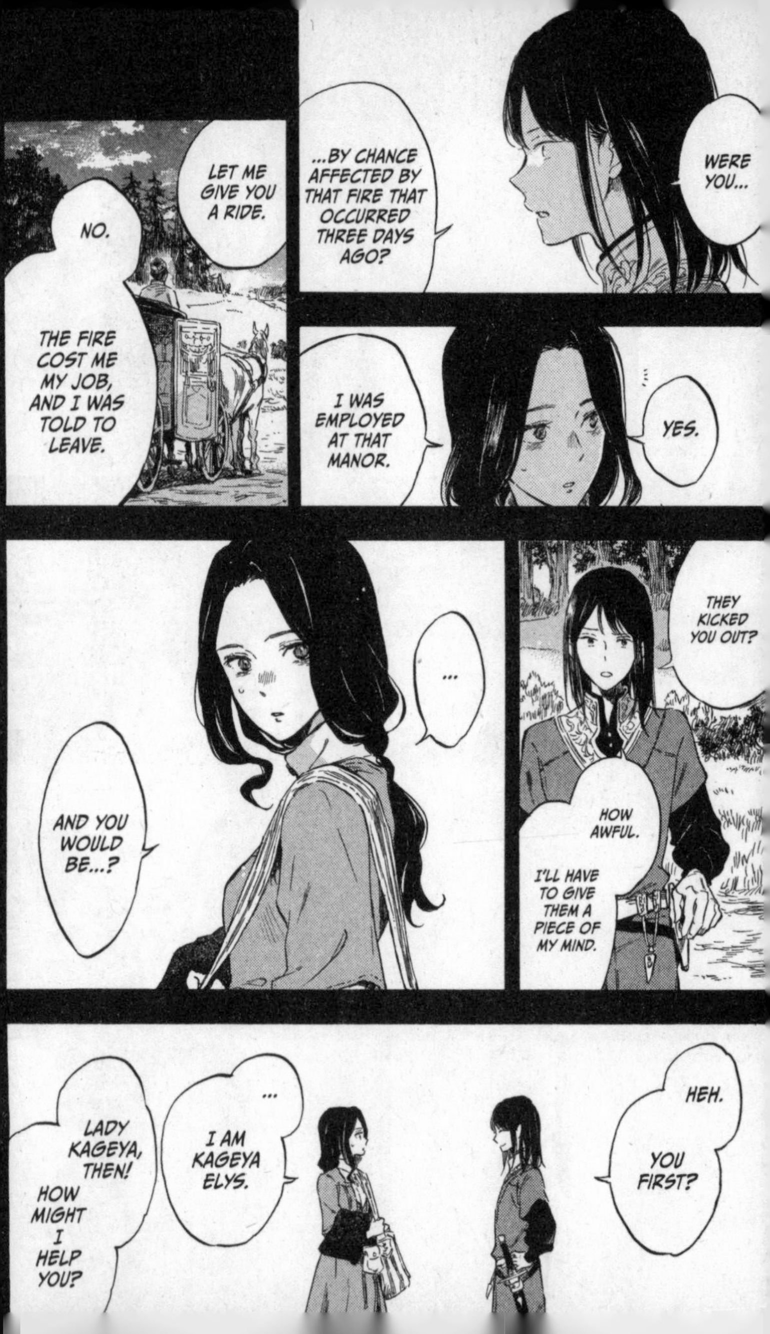
WERE YOU...
...BY CHANCE AFFECTED BY THAT FIRE THAT OCCURRED THREE DAYS AGO?
YES.
I WAS EMPLOYED AT THAT MANOR.
LET ME GIVE YOU A RIDE.
NO.
THE FIRE COST ME MY JOB, AND I WAS TOLD TO LEAVE.
THEY KICKED YOU OUT?
HOW AWFUL.
I'LL HAVE TO GIVE THEM A PIECE OF MY MIND.
...
AND YOU WOULD BE...?
HEH.
YOU FIRST?
...
I AM KAGEYA ELYS.
LADY KAGEYA, THEN! HOW MIGHT I HELP YOU?

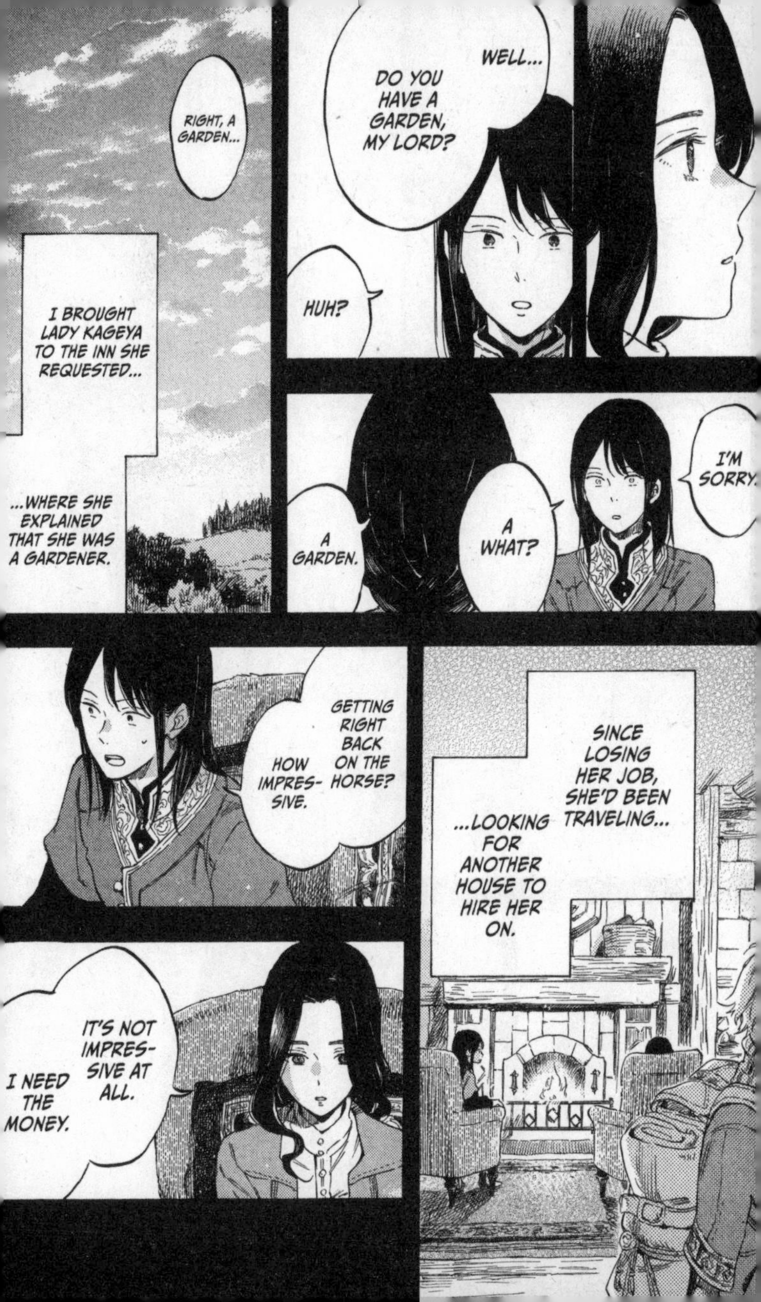
WELL...
DO YOU HAVE A GARDEN, MY LORD?
HUH?
I'M SORRY.
A WHAT?
A GARDEN.
RIGHT, A GARDEN...
I BROUGHT LADY KAGEYA TO THE INN SHE REQUESTED...
...WHERE SHE EXPLAINED THAT SHE WAS A GARDENER.
SINCE LOSING HER JOB, SHE'D BEEN TRAVELING...
...LOOKING FOR ANOTHER HOUSE TO HIRE HER ON.
GETTING RIGHT BACK ON THE HORSE?
HOW IMPRES-SIVE.
IT'S NOT IMPRES-SIVE AT ALL.
I NEED THE MONEY.

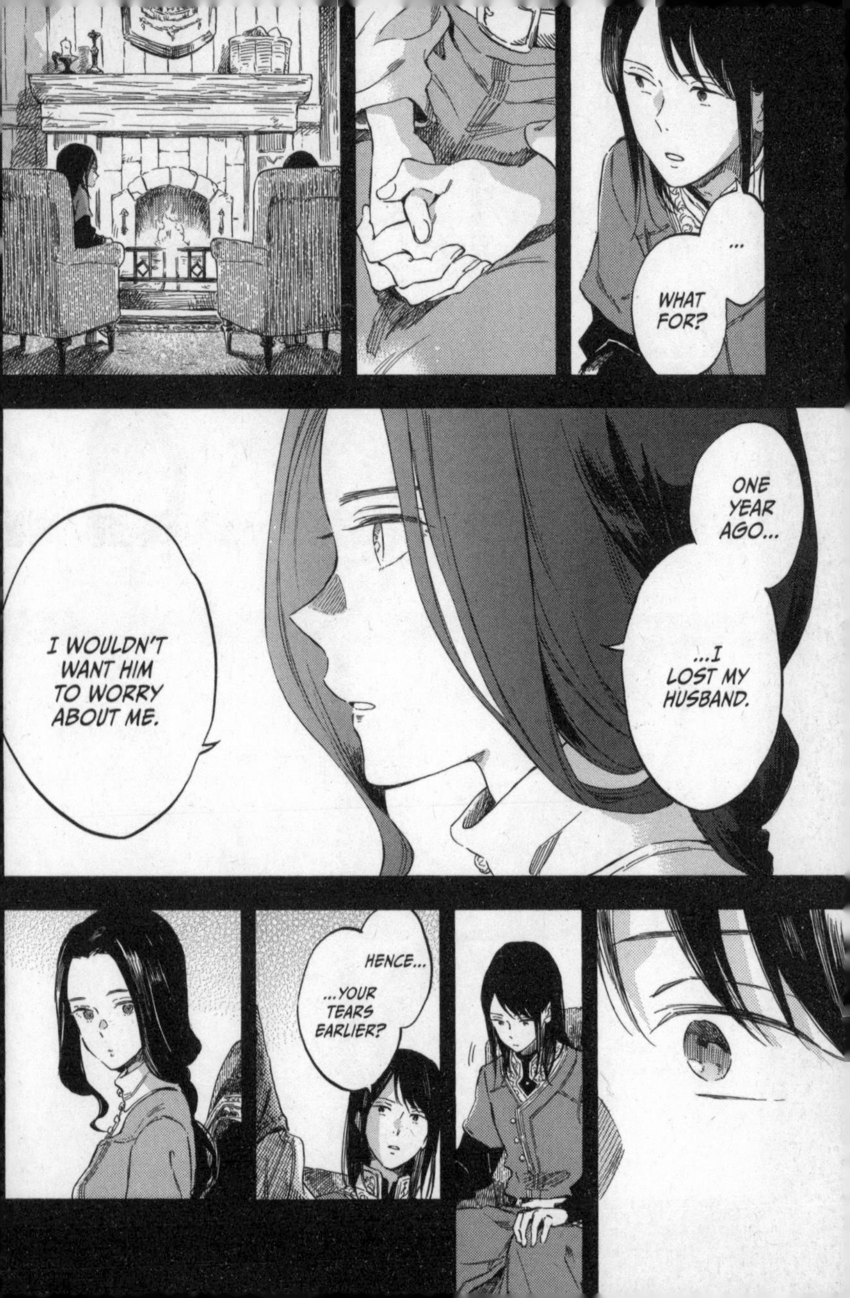
...
WHAT FOR?
ONE YEAR AGO...
...I LOST MY HUSBAND.
I WOULDN'T WANT HIM TO WORRY ABOUT ME.
HENCE...
...YOUR TEARS EARLIER?

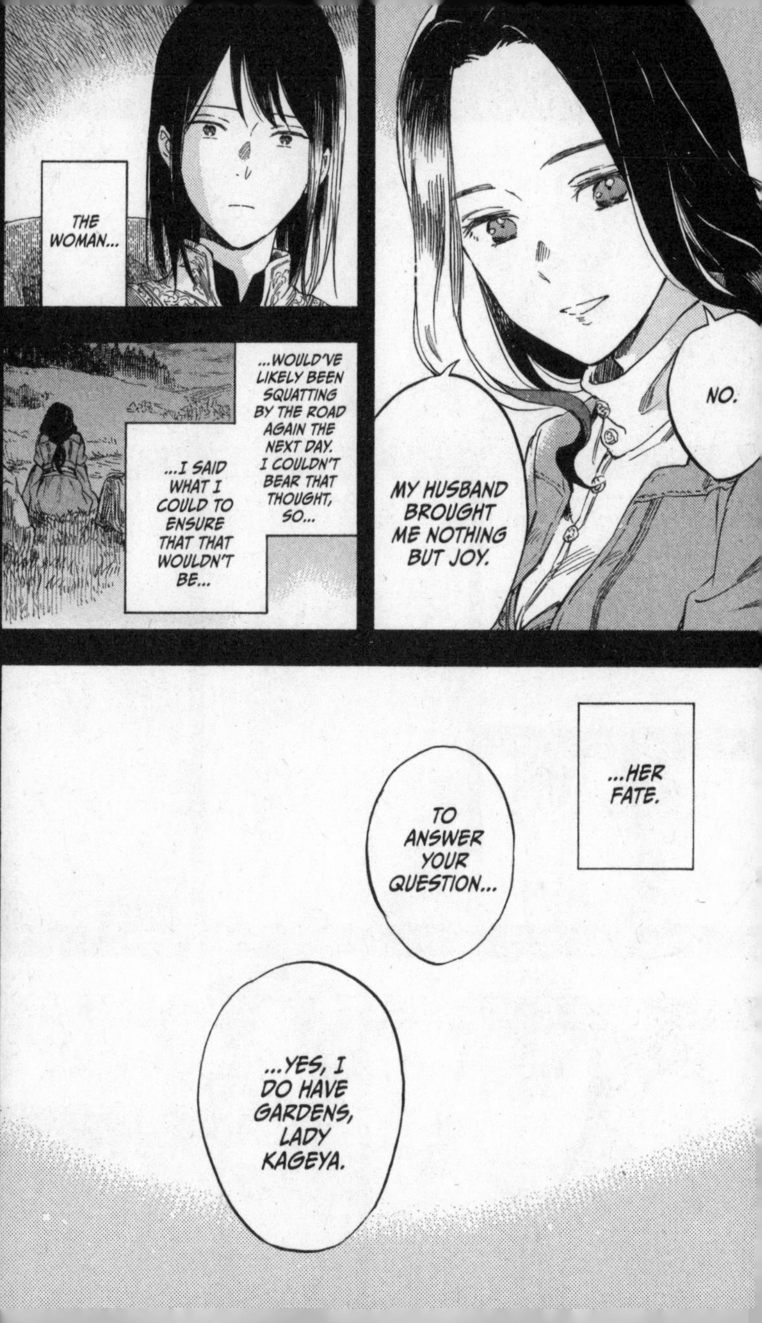
NO.
MY HUSBAND BROUGHT ME NOTHING BUT JOY.
THE WOMAN...
...WOULD'VE LIKELY BEEN SQUATTING BY THE ROAD AGAIN THE NEXT DAY. I COULDN'T BEAR THAT THOUGHT, SO...
...I SAID WHAT I COULD TO ENSURE THAT THAT WOULDN'T BE...
...HER FATE.
TO ANSWER YOUR QUESTION...
...YES, I DO HAVE GARDENS, LADY KAGEYA.

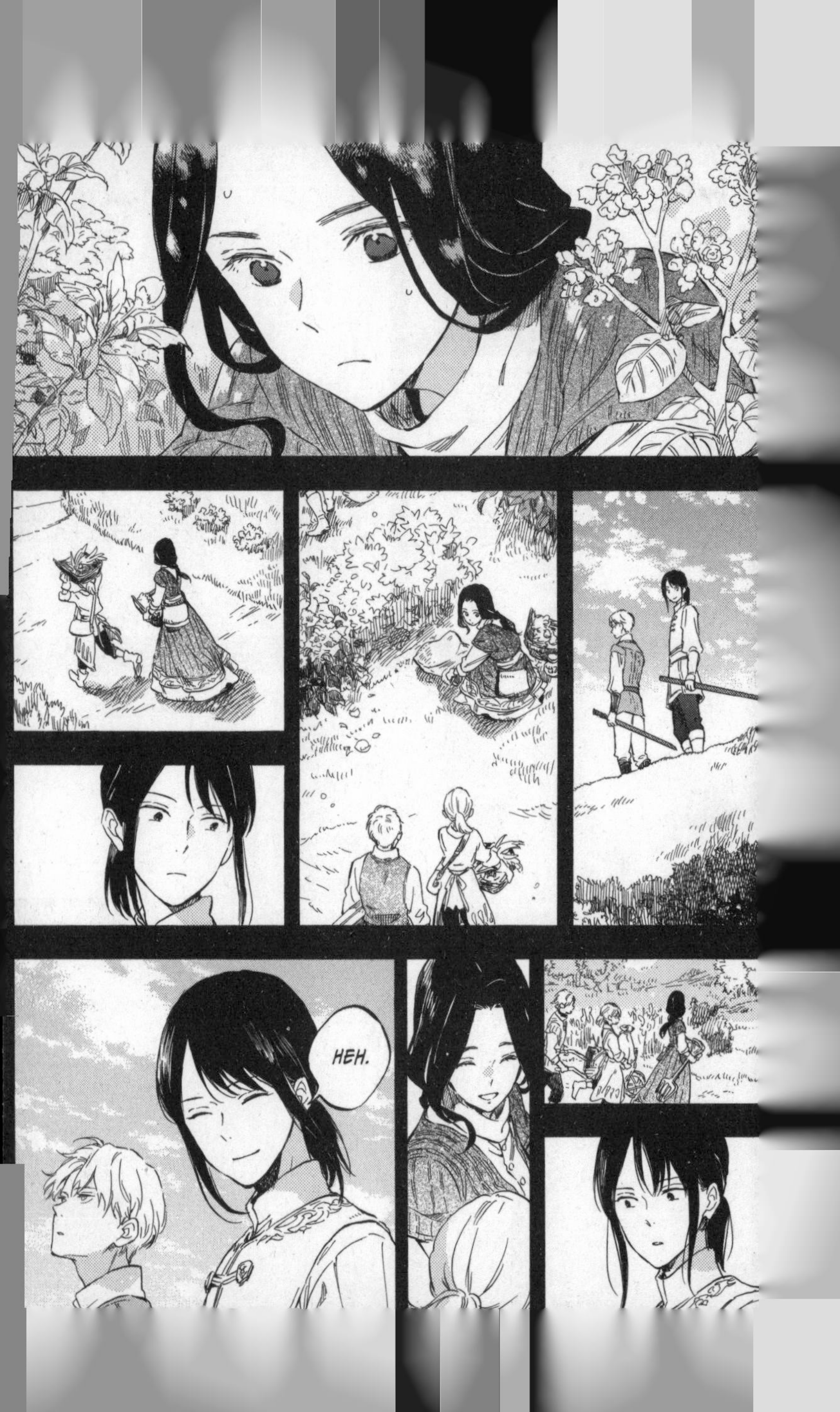
HEH.

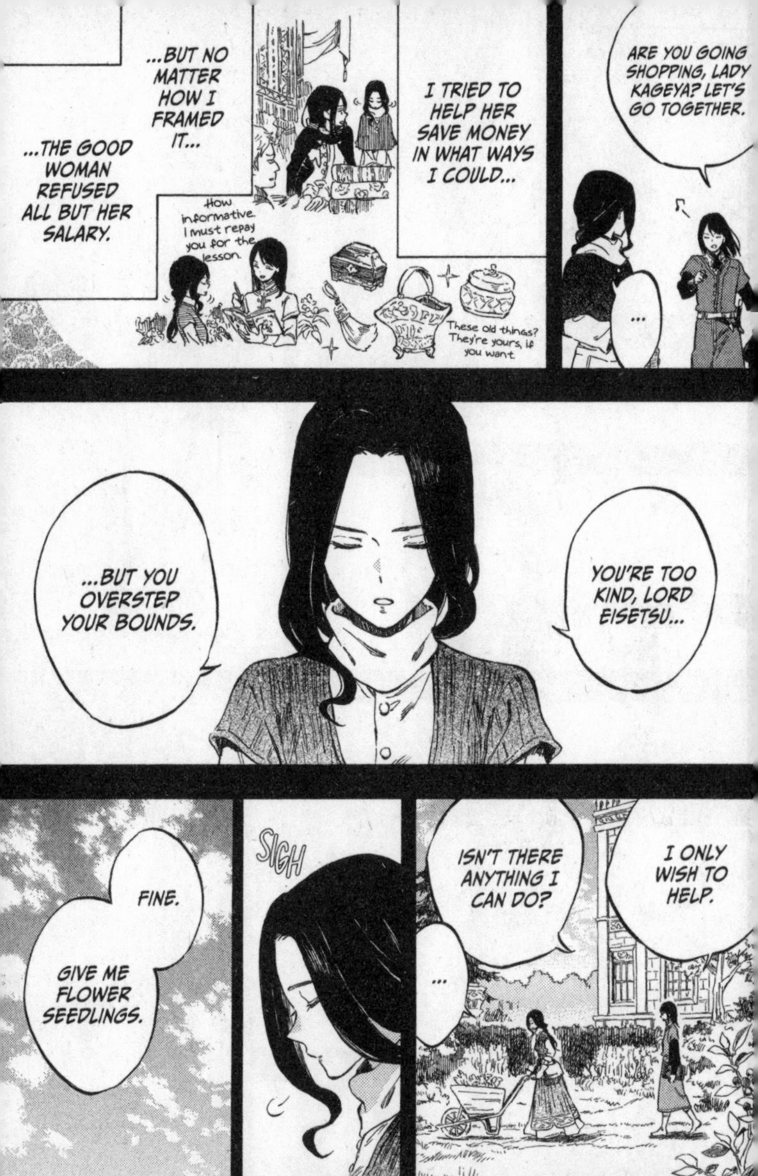
ARE YOU GOING SHOPPING, LADY KAGEYA? LET'S GO TOGETHER.
...
I TRIED TO HELP HER SAVE MONEY IN WHAT WAYS I COULD...
These old things? They're yours, if you want.
How informative. I must repay you for the lesson.
...BUT NO MATTER HOW I FRAMED IT...
...THE GOOD WOMAN REFUSED ALL BUT HER SALARY.
YOU'RE TOO KIND, LORD EISETSU...
...BUT YOU OVERSTEP YOUR BOUNDS.
I ONLY WISH TO HELP.
ISN'T THERE ANYTHING I CAN DO?
...
SIGH
FINE.
GIVE ME FLOWER SEEDLINGS.

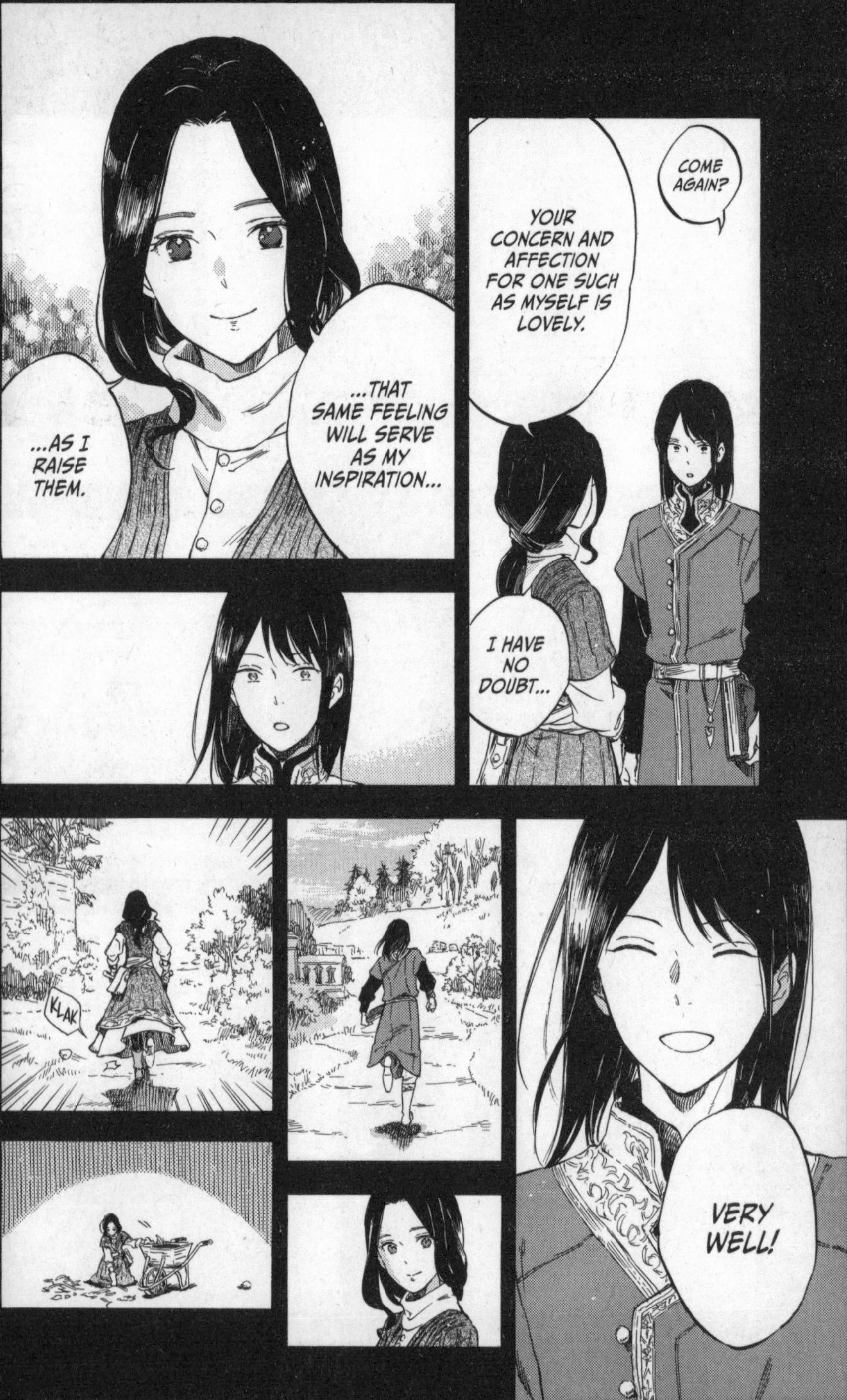
COME AGAIN?
YOUR CONCERN AND AFFECTION FOR ONE SUCH AS MYSELF IS LOVELY.
I HAVE NO DOUBT...
...THAT SAME FEELING WILL SERVE AS MY INSPIRATION...
...AS I RAISE THEM.
VERY WELL!
KLAK

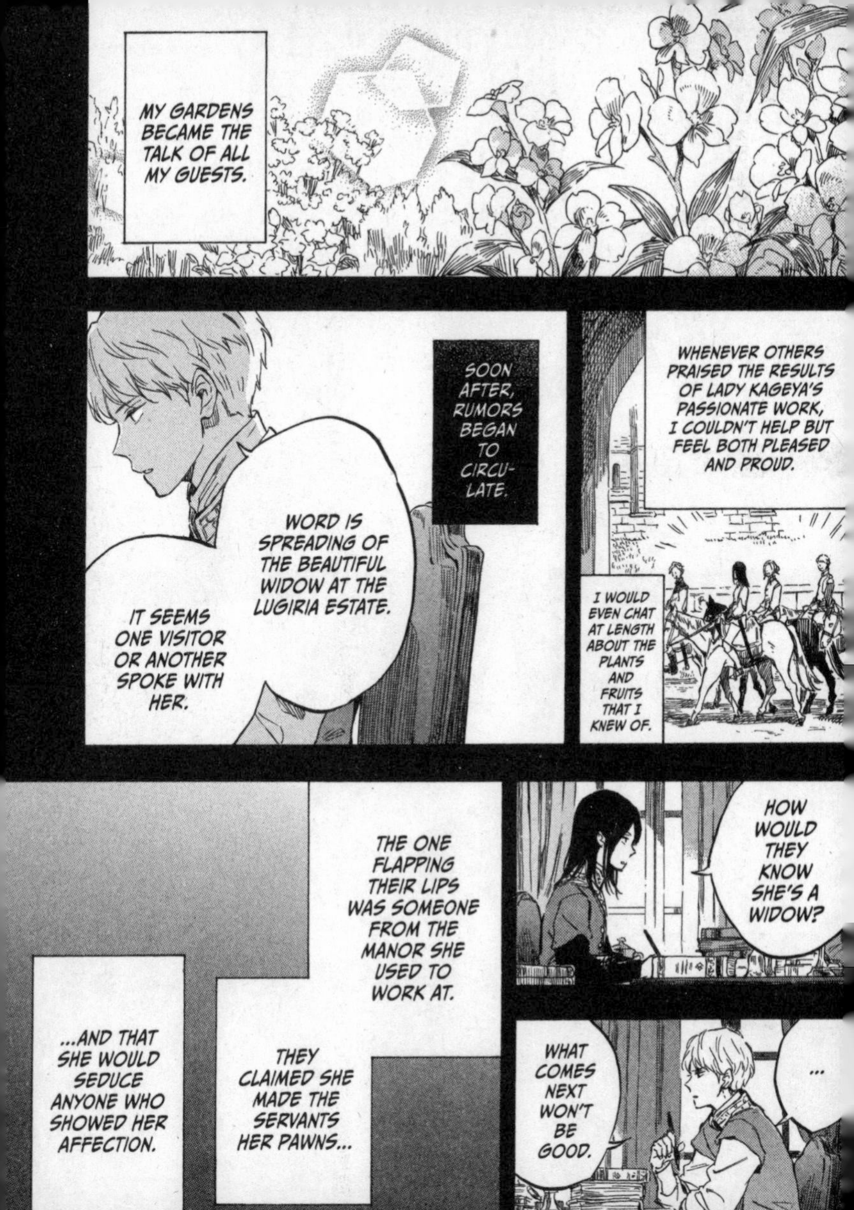
MY GARDENS BECAME THE TALK OF ALL MY GUESTS.
WHENEVER OTHERS PRAISED THE RESULTS OF LADY KAGEYA'S PASSIONATE WORK, I COULDN'T HELP BUT FEEL BOTH PLEASED AND PROUD.
I WOULD EVEN CHAT AT LENGTH ABOUT THE PLANTS AND FRUITS THAT I KNEW OF.
SOON AFTER, RUMORS BEGAN TO CIRCU-LATE.
WORD IS SPREADING OF THE BEAUTIFUL WIDOW AT THE LUGIRIA ESTATE.
IT SEEMS ONE VISITOR OR ANOTHER SPOKE WITH HER.
HOW WOULD THEY KNOW SHE'S A WIDOW?
...
WHAT COMES NEXT WON'T BE GOOD.
THE ONE FLAPPING THEIR LIPS WAS SOMEONE FROM THE MANOR SHE USED TO WORK AT.
THEY CLAIMED SHE MADE THE SERVANTS HER PAWNS...
...AND THAT SHE WOULD SEDUCE ANYONE WHO SHOWED HER AFFECTION.

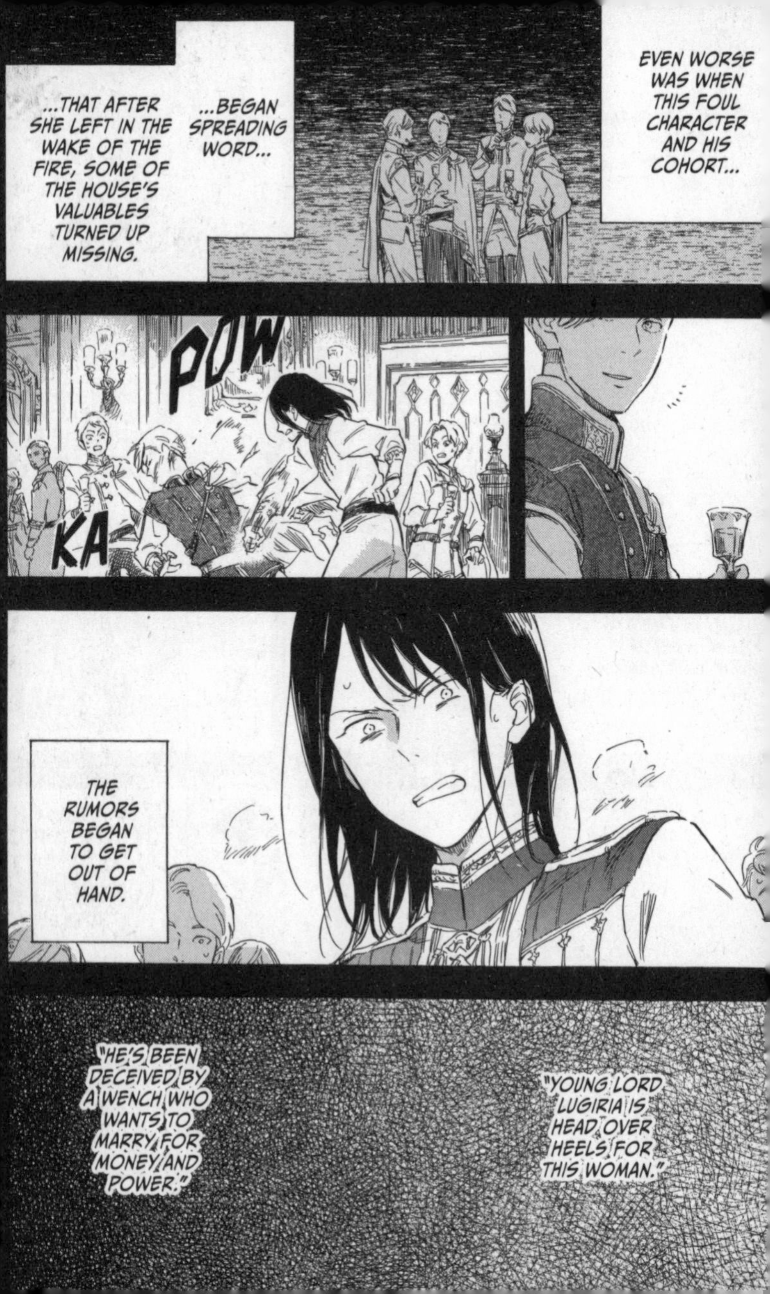
EVEN WORSE WAS WHEN THIS FOUL CHARACTER AND HIS COHORT...
...BEGAN SPREADING WORD...
...THAT AFTER SHE LEFT IN THE WAKE OF THE FIRE, SOME OF THE HOUSE'S VALUABLES TURNED UP MISSING.
...
POW
KA
THE RUMORS BEGAN TO GET OUT OF HAND.
"YOUNG LORD LUGIRIA IS HEAD OVER HEELS FOR THIS WOMAN."
"HE'S BEEN DECEIVED BY A WENCH WHO WANTS TO MARRY FOR MONEY AND POWER."

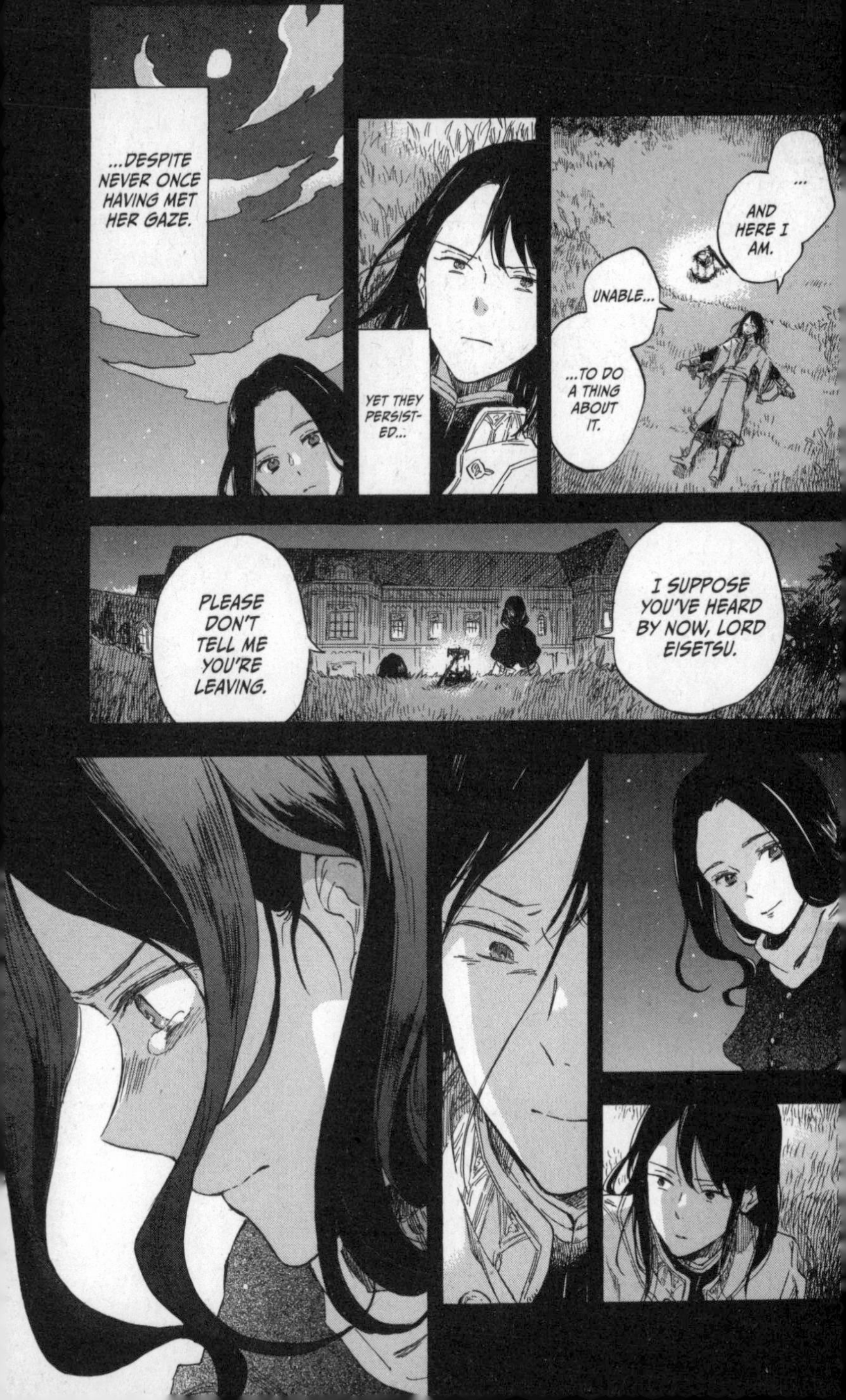
...
AND HERE I AM.
UNABLE...
...TO DO A THING ABOUT IT.
YET THEY PERSIST-ED...
...DESPITE NEVER ONCE HAVING MET HER GAZE.
I SUPPOSE YOU'VE HEARD BY NOW, LORD EISETSU.
PLEASE DON'T TELL ME YOU'RE LEAVING.

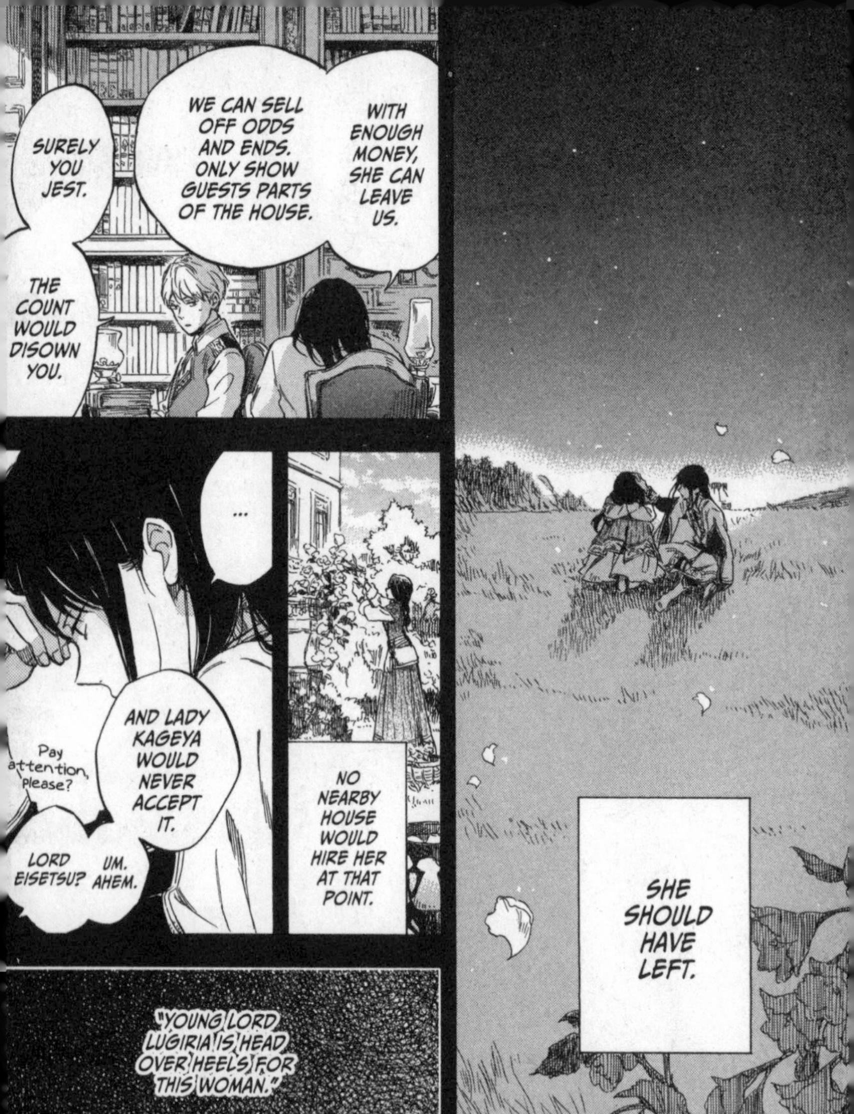
SHE SHOULD HAVE LEFT.
WITH ENOUGH MONEY, SHE CAN LEAVE US.
WE CAN SELL OFF ODDS AND ENDS. ONLY SHOW GUESTS PARTS OF THE HOUSE.
SURELY YOU JEST.
THE COUNT WOULD DISOWN YOU.
NO NEARBY HOUSE WOULD HIRE HER AT THAT POINT.
...
AND LADY KAGEYA WOULD NEVER ACCEPT IT.
UM. AHEM.
Pay attention, please?
LORD EISETSU?
"YOUNG LORD LUGIRIA IS HEAD OVER HEELS FOR THIS WOMAN."

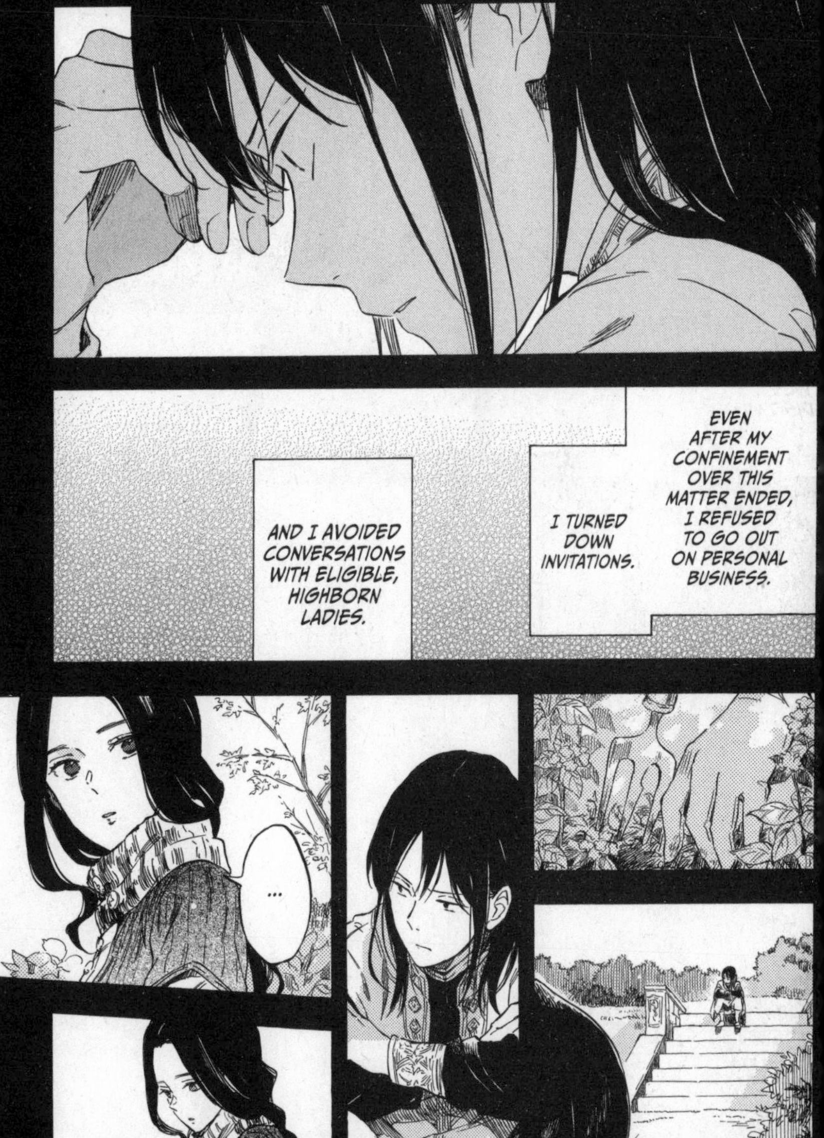
EVEN AFTER MY CONFINEMENT OVER THIS MATTER ENDED, I REFUSED TO GO OUT ON PERSONAL BUSINESS.
I TURNED DOWN INVITATIONS.
AND I AVOIDED CONVERSATIONS WITH ELIGIBLE, HIGHBORN LADIES.
...

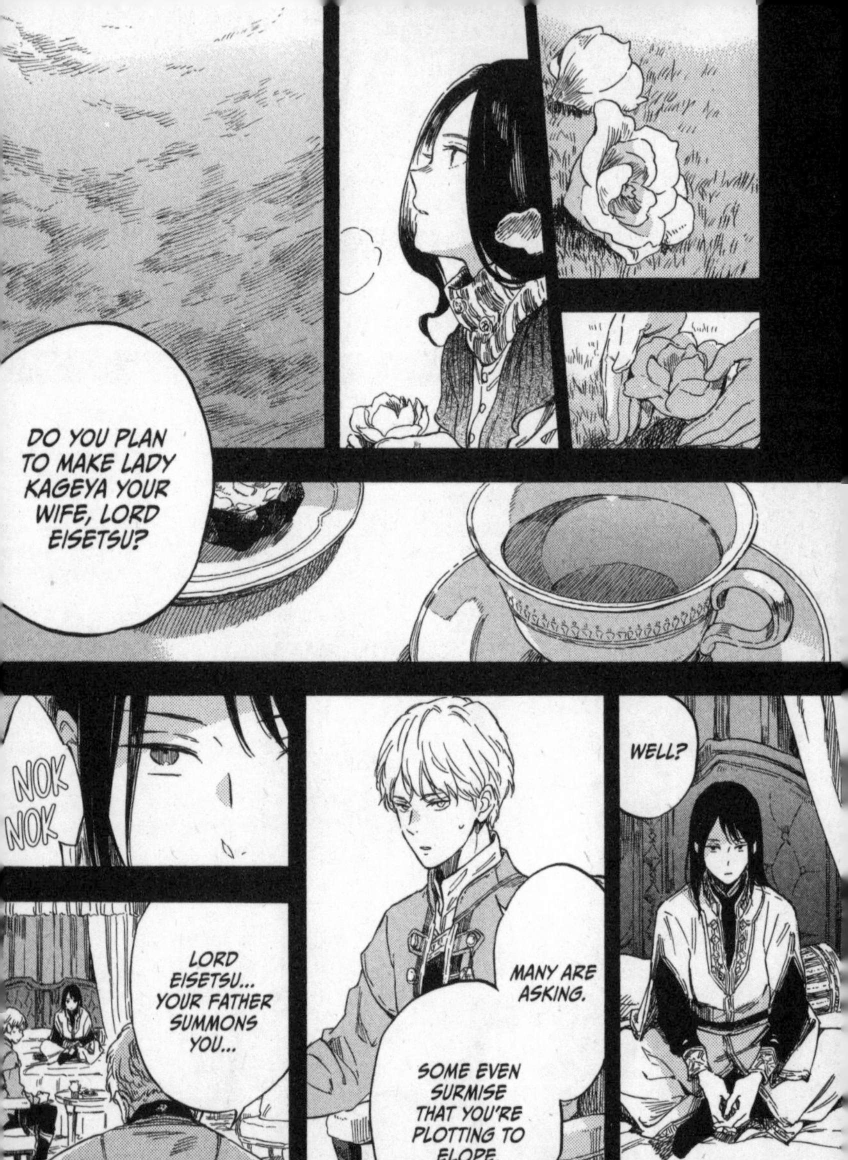
DO YOU PLAN TO MAKE LADY KAGEYA YOUR WIFE, LORD EISETSU?
WELL?
MANY ARE ASKING.
SOME EVEN SURMISE THAT YOU'RE PLOTTING TO ELOPE.
NOK NOK
LORD EISETSU... YOUR FATHER SUMMONS YOU...

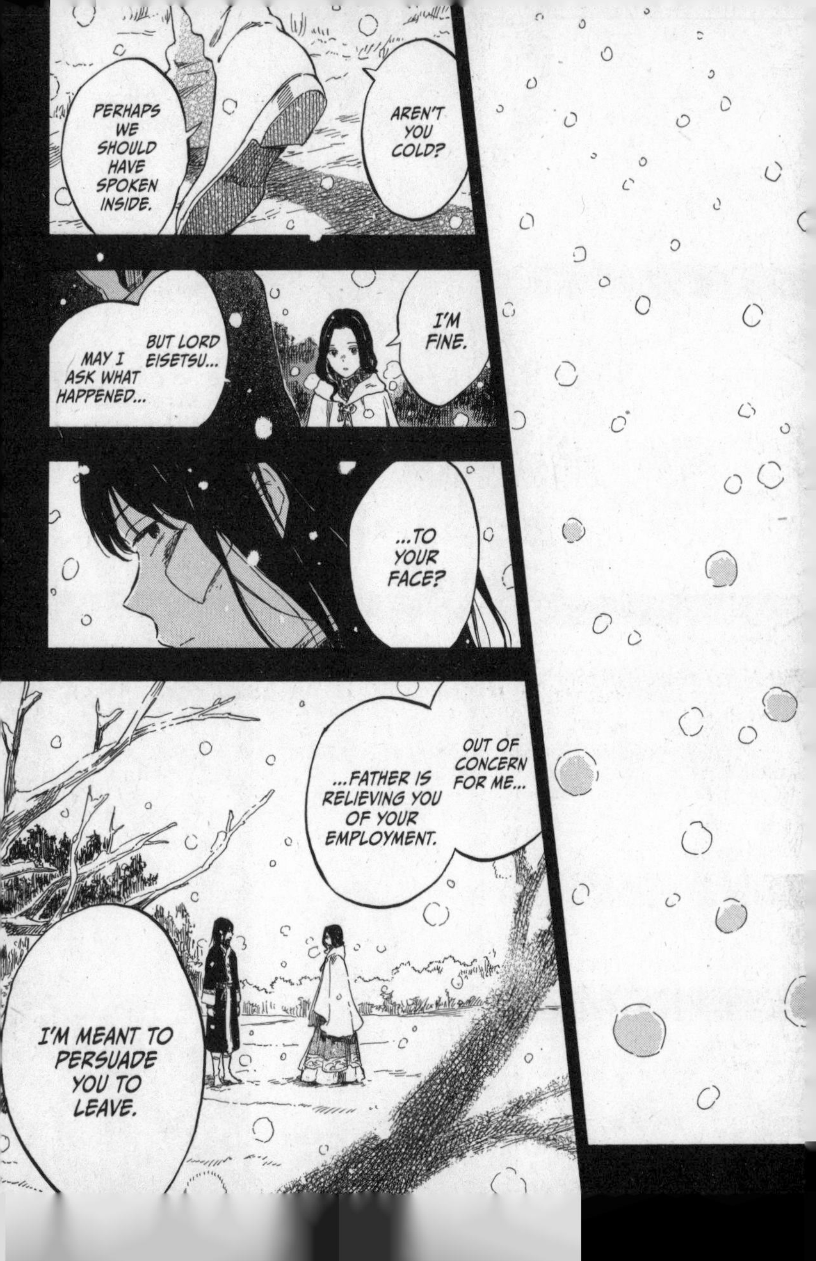
AREN'T YOU COLD?
PERHAPS WE SHOULD HAVE SPOKEN INSIDE.
I'M FINE.
BUT LORD EISETSU...
MAY I ASK WHAT HAPPENED...
...TO YOUR FACE?
OUT OF CONCERN FOR ME...
...FATHER IS RELIEVING YOU OF YOUR EMPLOYMENT.
I'M MEANT TO PERSUADE YOU TO LEAVE.

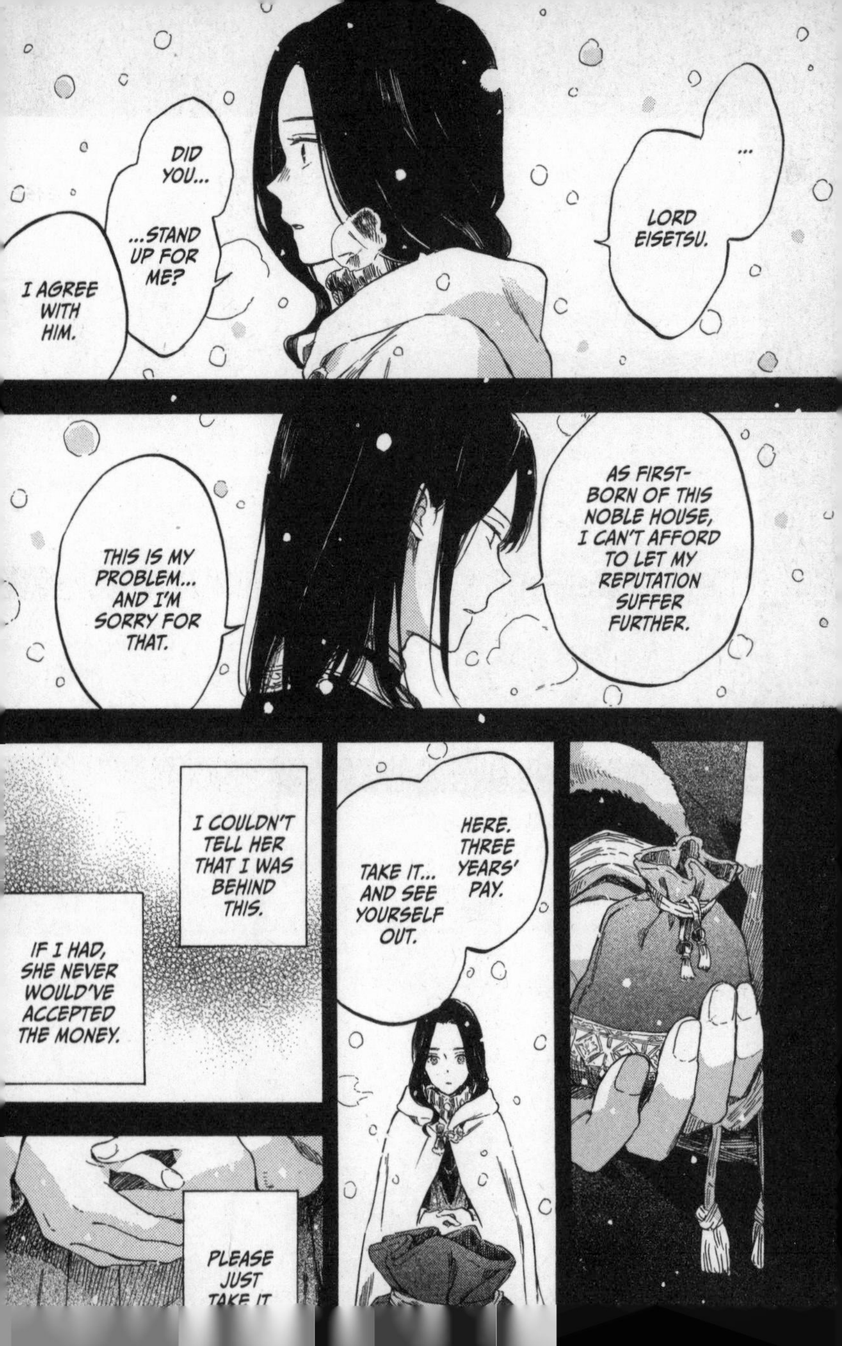
...
LORD EISETSU.
DID YOU...
...STAND UP FOR ME?
I AGREE WITH HIM.
AS FIRST-BORN OF THIS NOBLE HOUSE, I CAN'T AFFORD TO LET MY REPUTATION SUFFER FURTHER.
THIS IS MY PROBLEM... AND I'M SORRY FOR THAT.
HERE. THREE YEARS' PAY.
TAKE IT... AND SEE YOURSELF OUT.
I COULDN'T TELL HER THAT I WAS BEHIND THIS.
IF I HAD, SHE NEVER WOULD'VE ACCEPTED THE MONEY.
PLEASE JUST TAKE IT

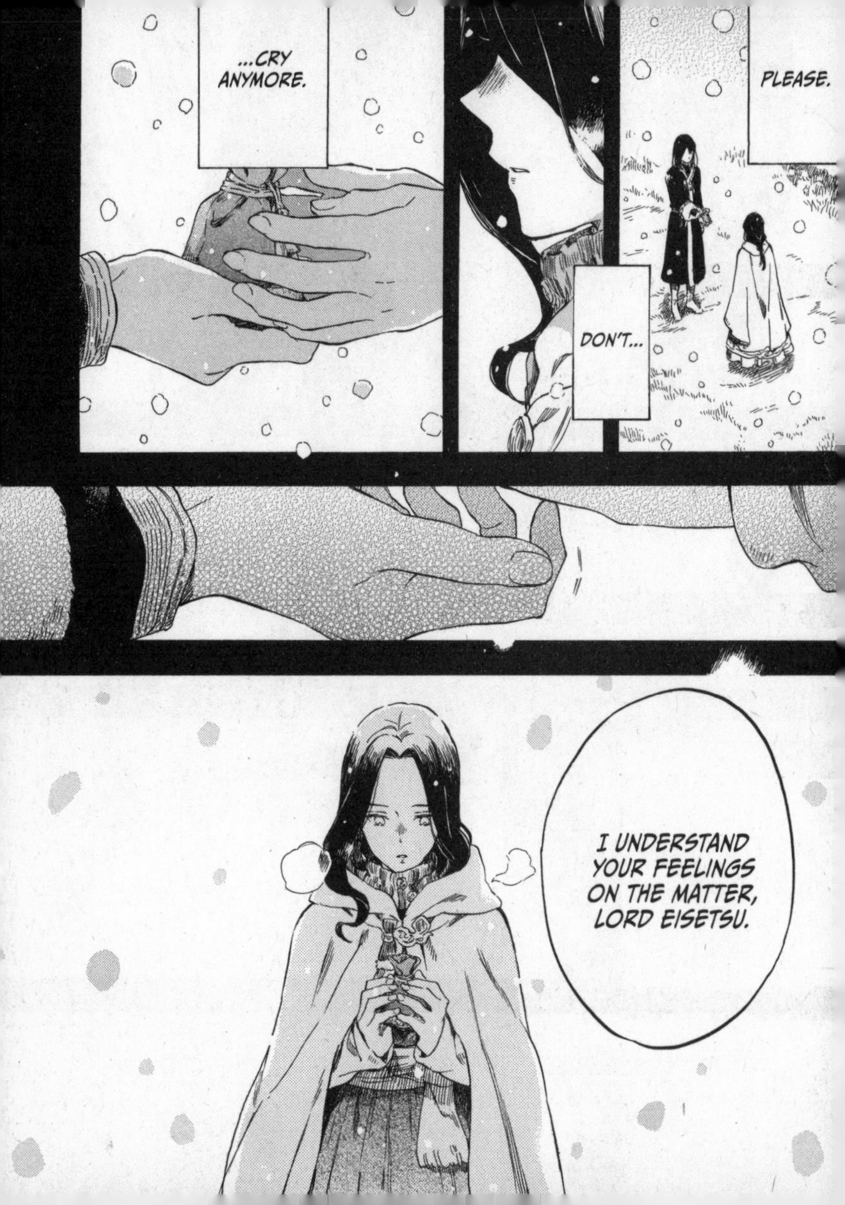
PLEASE.
DON'T...
...CRY ANYMORE.
I UNDERSTAND YOUR FEELINGS ON THE MATTER, LORD EISETSU.

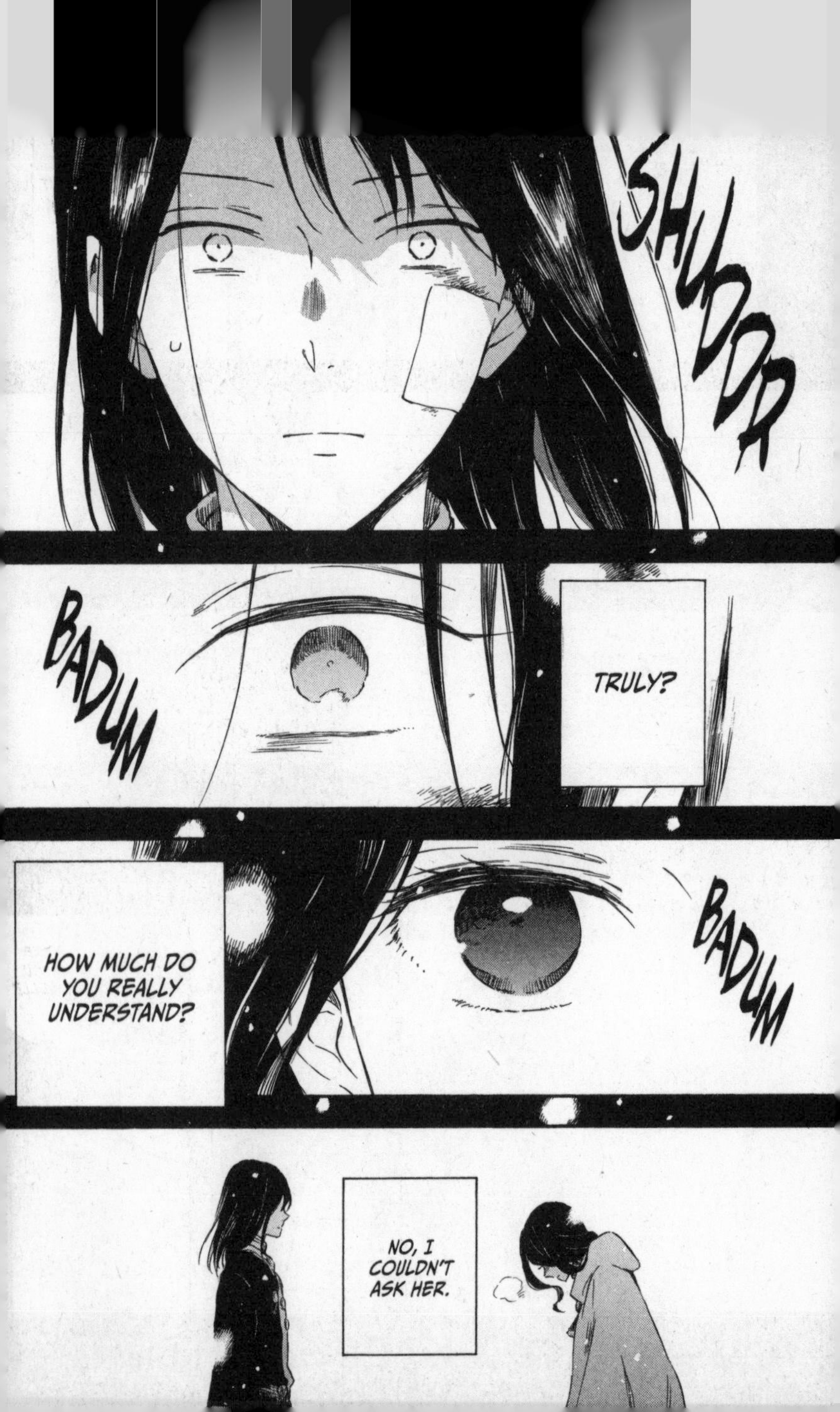
SHUDDR
TRULY?
BADUM
BADUM
HOW MUCH DO YOU REALLY UNDERSTAND?
NO, I COULDN'T ASK HER.

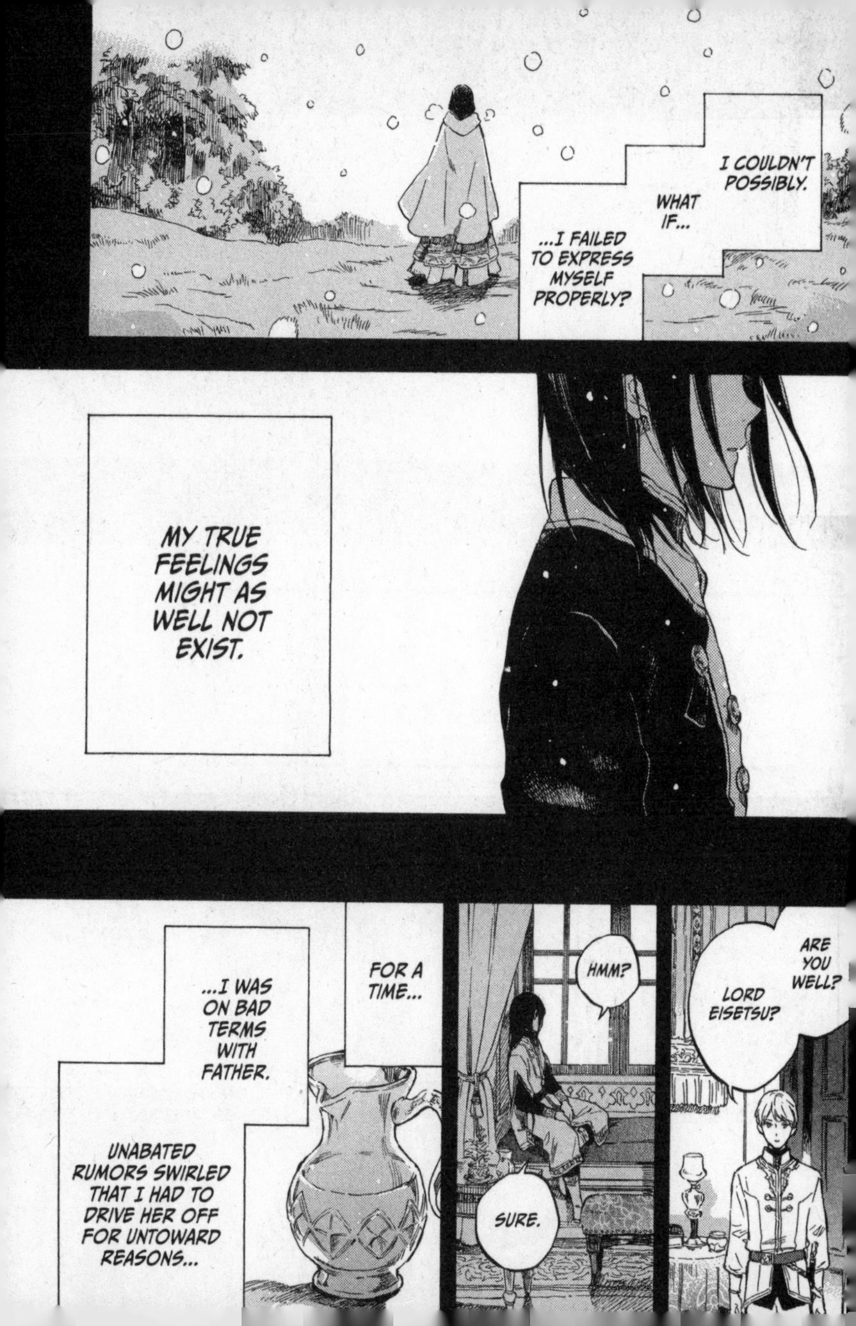
I COULDN'T POSSIBLY.
WHAT IF...
...I FAILED TO EXPRESS MYSELF PROPERLY?
MY TRUE FEELINGS MIGHT AS WELL NOT EXIST.
ARE YOU WELL?
LORD EISETSU?
HMM?
SURE.
FOR A TIME...
...I WAS ON BAD TERMS WITH FATHER.
UNABATED RUMORS SWIRLED THAT I HAD TO DRIVE HER OFF FOR UNTOWARD REASONS...

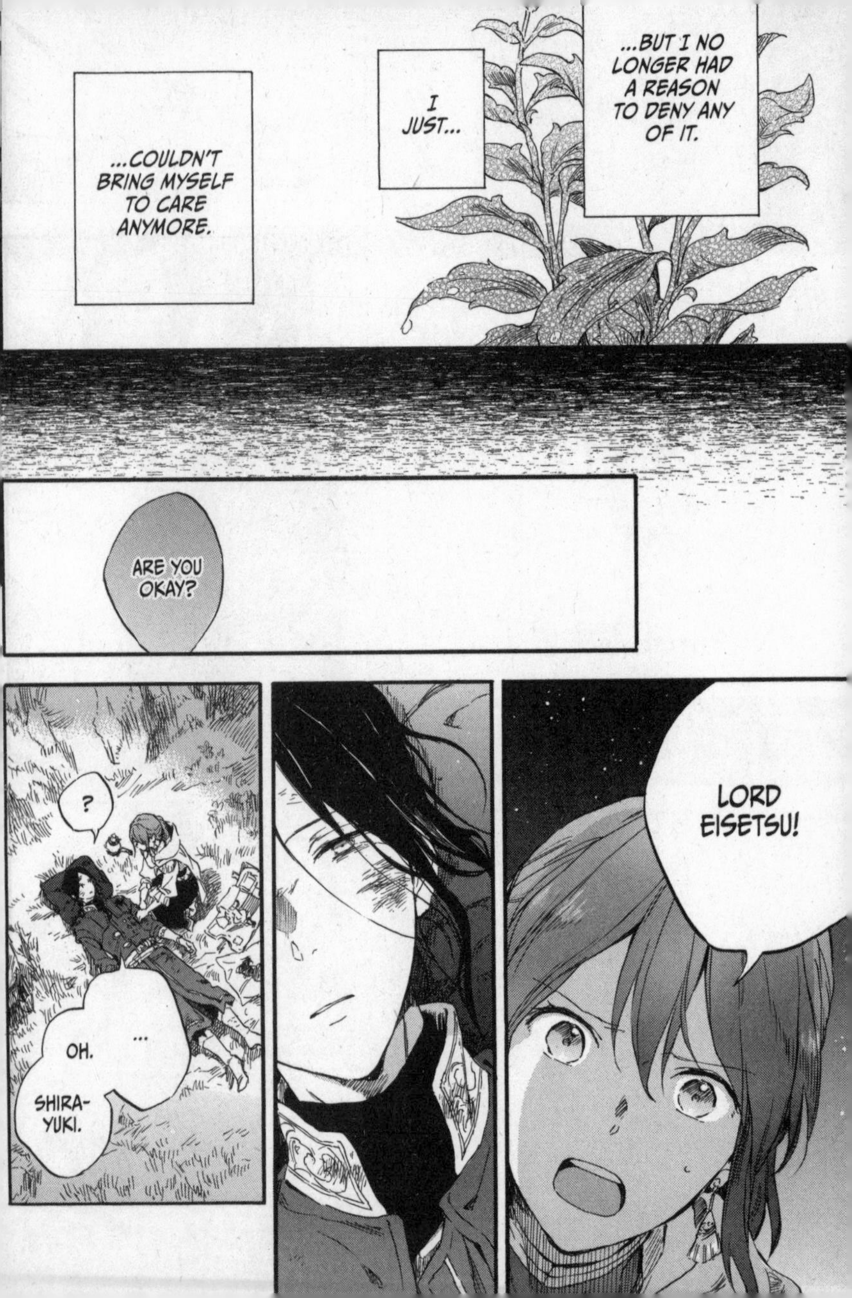
...BUT I NO LONGER HAD A REASON TO DENY ANY OF IT.
I JUST...
...COULDN'T BRING MYSELF TO CARE ANYMORE.
ARE YOU OKAY?
LORD EISETSU!
?
...
OH.
SHIRA-YUKI.

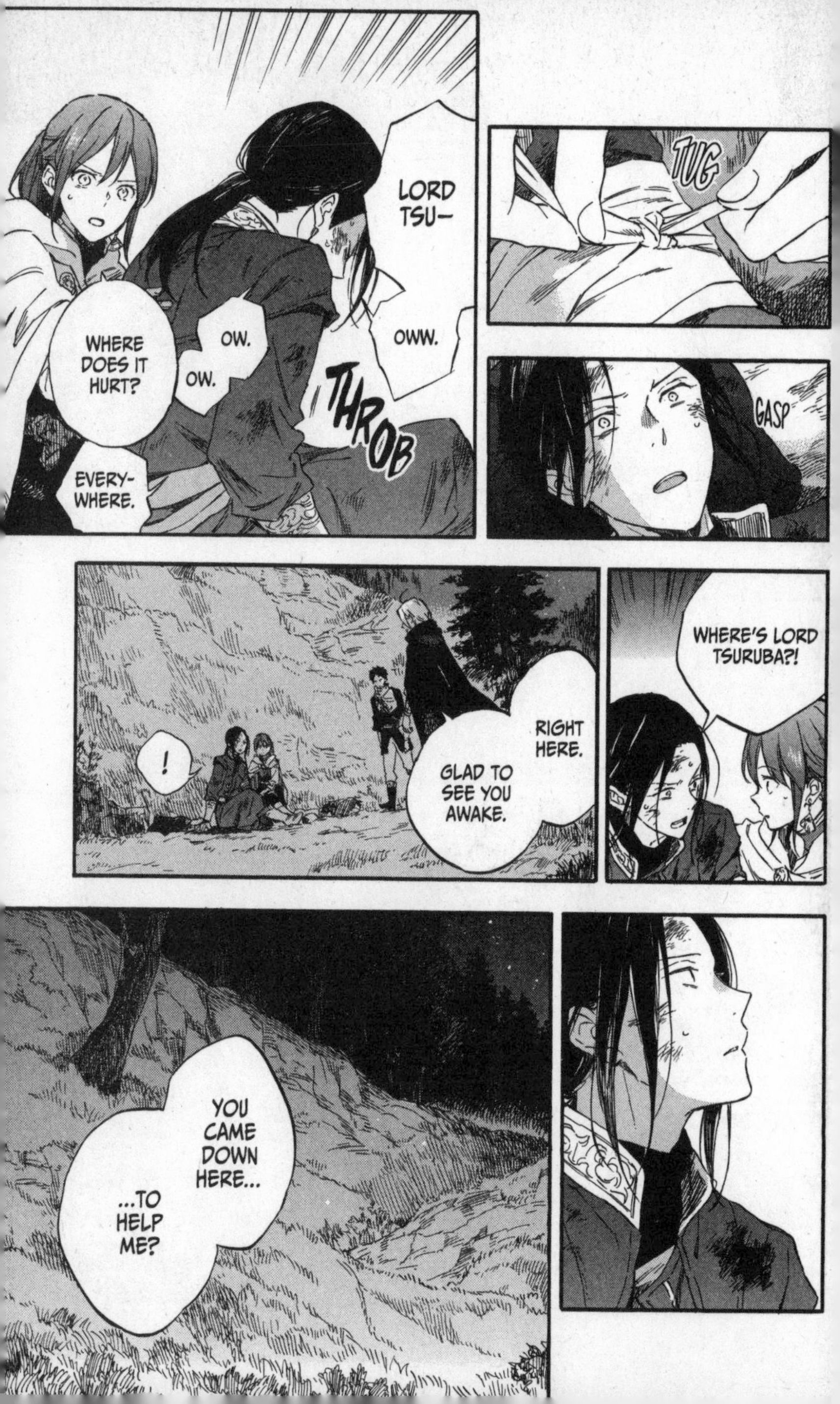
TUG
GASP
LORD TSU–
OWW.
THROB
OW.
OW.
WHERE DOES IT HURT?
EVERY-WHERE.
WHERE'S LORD TSURUBA?!
RIGHT HERE.
GLAD TO SEE YOU AWAKE.
!
YOU CAME DOWN HERE...
...TO HELP ME?

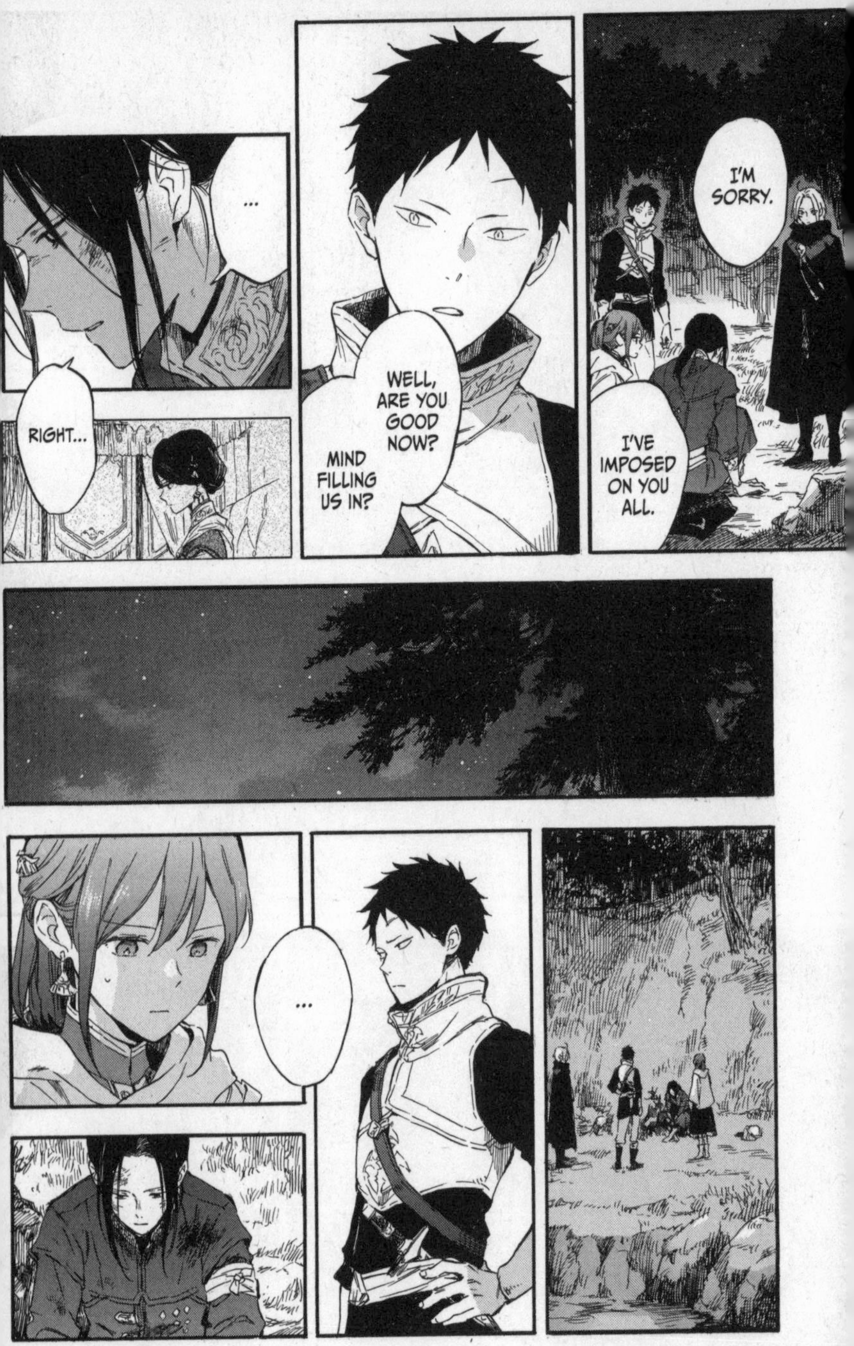
I'M SORRY.
I'VE IMPOSED ON YOU ALL.
WELL, ARE YOU GOOD NOW?
MIND FILLING US IN?
...
RIGHT...
...

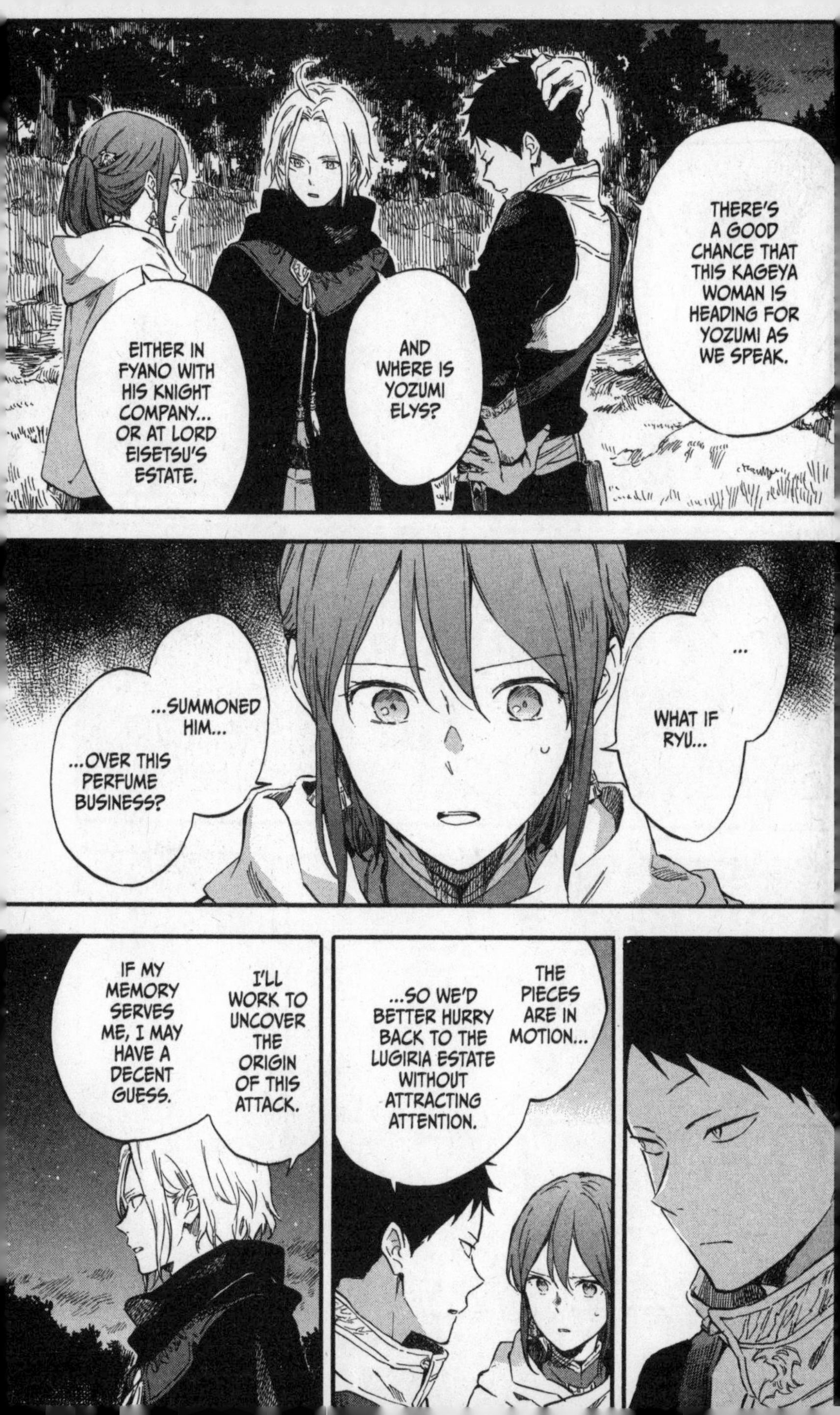
THERE'S A GOOD CHANCE THAT THIS KAGEYA WOMAN IS HEADING FOR YOZUMI AS WE SPEAK.
AND WHERE IS YOZUMI ELYS?
EITHER IN FYANO WITH HIS KNIGHT COMPANY... OR AT LORD EISETSU'S ESTATE.
...
WHAT IF RYU...
...SUMMONED HIM...
...OVER THIS PERFUME BUSINESS?
THE PIECES ARE IN MOTION...
...SO WE'D BETTER HURRY BACK TO THE LUGIRIA ESTATE WITHOUT ATTRACTING ATTENTION.
I'LL WORK TO UNCOVER THE ORIGIN OF THIS ATTACK.
IF MY MEMORY SERVES ME, I MAY HAVE A DECENT GUESS.

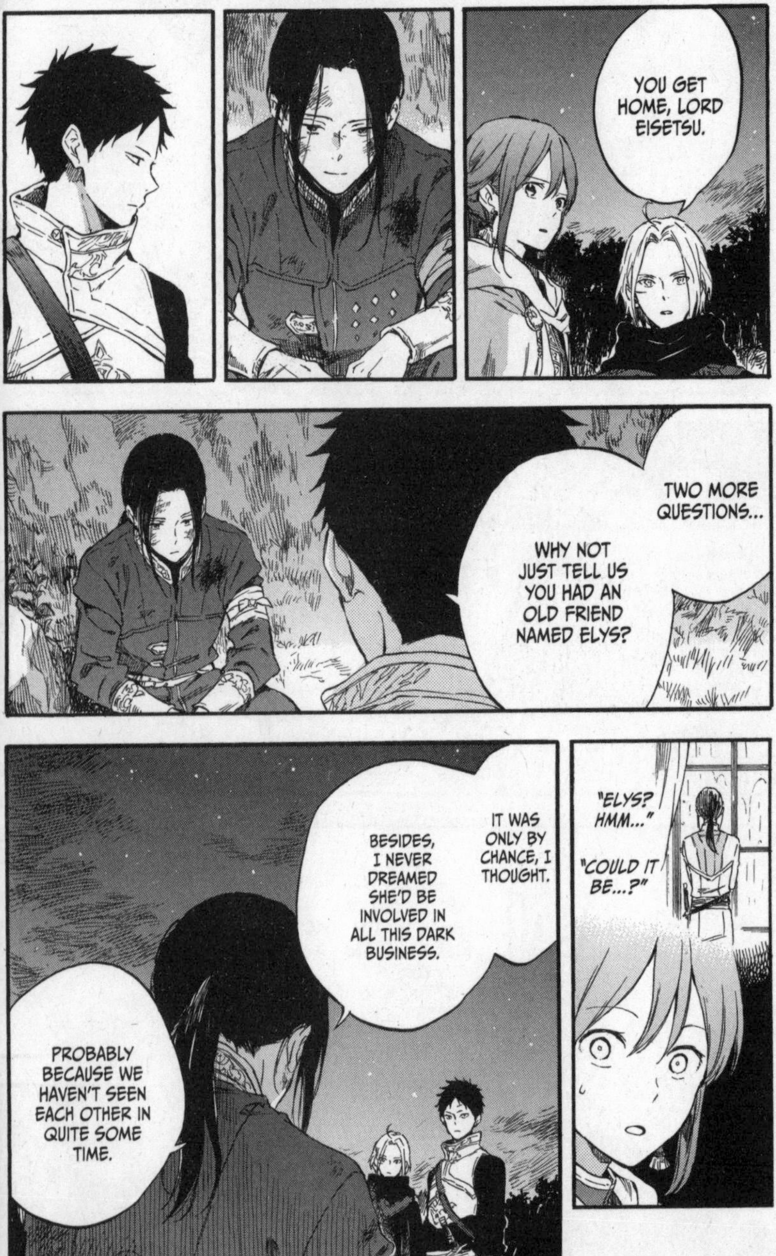
YOU GET HOME, LORD EISETSU.
TWO MORE QUESTIONS...
WHY NOT JUST TELL US YOU HAD AN OLD FRIEND NAMED ELYS?
"ELYS? HMM..."
"COULD IT BE...?"
IT WAS ONLY BY CHANCE, I THOUGHT.
BESIDES, I NEVER DREAMED SHE'D BE INVOLVED IN ALL THIS DARK BUSINESS.
PROBABLY BECAUSE WE HAVEN'T SEEN EACH OTHER IN QUITE SOME TIME.

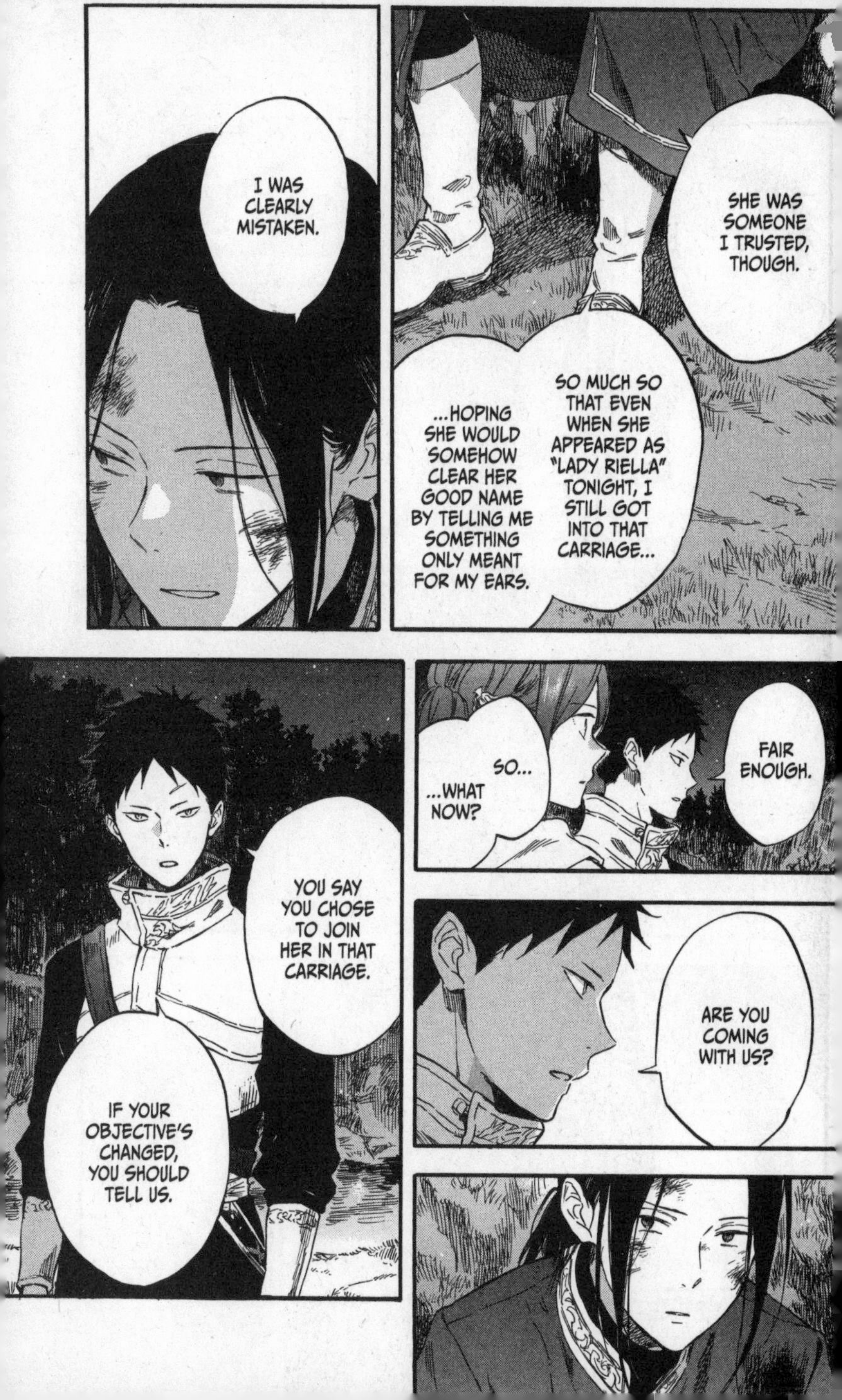
SHE WAS SOMEONE I TRUSTED, THOUGH.
SO MUCH SO THAT EVEN WHEN SHE APPEARED AS "LADY RIELLA" TONIGHT, I STILL GOT INTO THAT CARRIAGE...
...HOPING SHE WOULD SOMEHOW CLEAR HER GOOD NAME BY TELLING ME SOMETHING ONLY MEANT FOR MY EARS.
I WAS CLEARLY MISTAKEN.
FAIR ENOUGH.
SO...
...WHAT NOW?
ARE YOU COMING WITH US?
YOU SAY YOU CHOSE TO JOIN HER IN THAT CARRIAGE.
IF YOUR OBJECTIVE'S CHANGED, YOU SHOULD TELL US.

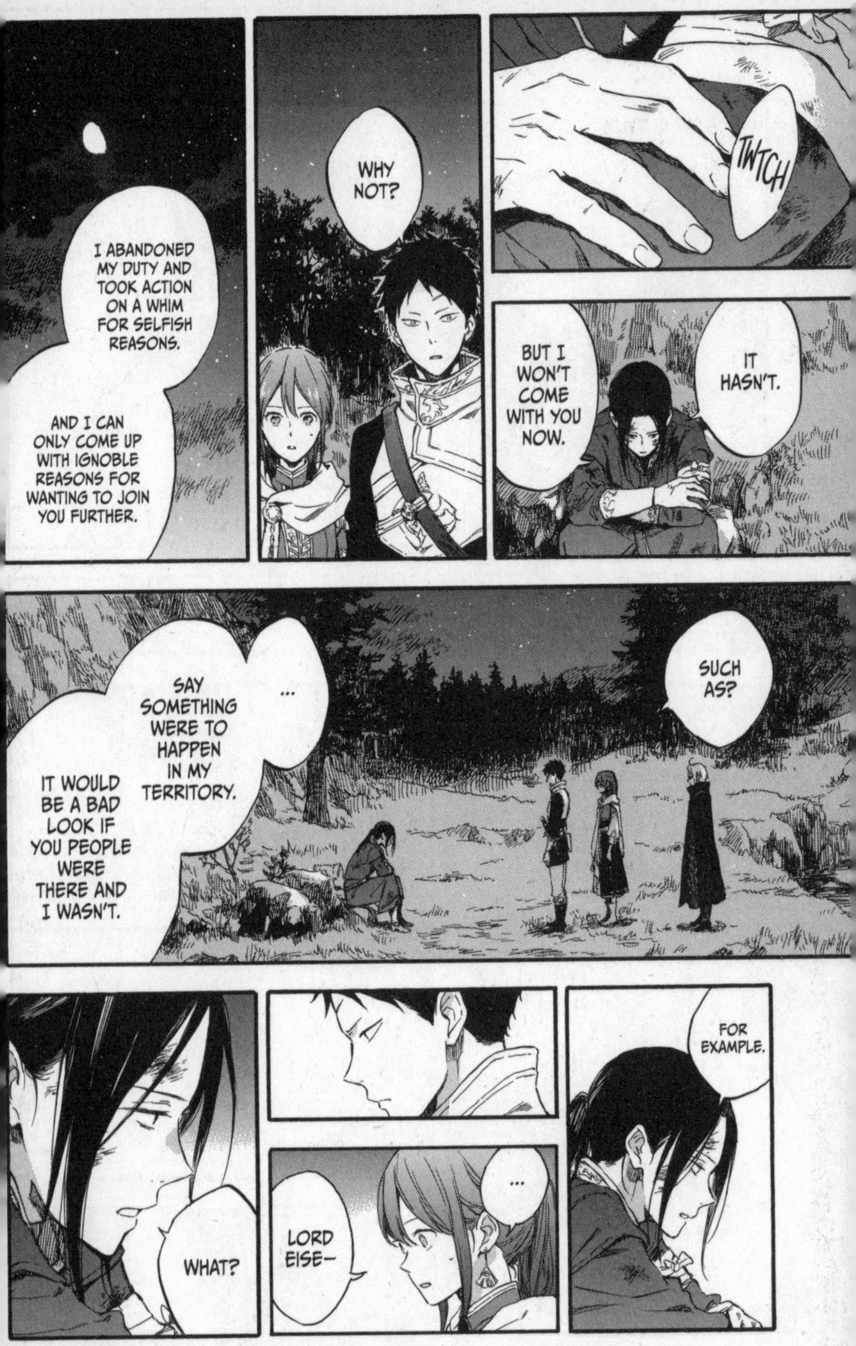
TWTCH
IT HASN'T.
BUT I WON'T COME WITH YOU NOW.
WHY NOT?
I ABANDONED MY DUTY AND TOOK ACTION ON A WHIM FOR SELFISH REASONS.
AND I CAN ONLY COME UP WITH IGNOBLE REASONS FOR WANTING TO JOIN YOU FURTHER.
SUCH AS?
...
SAY SOMETHING WERE TO HAPPEN IN MY TERRITORY.
IT WOULD BE A BAD LOOK IF YOU PEOPLE WERE THERE AND I WASN'T.
FOR EXAMPLE.
...
LORD EISE—
WHAT?

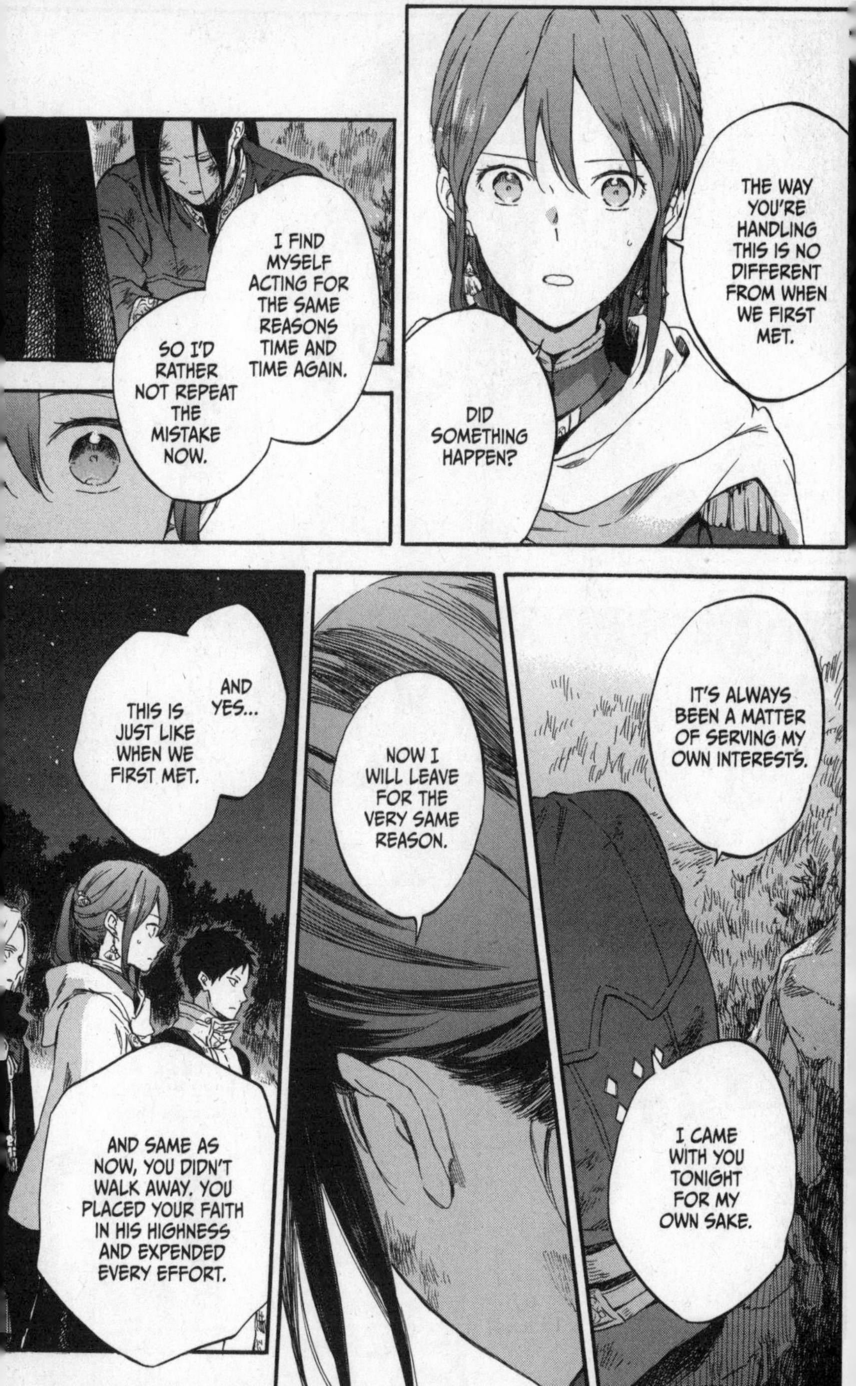
THE WAY YOU'RE HANDLING THIS IS NO DIFFERENT FROM WHEN WE FIRST MET.
DID SOMETHING HAPPEN?
I FIND MYSELF ACTING FOR THE SAME REASONS TIME AND TIME AGAIN.
SO I'D RATHER NOT REPEAT THE MISTAKE NOW.
IT'S ALWAYS BEEN A MATTER OF SERVING MY OWN INTERESTS.
I CAME WITH YOU TONIGHT FOR MY OWN SAKE.
NOW I WILL LEAVE FOR THE VERY SAME REASON.
AND YES...
THIS IS JUST LIKE WHEN WE FIRST MET.
AND SAME AS NOW, YOU DIDN'T WALK AWAY. YOU PLACED YOUR FAITH IN HIS HIGHNESS AND EXPENDED EVERY EFFORT.

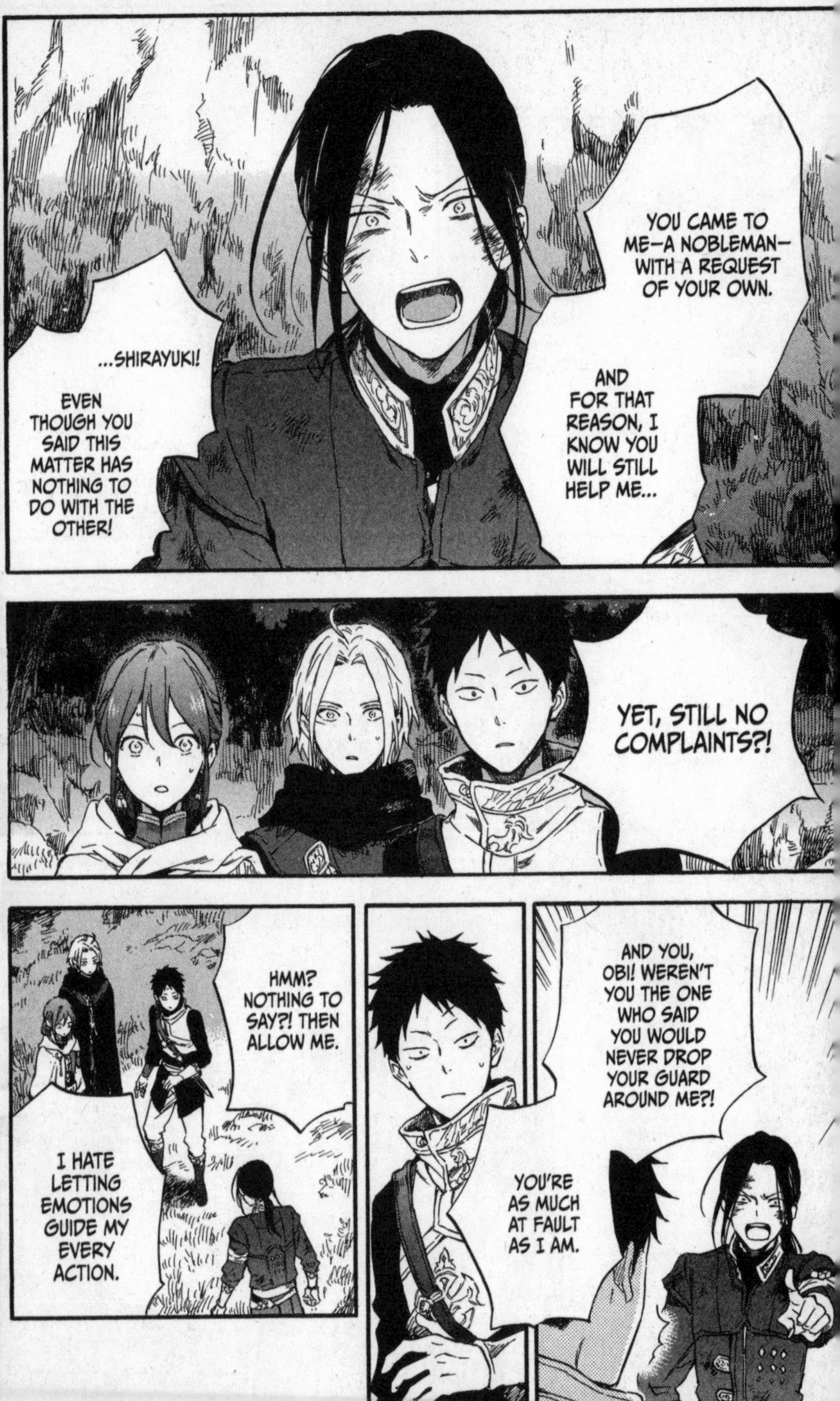
YOU CAME TO ME—A NOBLEMAN—WITH A REQUEST OF YOUR OWN.
AND FOR THAT REASON, I KNOW YOU WILL STILL HELP ME...
...SHIRAYUKI!
EVEN THOUGH YOU SAID THIS MATTER HAS NOTHING TO DO WITH THE OTHER!
YET, STILL NO COMPLAINTS?!
AND YOU, OBI! WEREN'T YOU THE ONE WHO SAID YOU WOULD NEVER DROP YOUR GUARD AROUND ME?!
YOU'RE AS MUCH AT FAULT AS I AM.
HMM? NOTHING TO SAY?! THEN ALLOW ME.
I HATE LETTING EMOTIONS GUIDE MY EVERY ACTION.

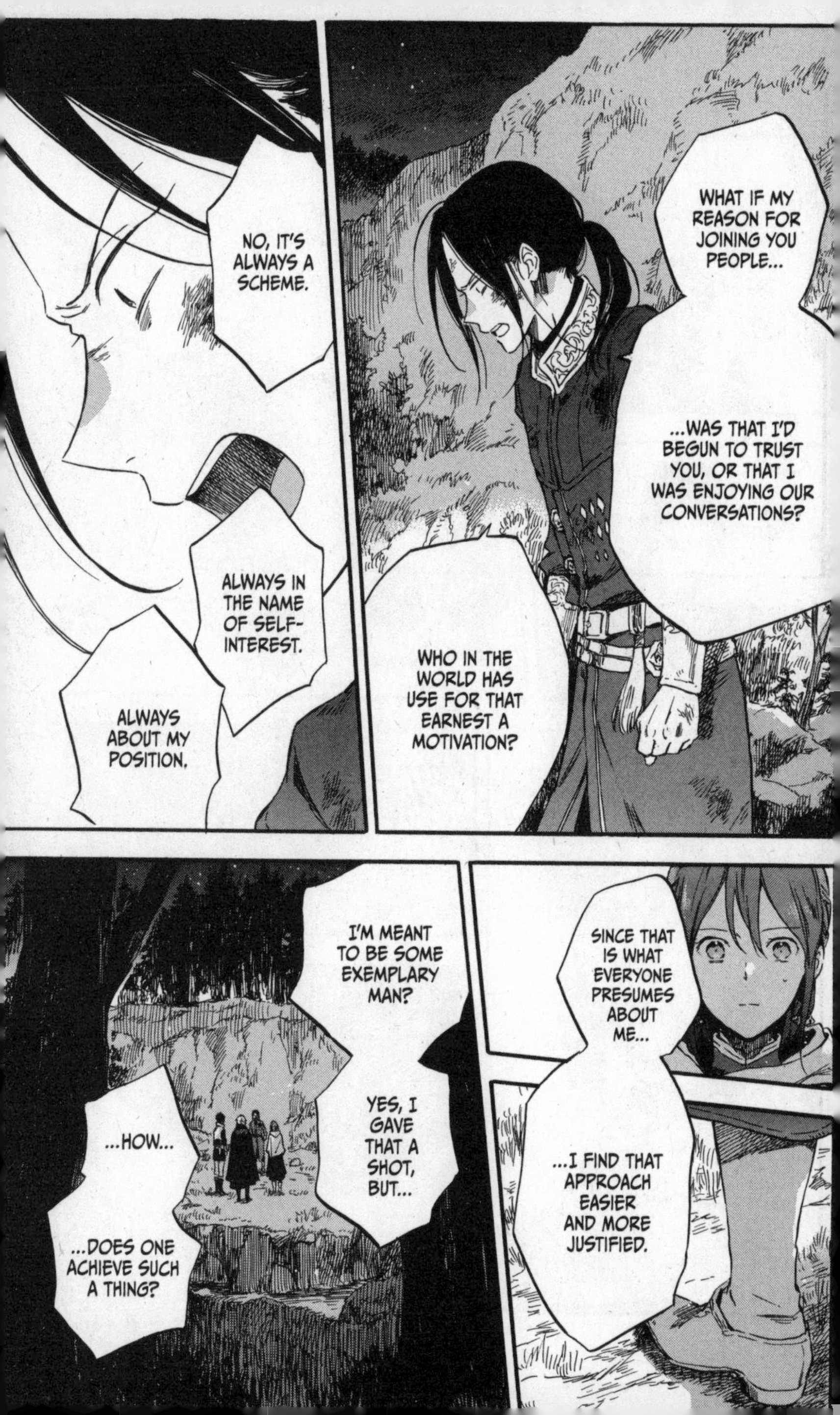
WHAT IF MY REASON FOR JOINING YOU PEOPLE...
...WAS THAT I'D BEGUN TO TRUST YOU, OR THAT I WAS ENJOYING OUR CONVERSATIONS?
WHO IN THE WORLD HAS USE FOR THAT EARNEST A MOTIVATION?
NO, IT'S ALWAYS A SCHEME.
ALWAYS IN THE NAME OF SELF-INTEREST.
ALWAYS ABOUT MY POSITION.
SINCE THAT IS WHAT EVERYONE PRESUMES ABOUT ME...
...I FIND THAT APPROACH EASIER AND MORE JUSTIFIED.
I'M MEANT TO BE SOME EXEMPLARY MAN?
YES, I GAVE THAT A SHOT, BUT...
...HOW...
...DOES ONE ACHIEVE SUCH A THING?

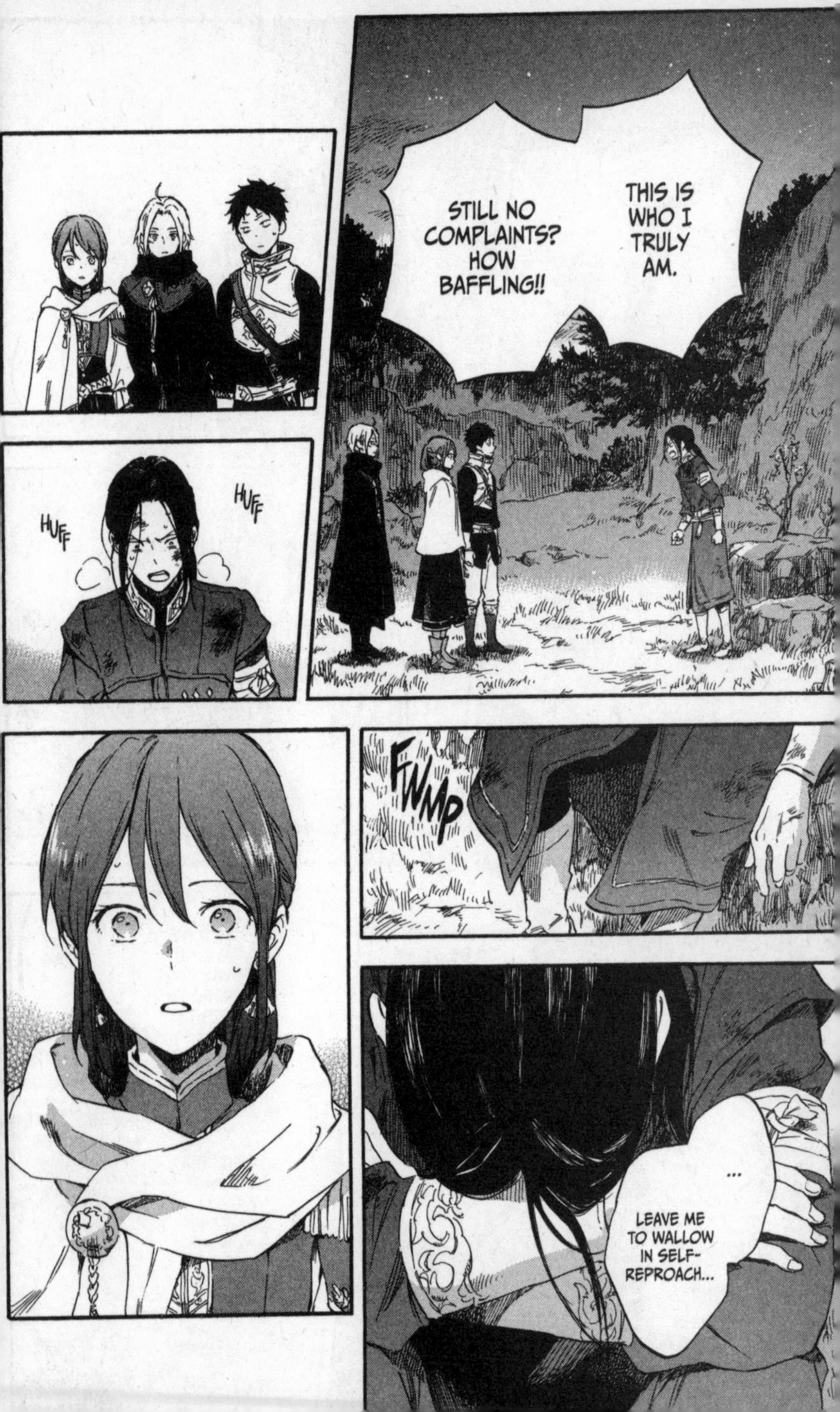
THIS IS WHO I TRULY AM.
STILL NO COMPLAINTS? HOW BAFFLING!!
HUFF
HUFF
FWMP
...
LEAVE ME TO WALLOW IN SELF-REPROACH...

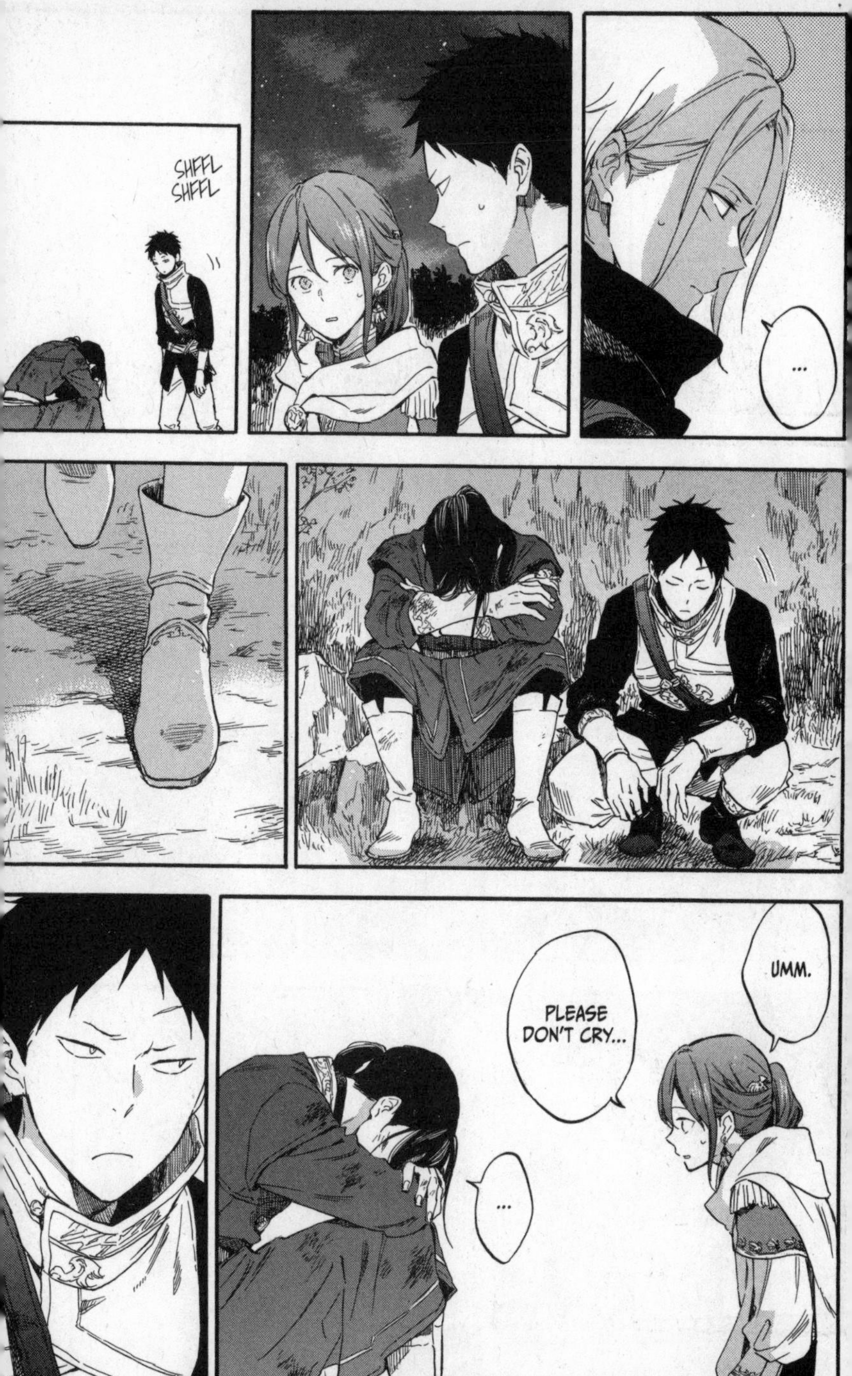
...
SHFFL SHFFL
UMM.
PLEASE DON'T CRY...
...

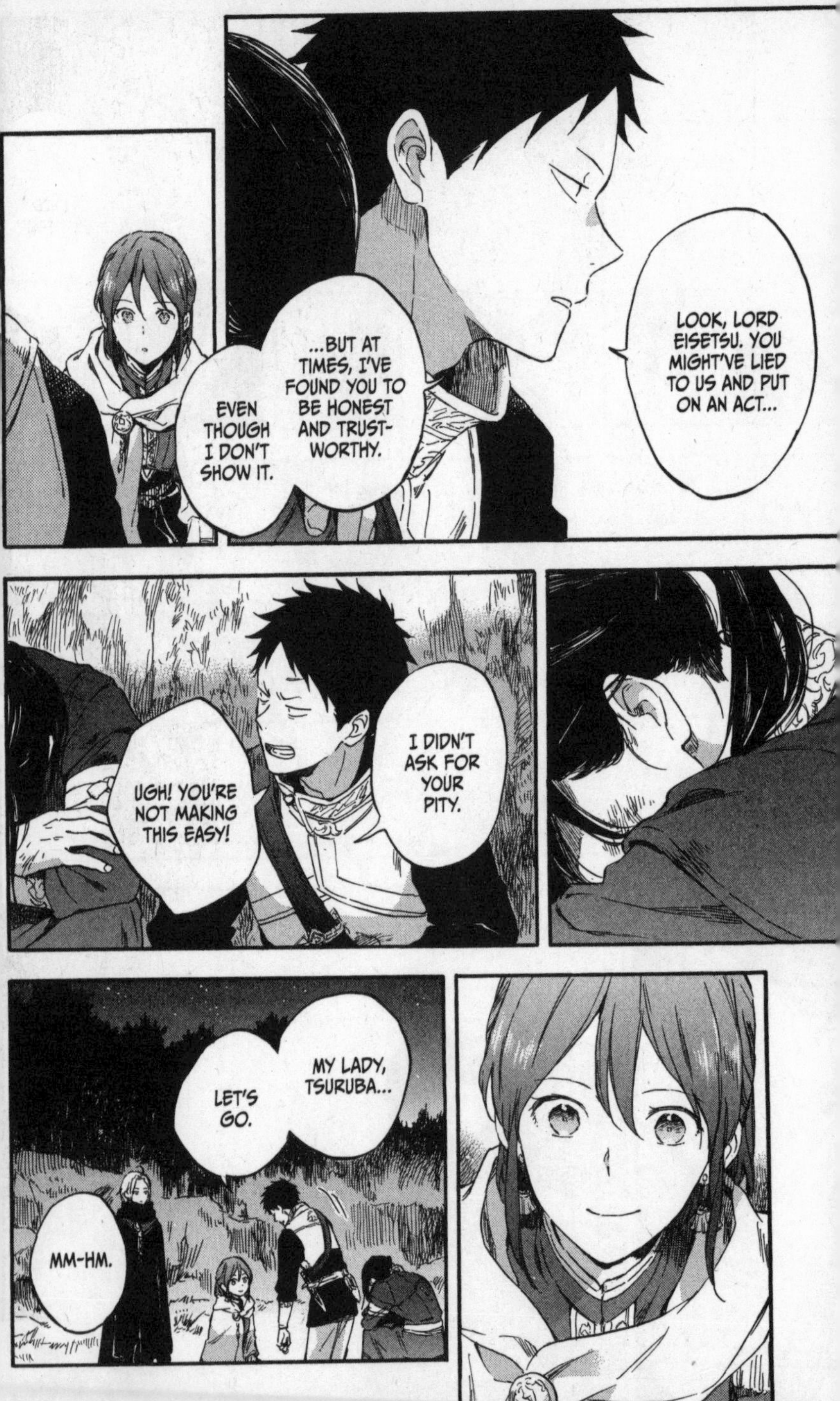
LOOK, LORD EISETSU. YOU MIGHT'VE LIED TO US AND PUT ON AN ACT...
...BUT AT TIMES, I'VE FOUND YOU TO BE HONEST AND TRUST-WORTHY.
EVEN THOUGH I DON'T SHOW IT.
I DIDN'T ASK FOR YOUR PITY.
UGH! YOU'RE NOT MAKING THIS EASY!
MY LADY, TSURUBA...
LET'S GO.
MM-HM.

LORD EISETSU?

IF YOU'RE REALLY NOT COMING WITH US, THEN...

"HERE. SLAP MY HAND."

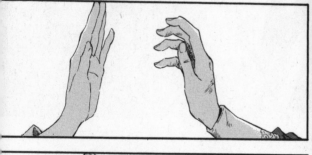

...

YOU NEED THEM.

TWTCH

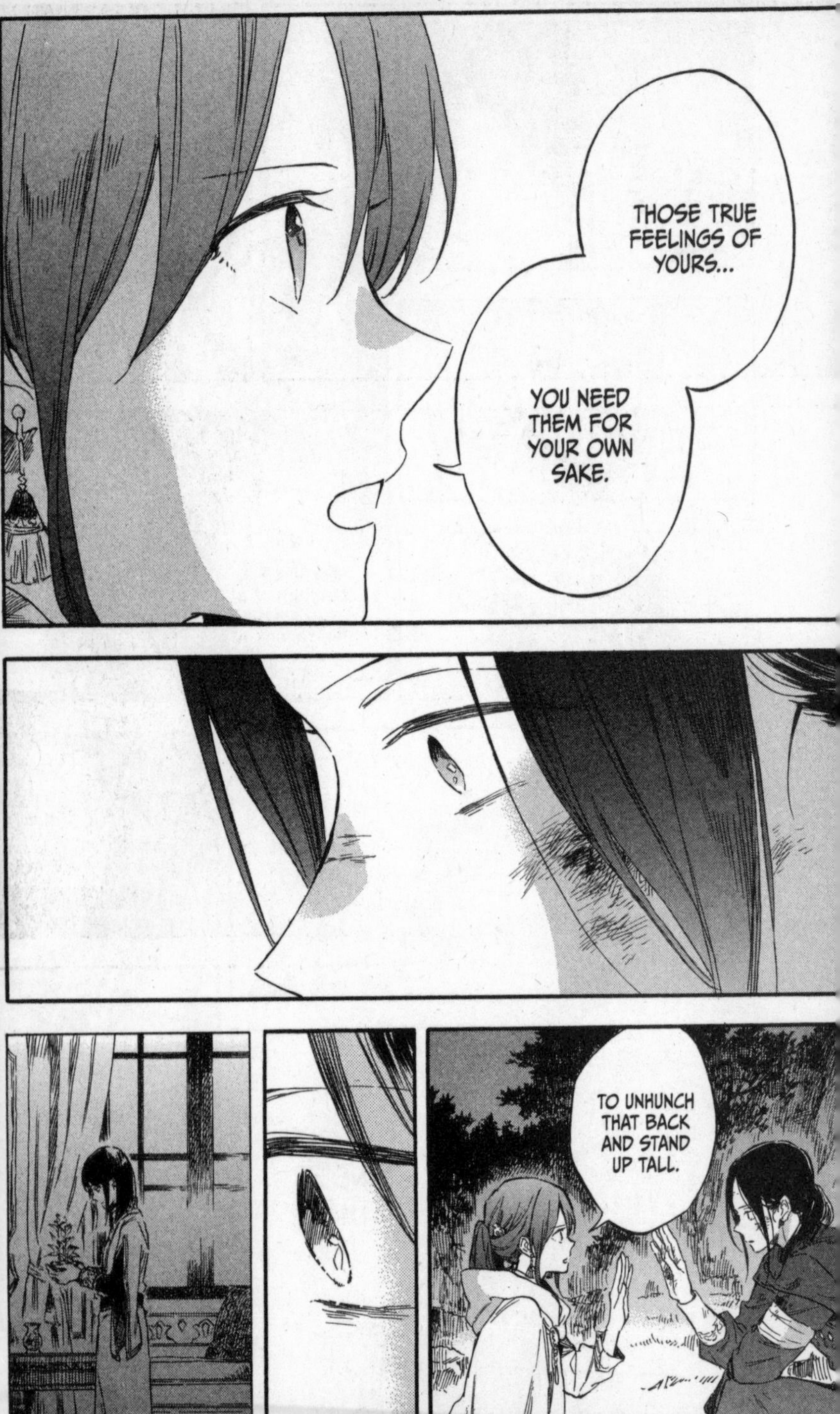
THOSE TRUE FEELINGS OF YOURS...
YOU NEED THEM FOR YOUR OWN SAKE.
TO UNHUNCH THAT BACK AND STAND UP TALL.

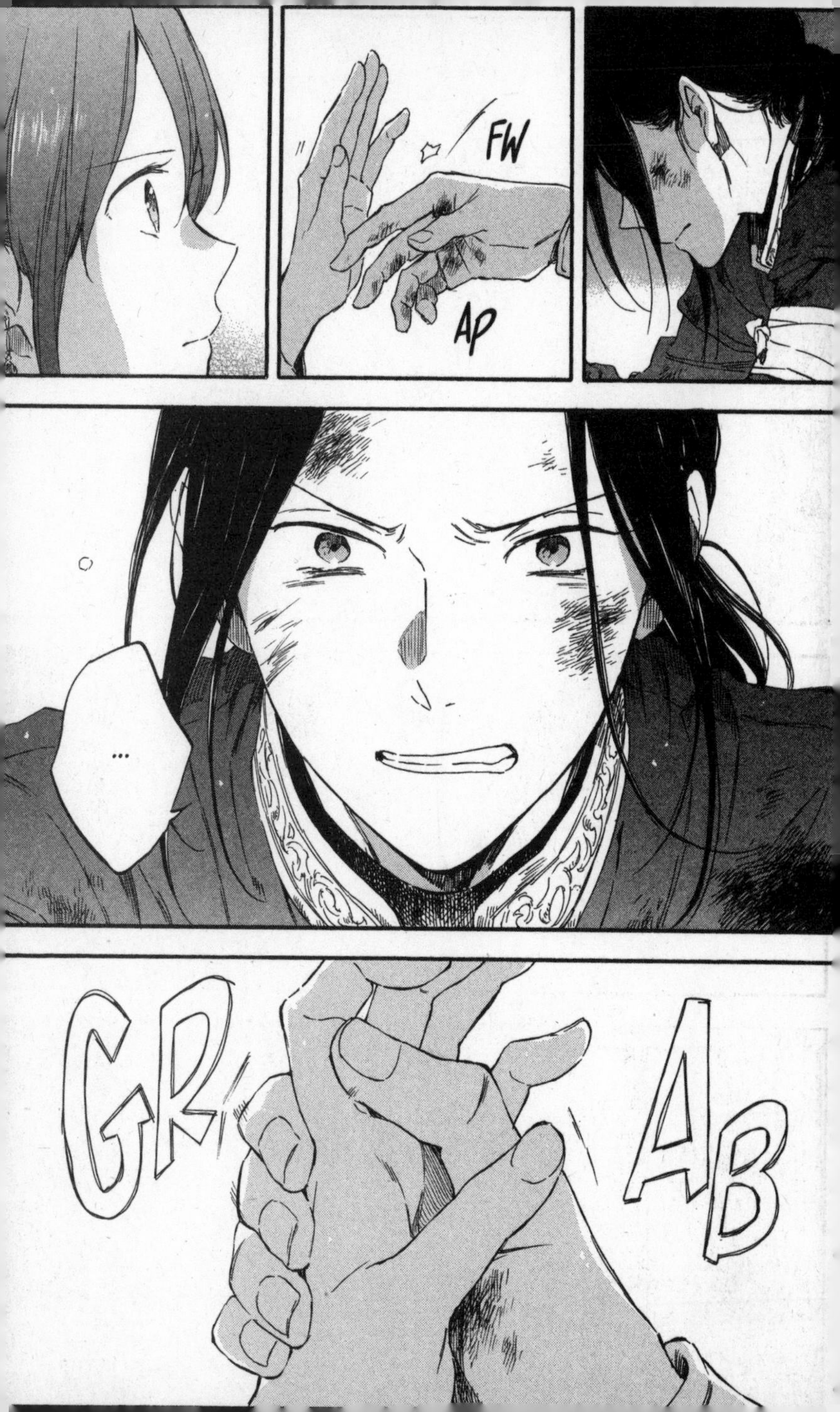
FW
AP
...
GR
AB

Chapter 122

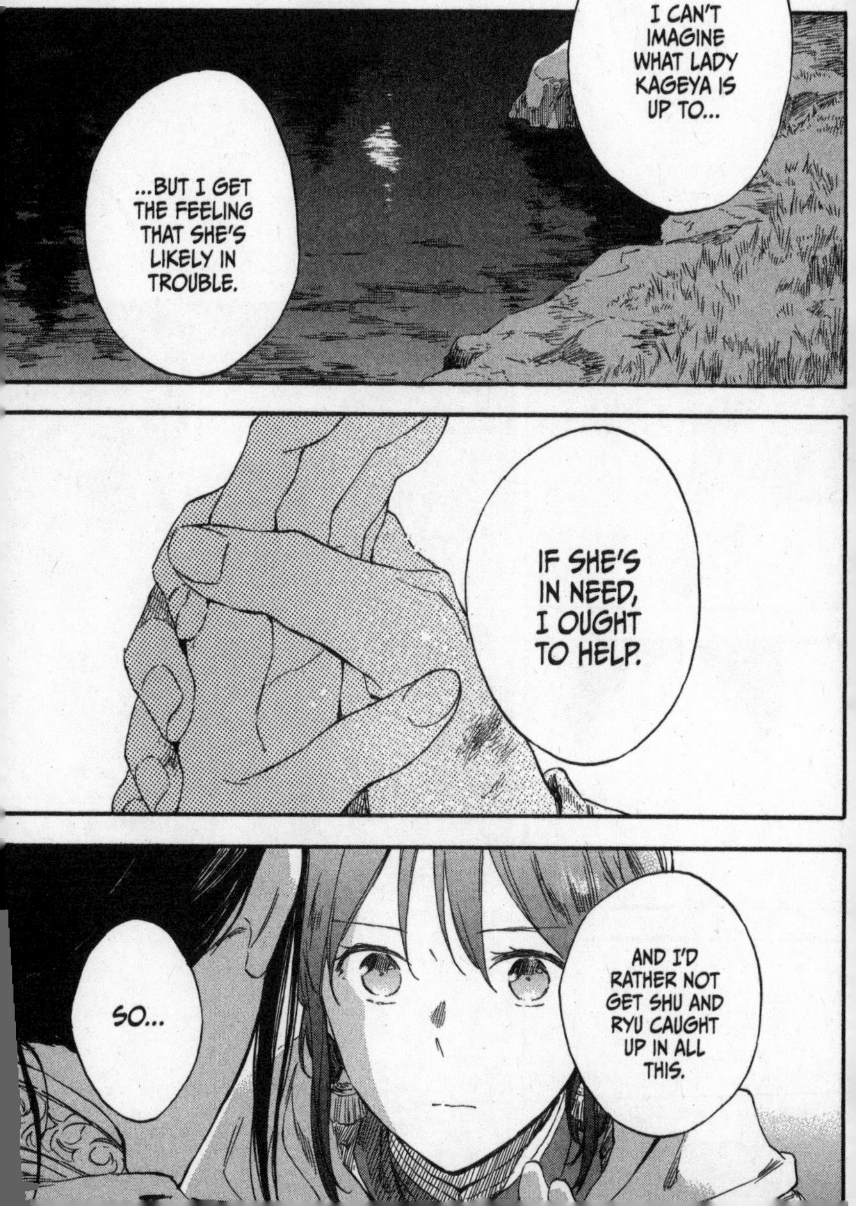
I CAN'T IMAGINE WHAT LADY KAGEYA IS UP TO...
...BUT I GET THE FEELING THAT SHE'S LIKELY IN TROUBLE.
IF SHE'S IN NEED, I OUGHT TO HELP.
AND I'D RATHER NOT GET SHU AND RYU CAUGHT UP IN ALL THIS.
SO...

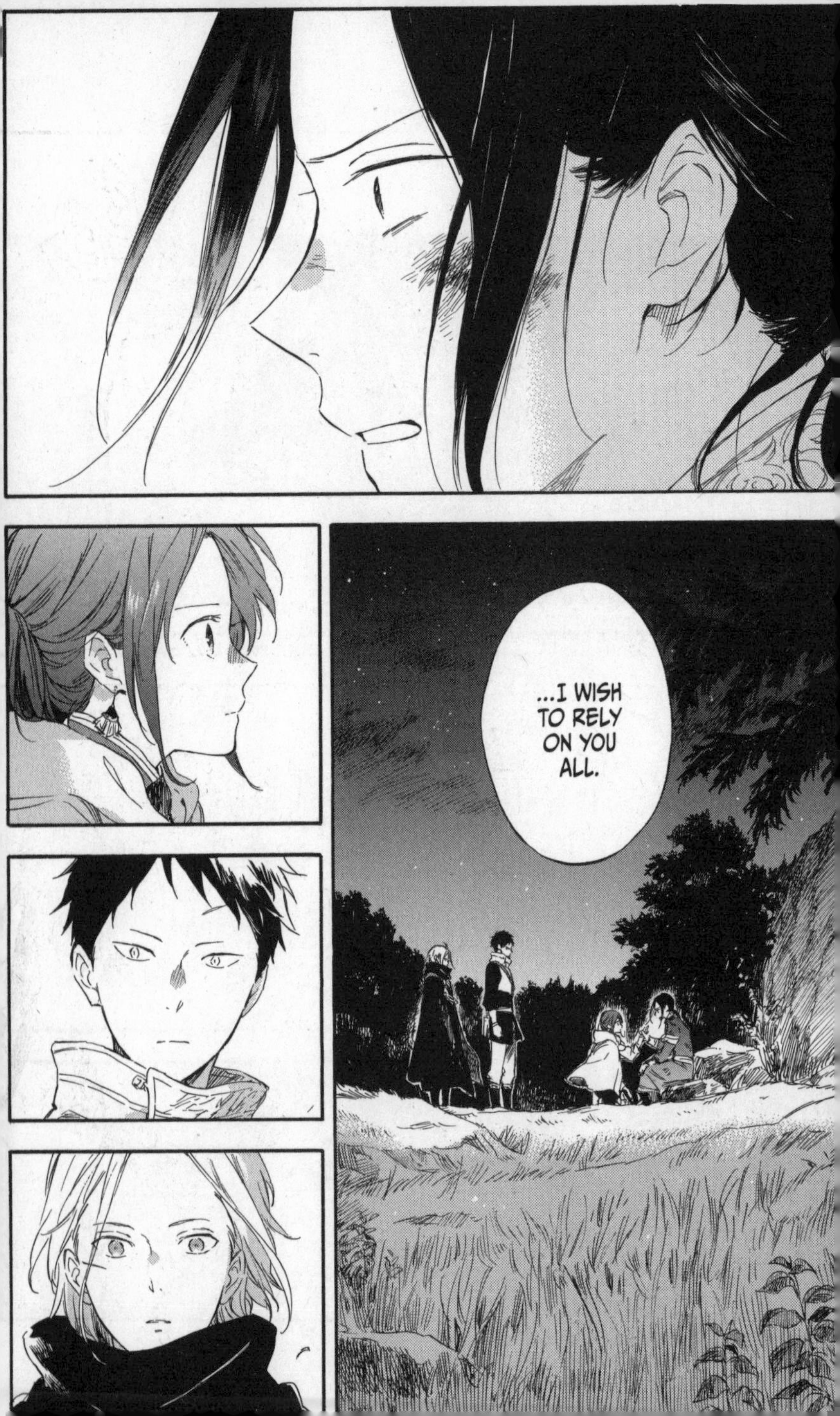
...I WISH TO RELY ON YOU ALL.

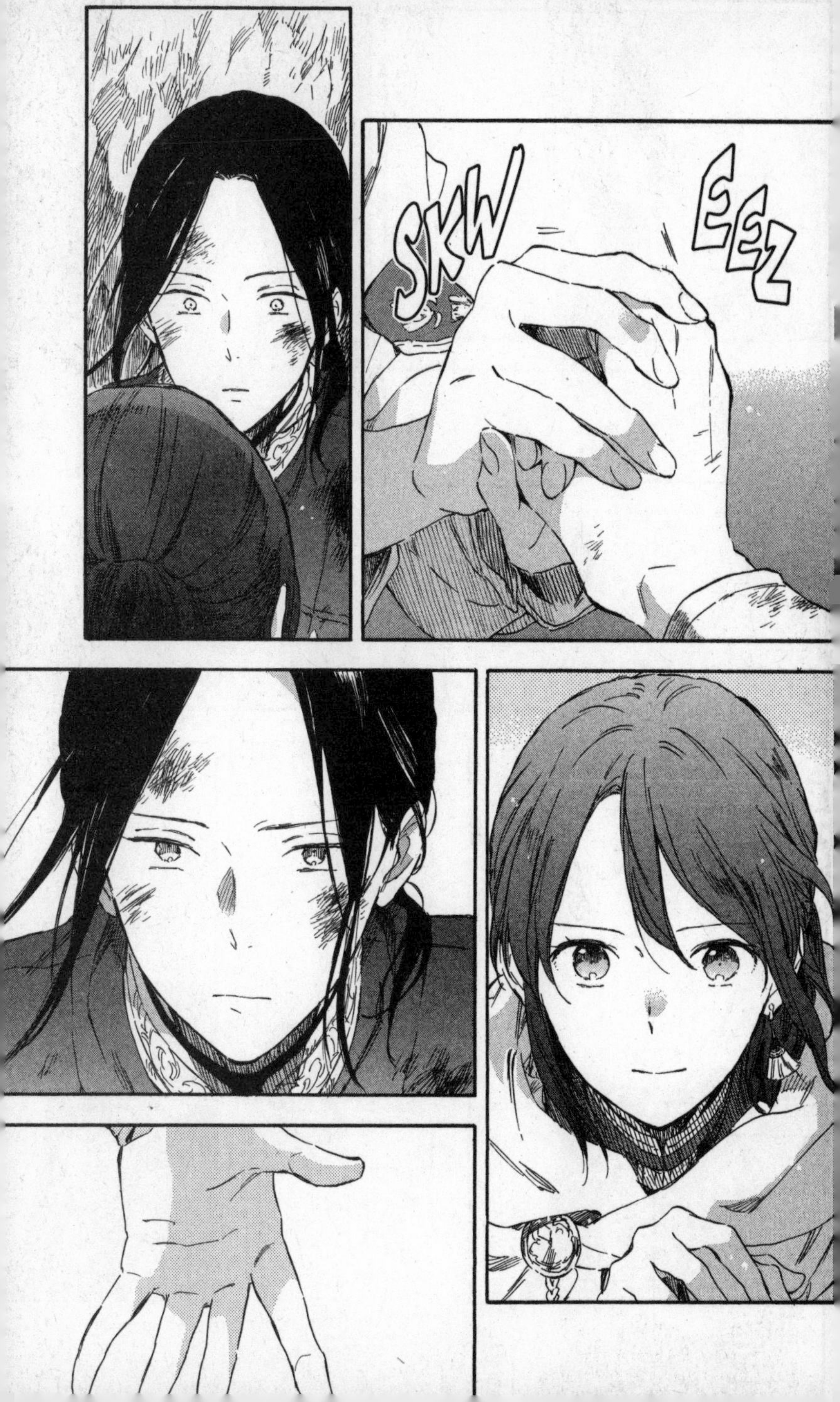
SKWEEZ

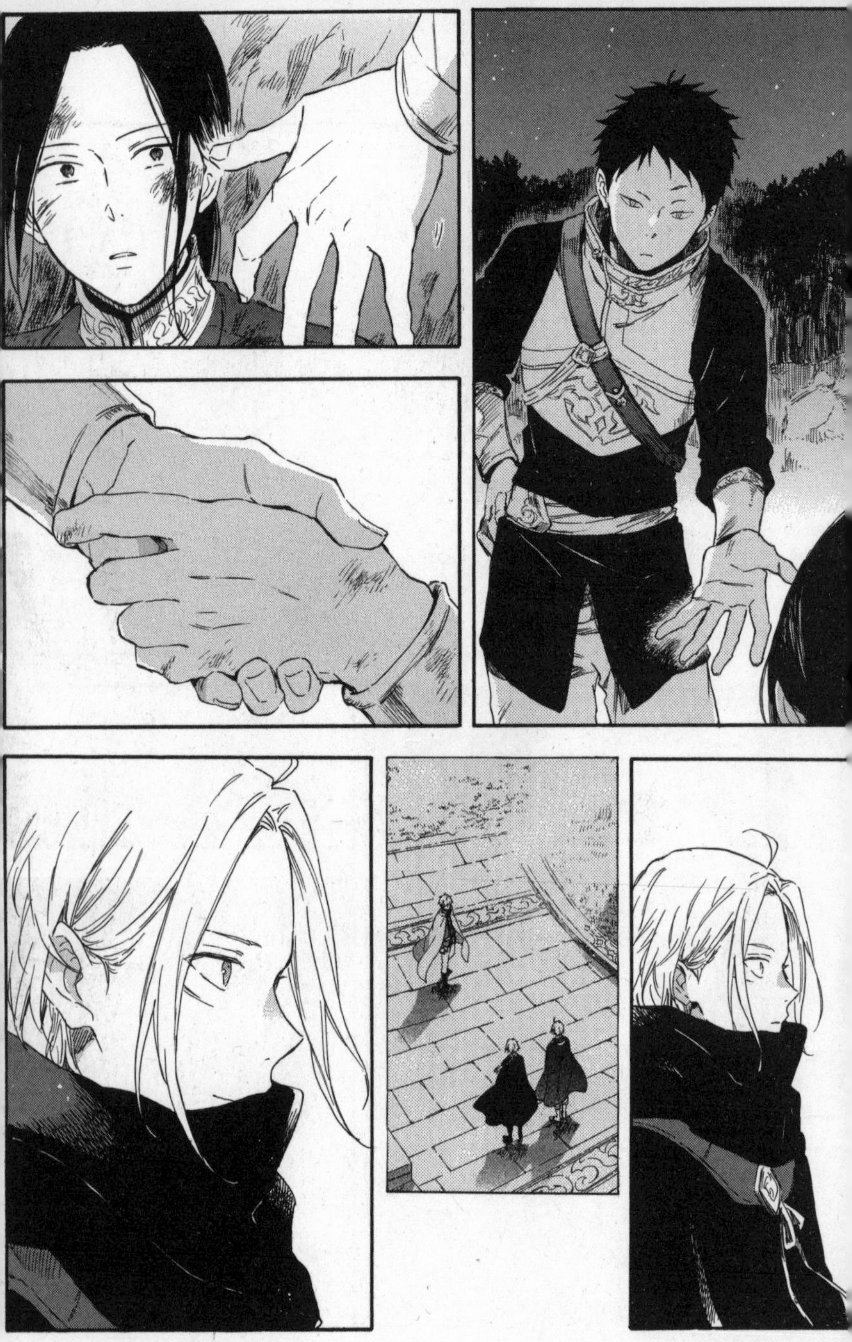

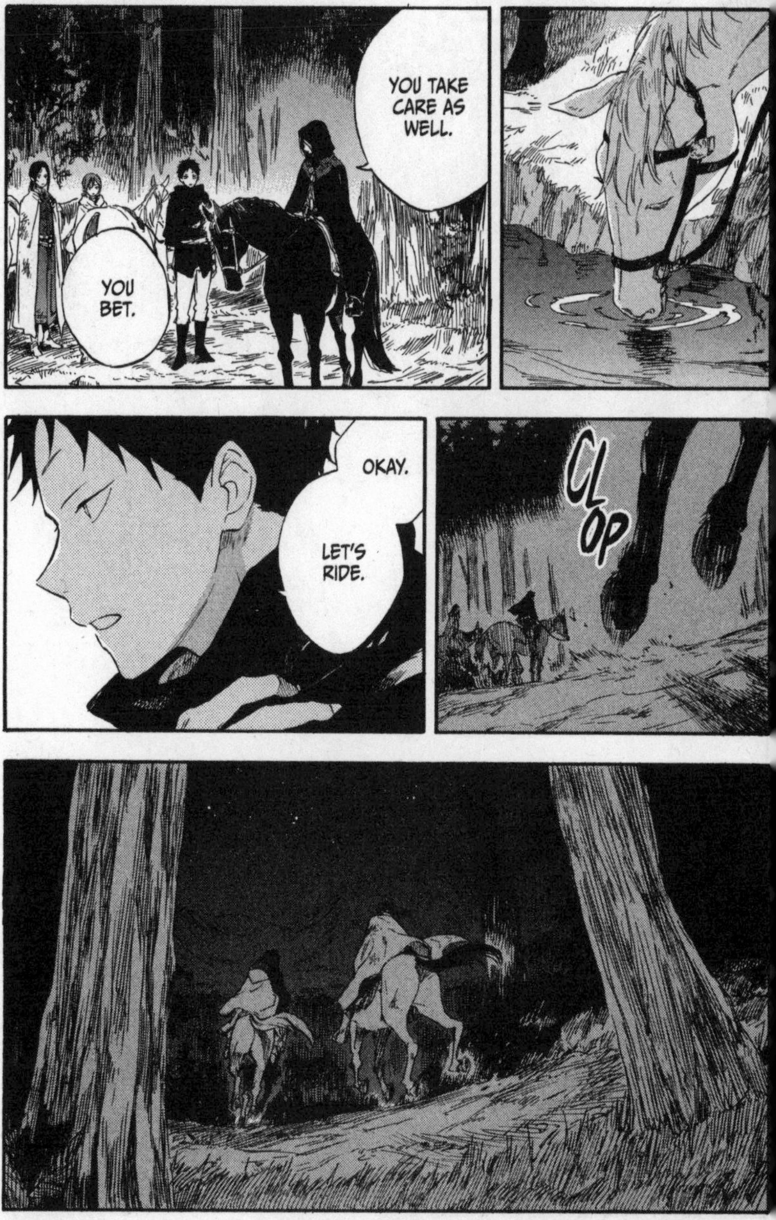
YOU TAKE CARE AS WELL.
YOU BET.
CLOP
OKAY.
LET'S RIDE.

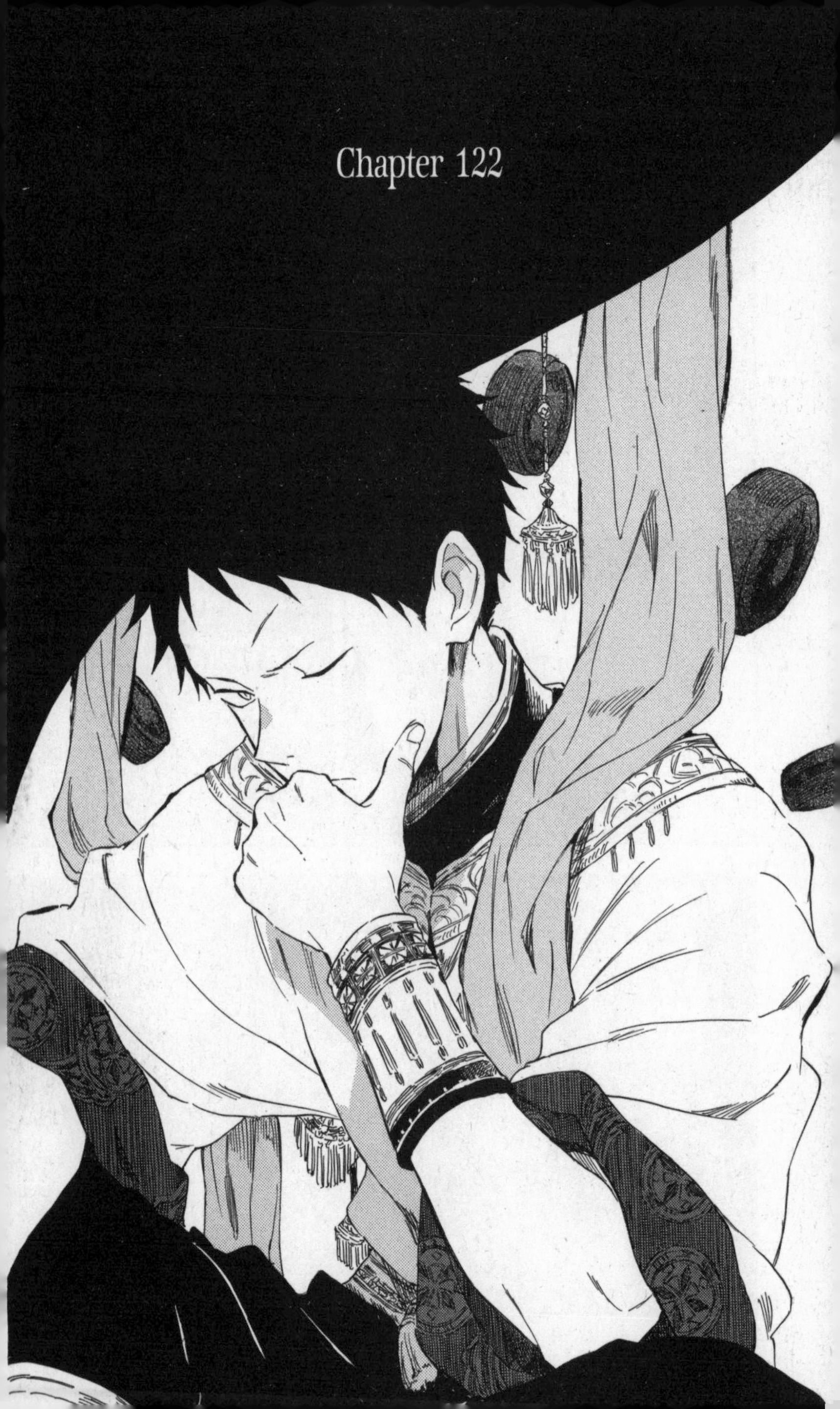
Chapter 122

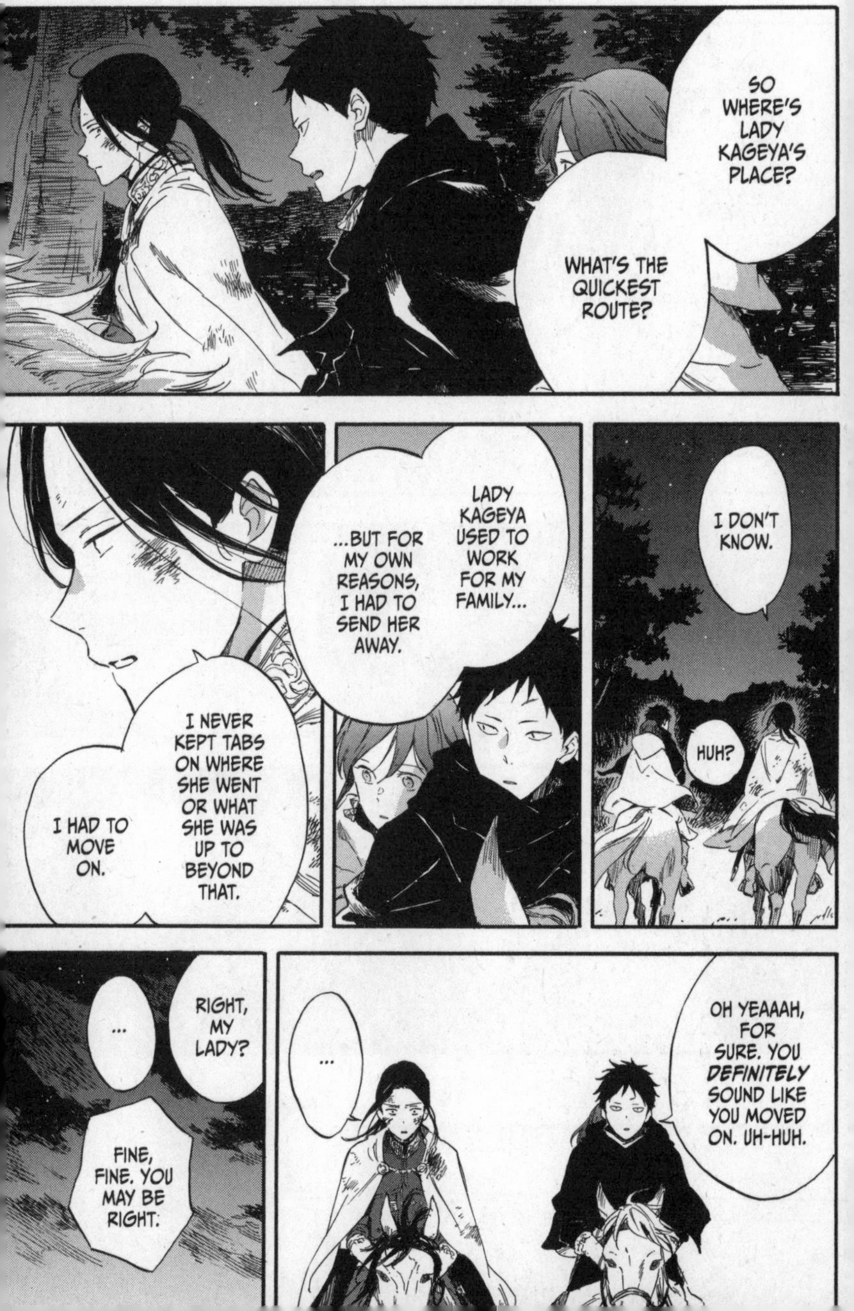
SO WHERE'S LADY KAGEYA'S PLACE?
WHAT'S THE QUICKEST ROUTE?
I DON'T KNOW.
HUH?
LADY KAGEYA USED TO WORK FOR MY FAMILY...
...BUT FOR MY OWN REASONS, I HAD TO SEND HER AWAY.
I NEVER KEPT TABS ON WHERE SHE WENT OR WHAT SHE WAS UP TO BEYOND THAT.
I HAD TO MOVE ON.
OH YEAAAH, FOR SURE. YOU *DEFINITELY* SOUND LIKE YOU MOVED ON. UH-HUH.
...
RIGHT, MY LADY?
...
FINE, FINE. YOU MAY BE RIGHT.

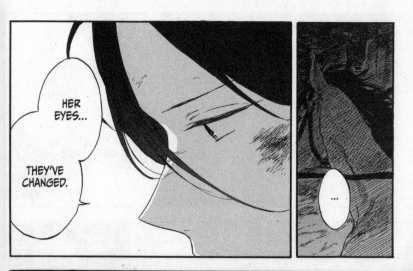

HER EYES...

THEY'VE CHANGED.

...

I WISH SHE MERELY HATED ME.

THEN HER CONTEMPT WOULD EXPLAIN THAT ICY GAZE.

BUT THAT'S TOO OPTIMISTIC OF A GUESS BY FAR.

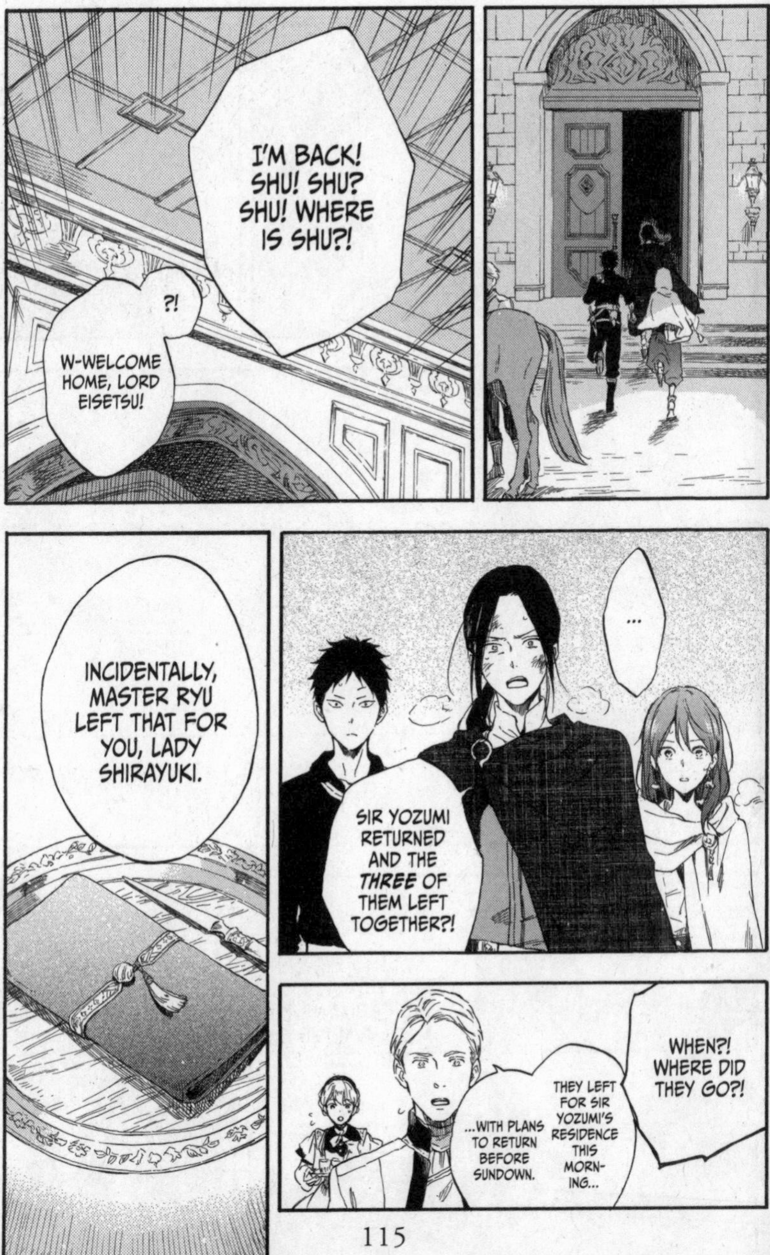
I'M BACK! SHU! SHU? SHU! WHERE IS SHU?!
?!
W-WELCOME HOME, LORD EISETSU!
...
SIR YOZUMI RETURNED AND THE *THREE* OF THEM LEFT TOGETHER?!
WHEN?! WHERE DID THEY GO?!
THEY LEFT FOR SIR YOZUMI'S RESIDENCE THIS MORN-ING...
...WITH PLANS TO RETURN BEFORE SUNDOWN.
INCIDENTALLY, MASTER RYU LEFT THAT FOR YOU, LADY SHIRAYUKI.

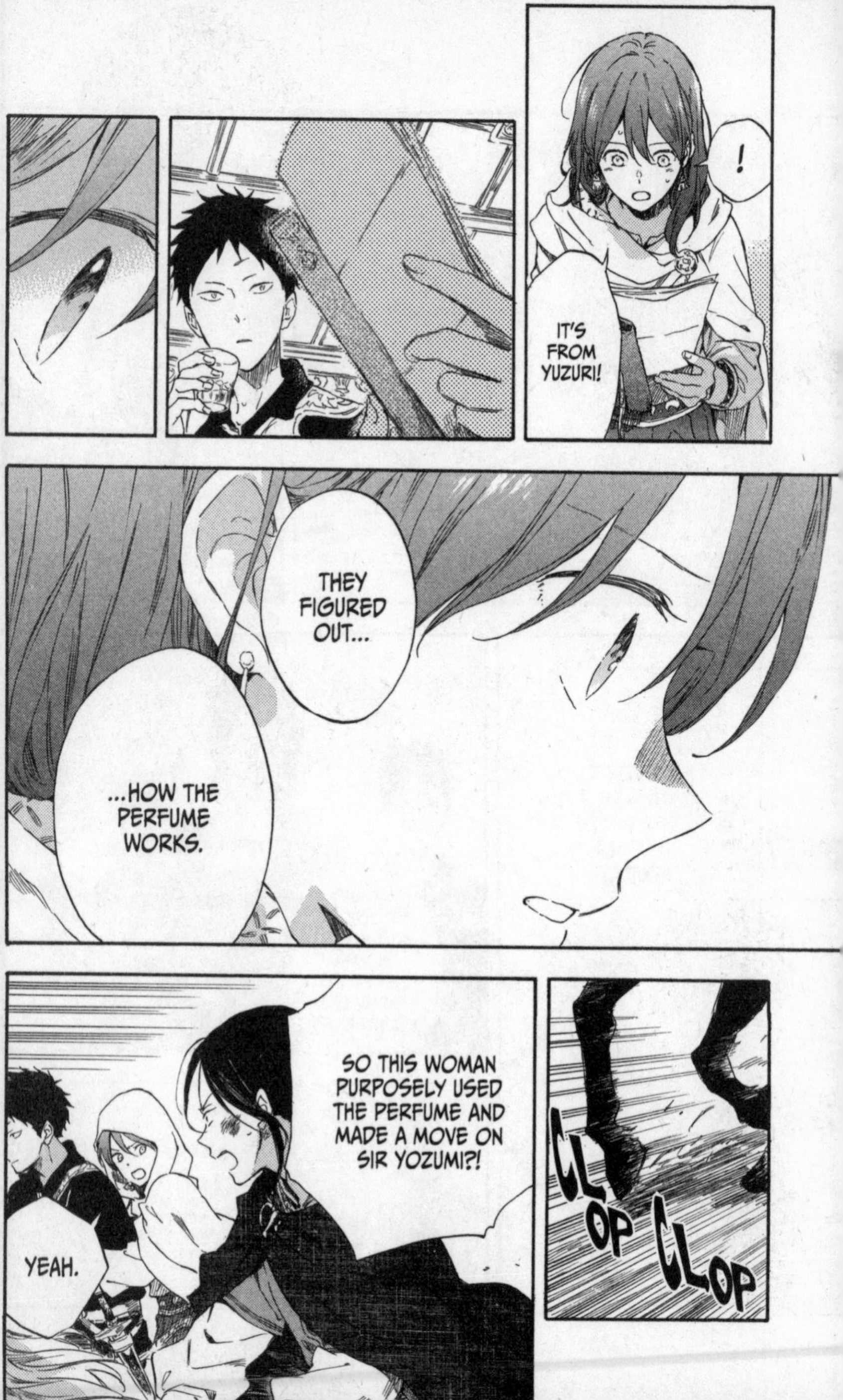
!
IT'S FROM YUZURI!
THEY FIGURED OUT...
...HOW THE PERFUME WORKS.
CLOP CLOP
SO THIS WOMAN PURPOSELY USED THE PERFUME AND MADE A MOVE ON SIR YOZUMI?!
YEAH.

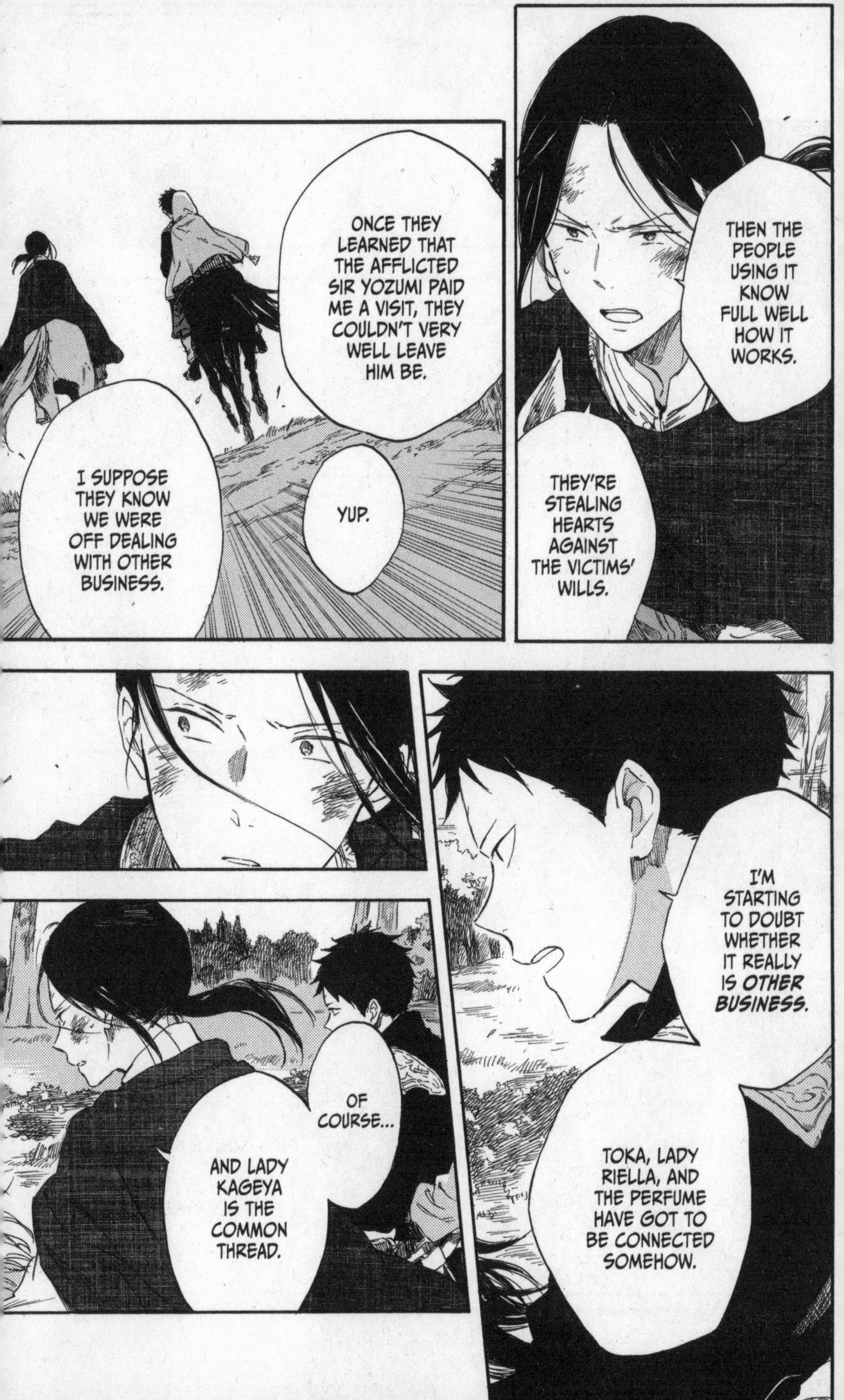
THEN THE PEOPLE USING IT KNOW FULL WELL HOW IT WORKS.
THEY'RE STEALING HEARTS AGAINST THE VICTIMS' WILLS.
ONCE THEY LEARNED THAT THE AFFLICTED SIR YOZUMI PAID ME A VISIT, THEY COULDN'T VERY WELL LEAVE HIM BE.
I SUPPOSE THEY KNOW WE WERE OFF DEALING WITH OTHER BUSINESS.
YUP.
I'M STARTING TO DOUBT WHETHER IT REALLY IS *OTHER BUSINESS.*
TOKA, LADY RIELLA, AND THE PERFUME HAVE GOT TO BE CONNECTED SOMEHOW.
OF COURSE...
AND LADY KAGEYA IS THE COMMON THREAD.

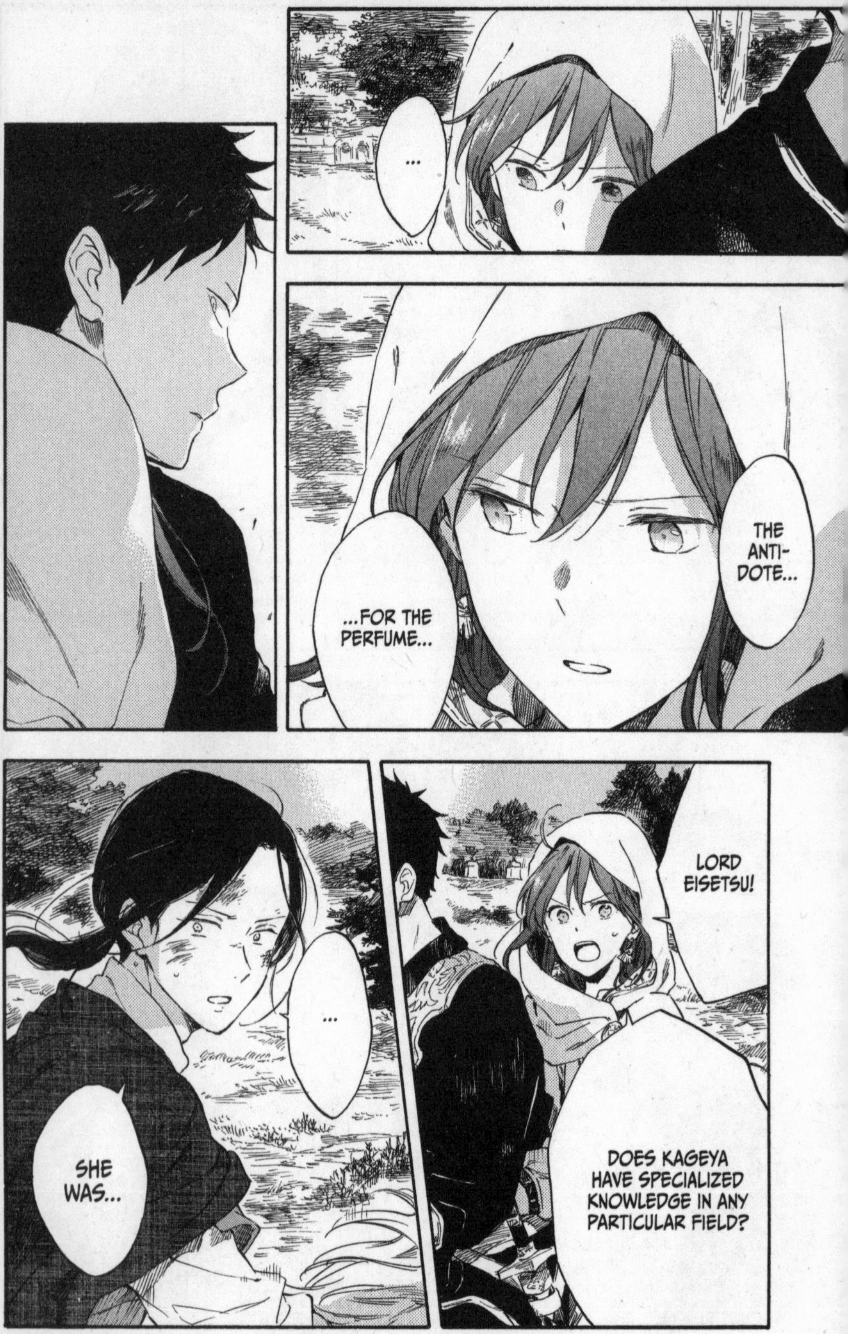
...
THE ANTI-DOTE...
...FOR THE PERFUME...
LORD EISETSU!
DOES KAGEYA HAVE SPECIALIZED KNOWLEDGE IN ANY PARTICULAR FIELD?
...
SHE WAS...

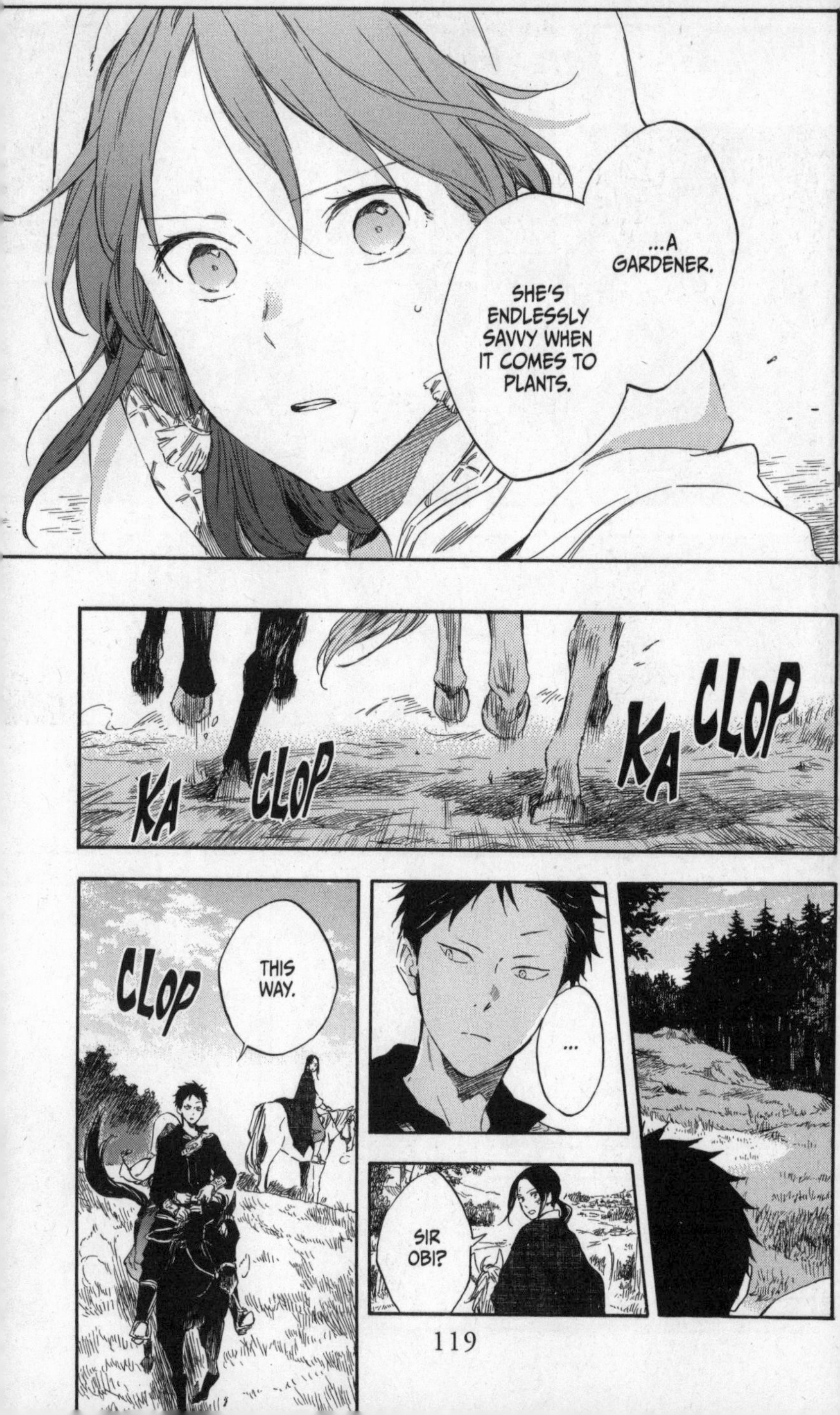
...A GARDENER.
SHE'S ENDLESSLY SAVVY WHEN IT COMES TO PLANTS.
KA CLOP
KA CLOP
...
SIR OBI?
THIS WAY.
CLOP

IT'S DARK DOWN HERE.

!

...

BLOOD.

WHAT?!

120

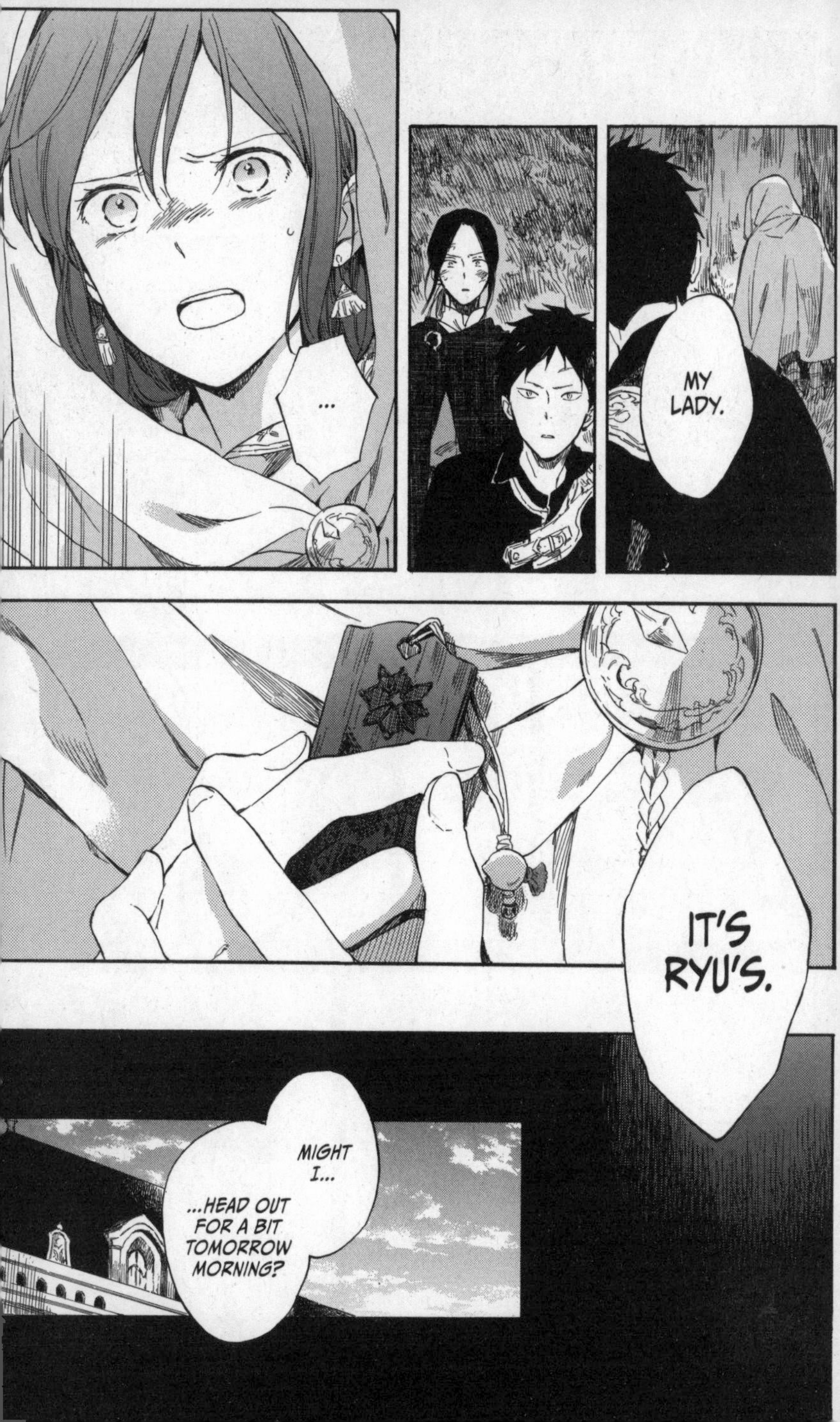
MY LADY.
...
IT'S RYU'S.
MIGHT I...
...HEAD OUT FOR A BIT TOMORROW MORNING?

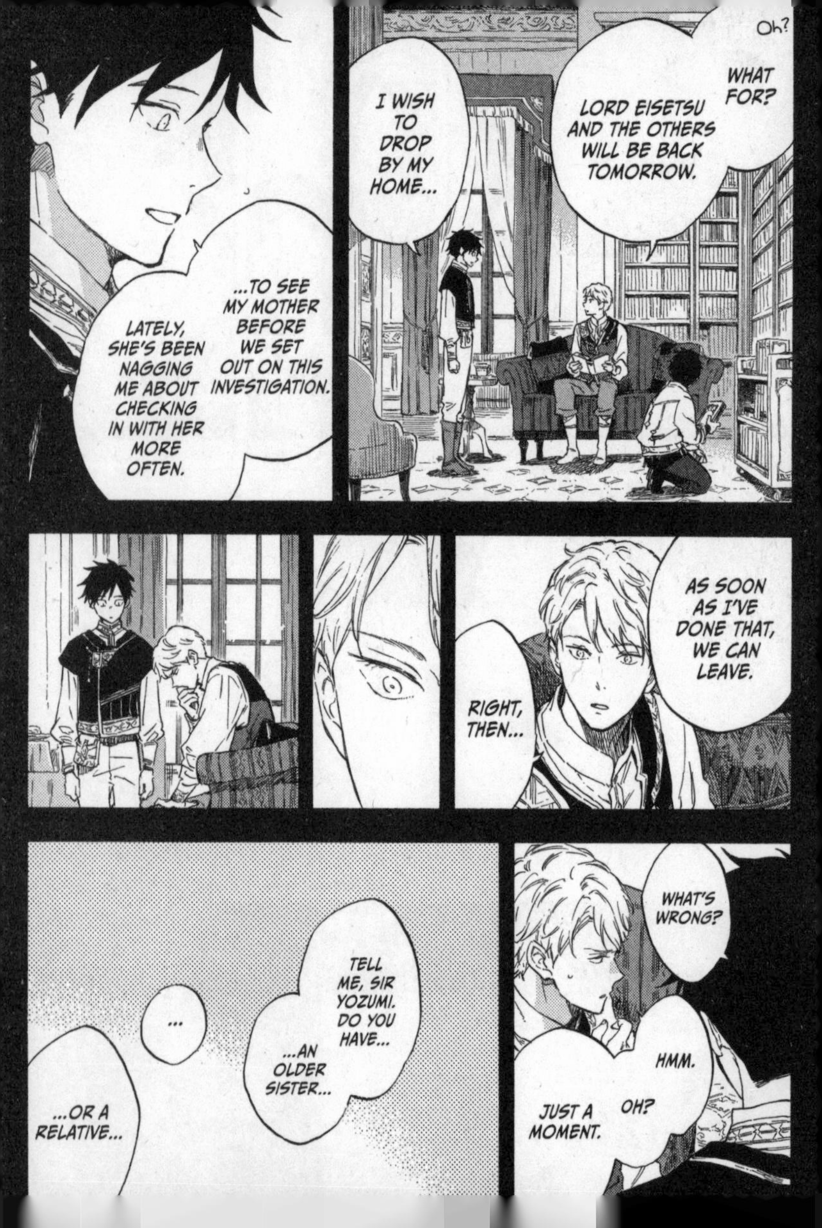
Oh?
WHAT FOR?
LORD EISETSU AND THE OTHERS WILL BE BACK TOMORROW.
I WISH TO DROP BY MY HOME...
...TO SEE MY MOTHER BEFORE WE SET OUT ON THIS INVESTIGATION.
LATELY, SHE'S BEEN NAGGING ME ABOUT CHECKING IN WITH HER MORE OFTEN.
AS SOON AS I'VE DONE THAT, WE CAN LEAVE.
RIGHT, THEN...
WHAT'S WRONG?
HMM.
OH?
JUST A MOMENT.
TELL ME, SIR YOZUMI. DO YOU HAVE...
...AN OLDER SISTER...
...
...OR A RELATIVE...

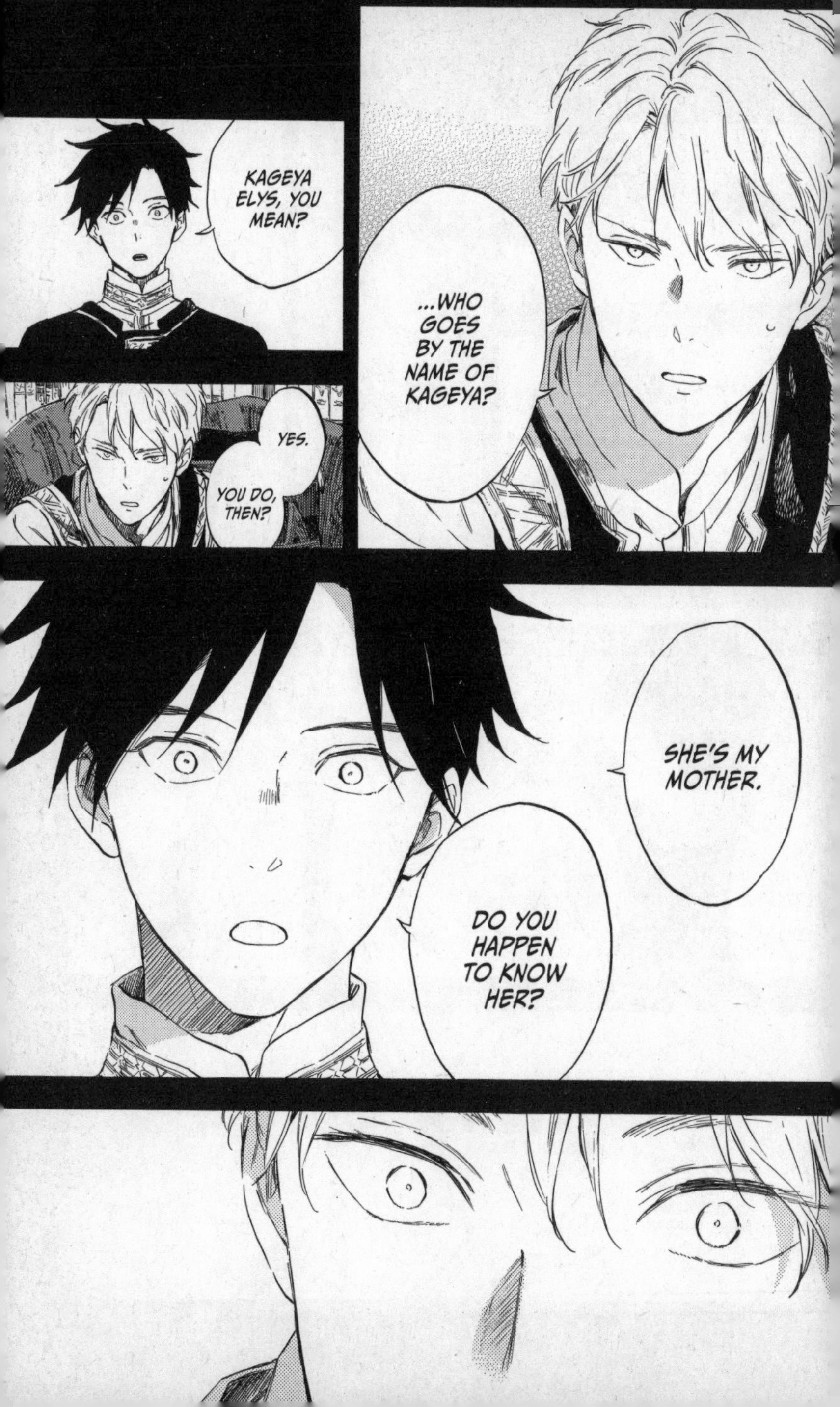
...WHO GOES BY THE NAME OF KAGEYA?
KAGEYA ELYS, YOU MEAN?
YES.
YOU DO, THEN?
SHE'S MY MOTHER.
DO YOU HAPPEN TO KNOW HER?

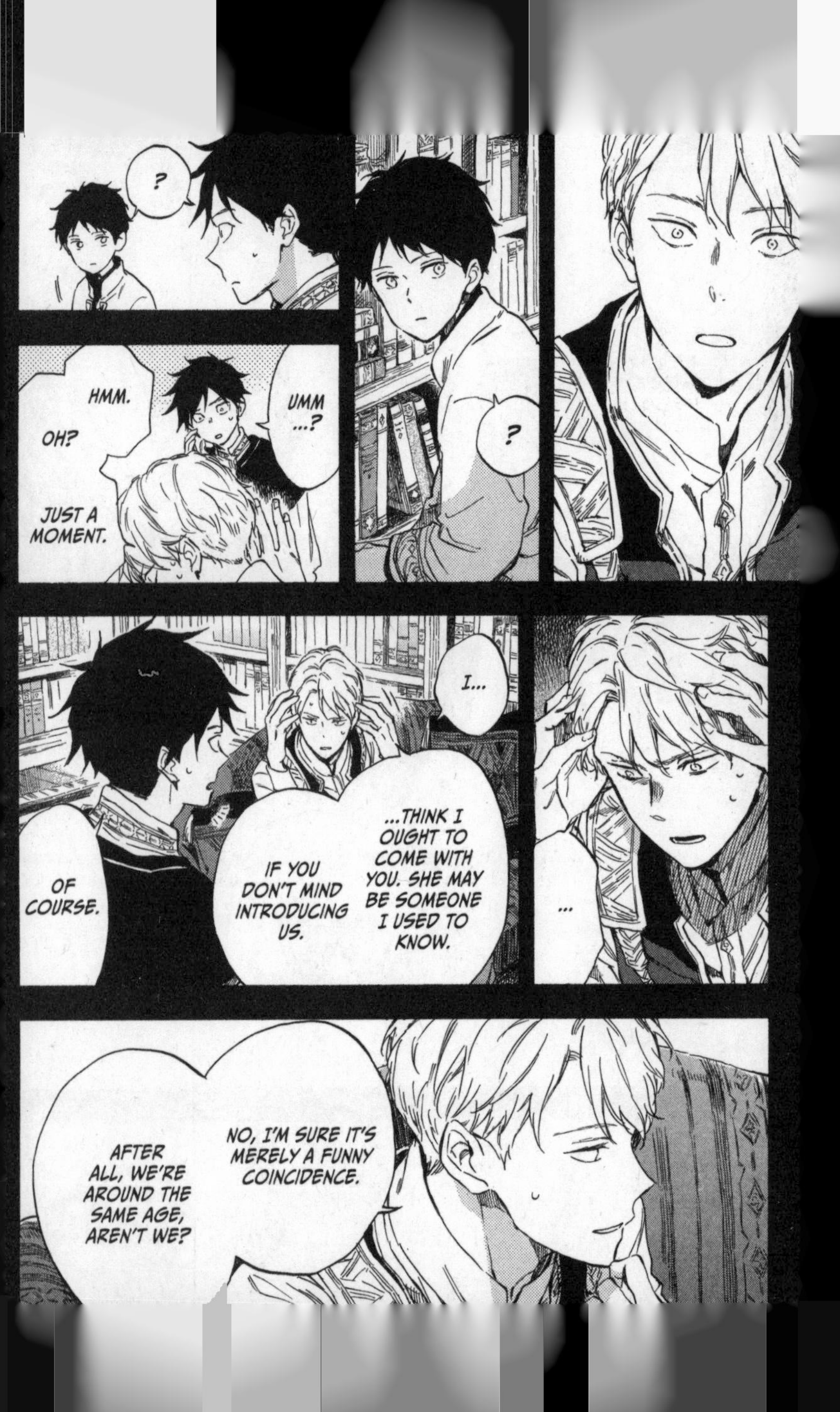
?
?
UMM ...?
HMM.
OH?
JUST A MOMENT.
...
I...
...THINK I OUGHT TO COME WITH YOU. SHE MAY BE SOMEONE I USED TO KNOW.
IF YOU DON'T MIND INTRODUCING US.
OF COURSE.
NO, I'M SURE IT'S MERELY A FUNNY COINCIDENCE.
AFTER ALL, WE'RE AROUND THE SAME AGE, AREN'T WE?

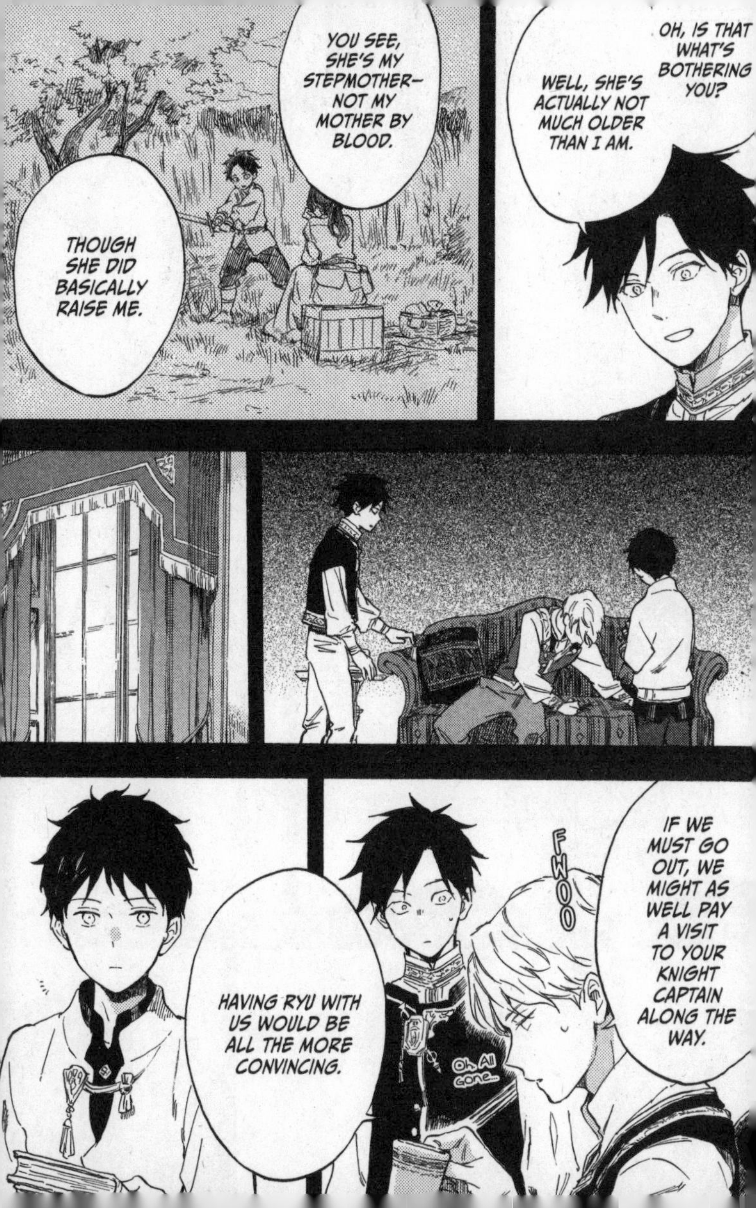
OH, IS THAT WHAT'S BOTHERING YOU?
WELL, SHE'S ACTUALLY NOT MUCH OLDER THAN I AM.
YOU SEE, SHE'S MY STEPMOTHER— NOT MY MOTHER BY BLOOD.
THOUGH SHE DID BASICALLY RAISE ME.
IF WE MUST GO OUT, WE MIGHT AS WELL PAY A VISIT TO YOUR KNIGHT CAPTAIN ALONG THE WAY.
FWOO
HAVING RYU WITH US WOULD BE ALL THE MORE CONVINCING.
Oh All Gone...

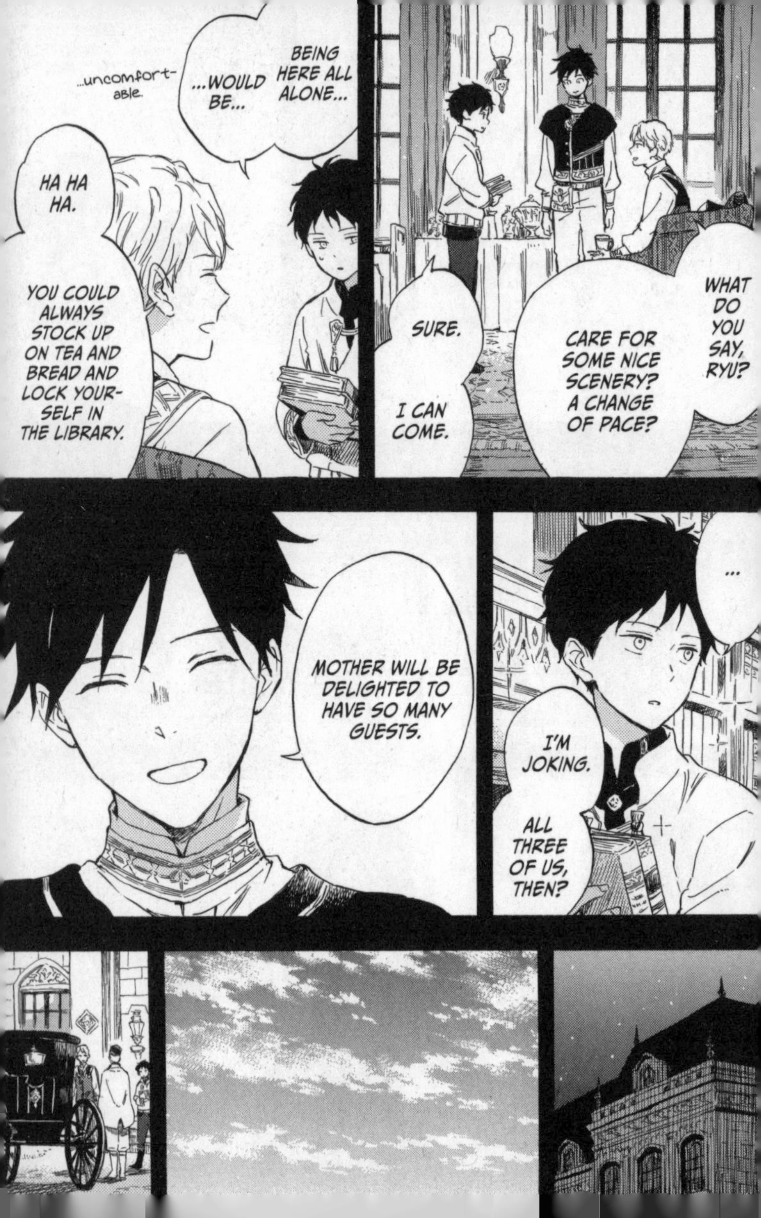
WHAT DO YOU SAY, RYU?
CARE FOR SOME NICE SCENERY? A CHANGE OF PACE?
SURE.
I CAN COME.
BEING HERE ALL ALONE...
...WOULD BE...
...uncomfort-able.
HA HA HA.
YOU COULD ALWAYS STOCK UP ON TEA AND BREAD AND LOCK YOURSELF IN THE LIBRARY.
...
I'M JOKING.
ALL THREE OF US, THEN?
MOTHER WILL BE DELIGHTED TO HAVE SO MANY GUESTS.

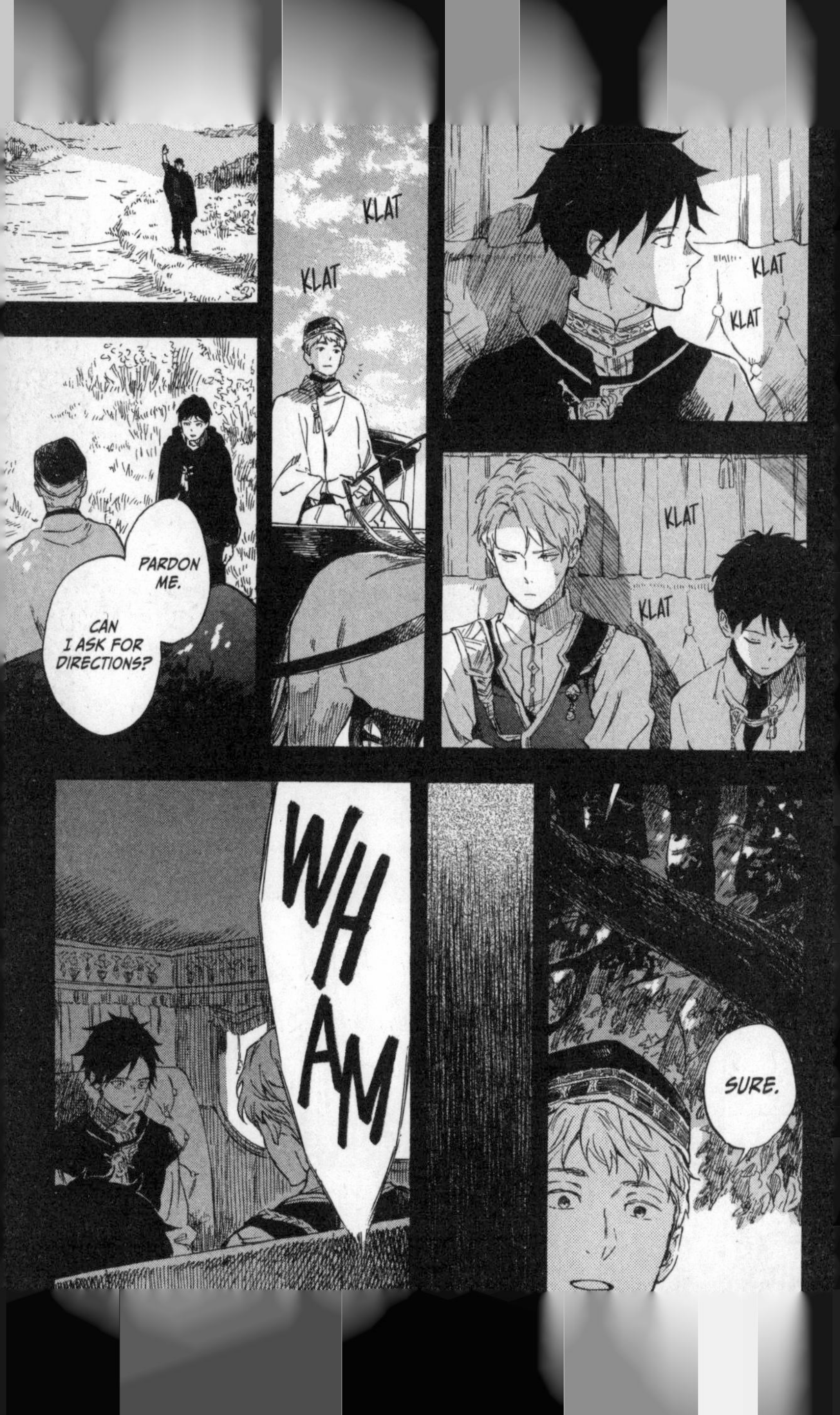
KLAT
KLAT
KLAT
KLAT
KLAT
KLAT
PARDON ME.
CAN I ASK FOR DIRECTIONS?
SURE.
WHAM

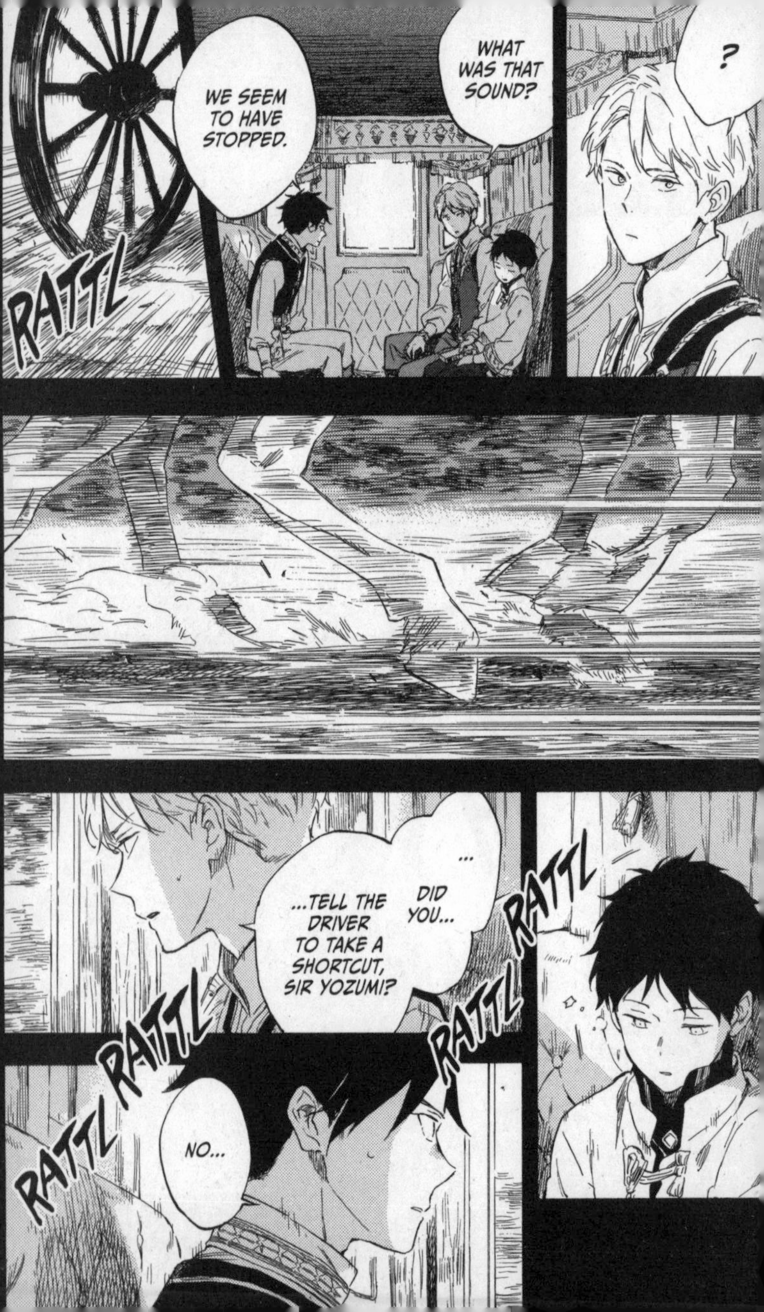
?
WHAT WAS THAT SOUND?
WE SEEM TO HAVE STOPPED.
RATTL
...
DID YOU...
...TELL THE DRIVER TO TAKE A SHORTCUT, SIR YOZUMI?
RATTL
RATTL
RATTL
RATTL
NO...

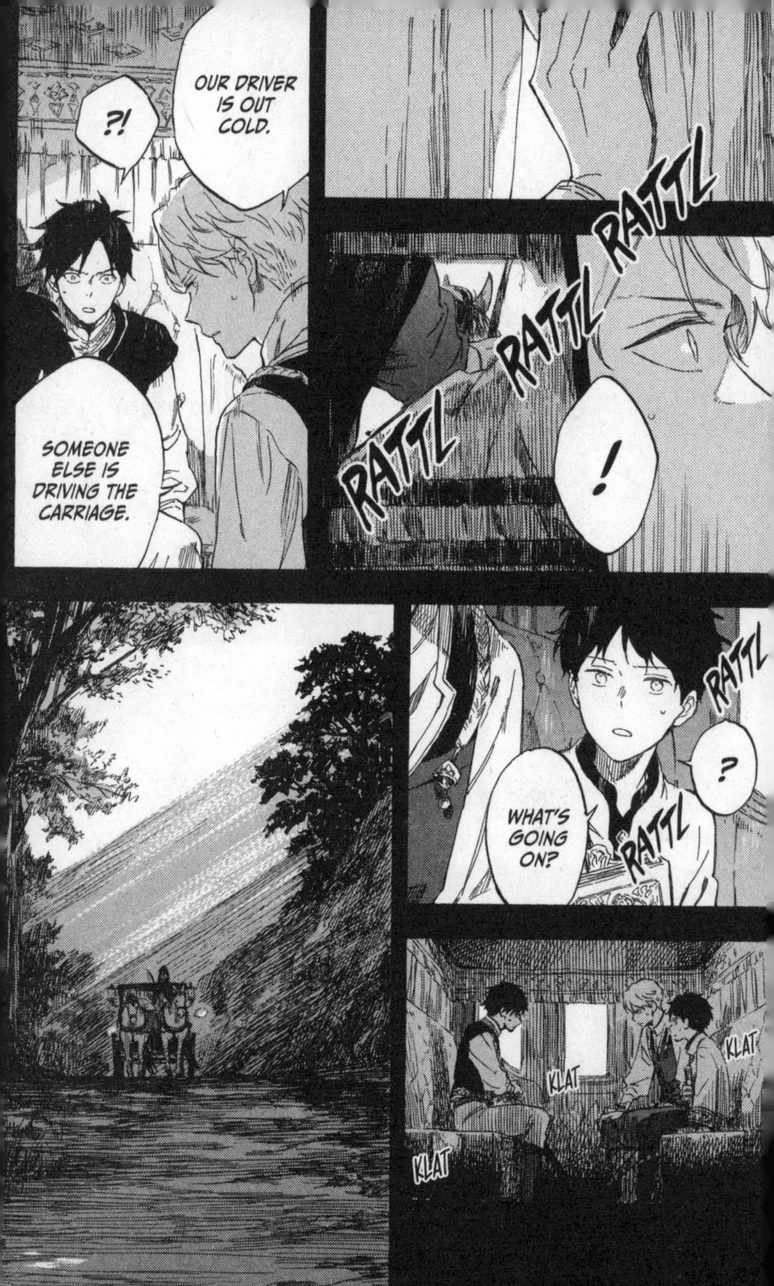
RATTL
RATTL
RATTL
!
RATTL
OUR DRIVER IS OUT COLD.
?!
SOMEONE ELSE IS DRIVING THE CARRIAGE.
RATTL
?
WHAT'S GOING ON?
RATTL
KLAT
KLAT
KLAT

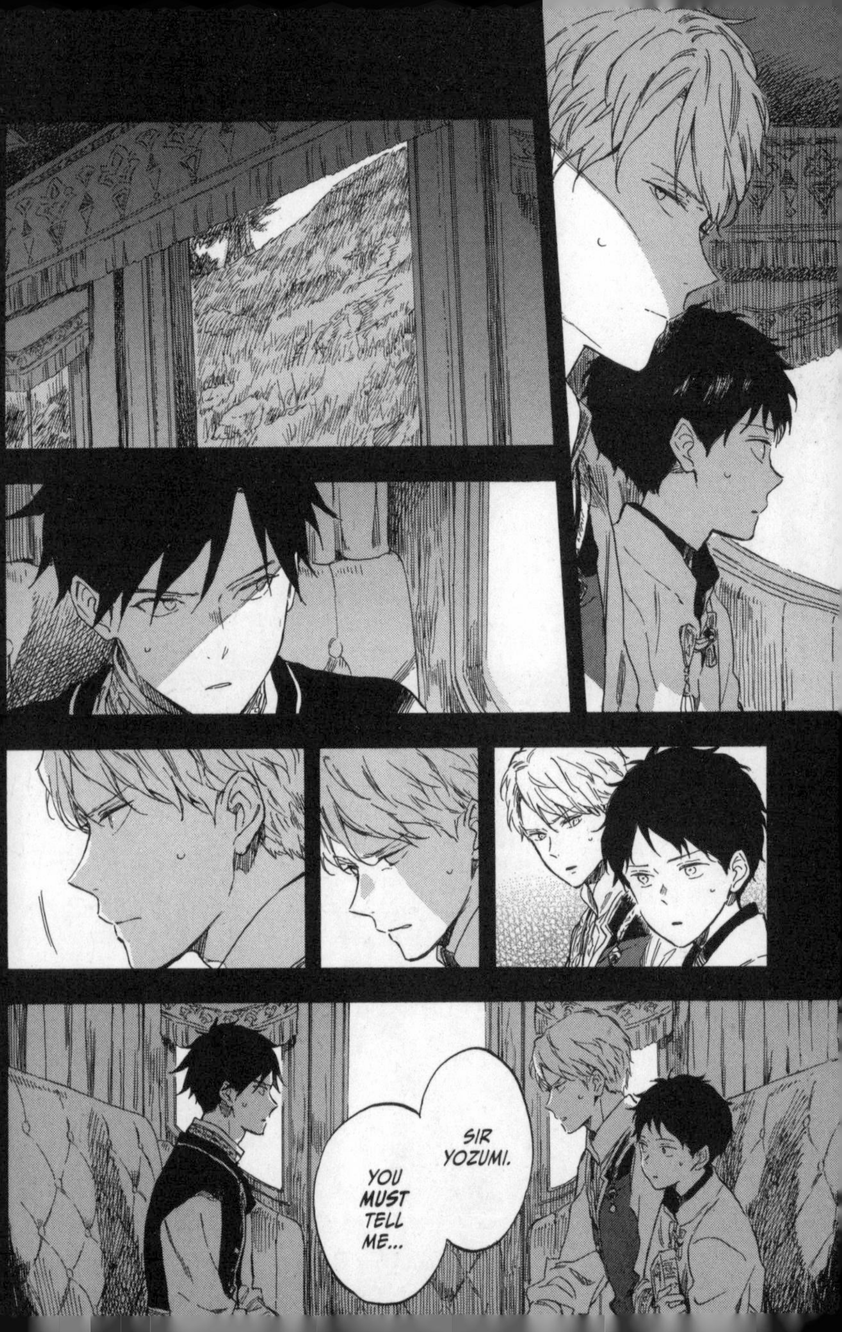
SIR YOZUMI.
YOU MUST TELL ME...

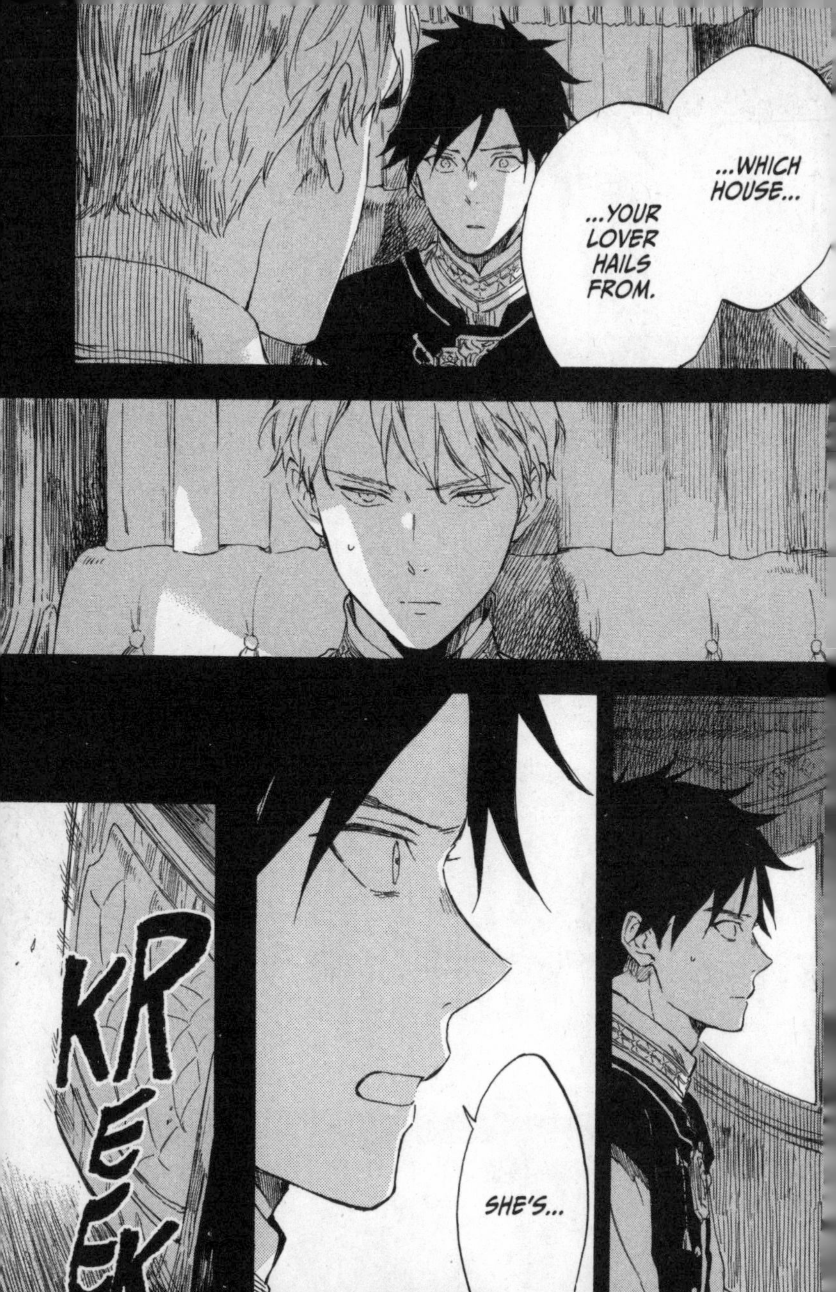
...WHICH HOUSE...
...YOUR LOVER HAILS FROM.
SHE'S...
KREEEK

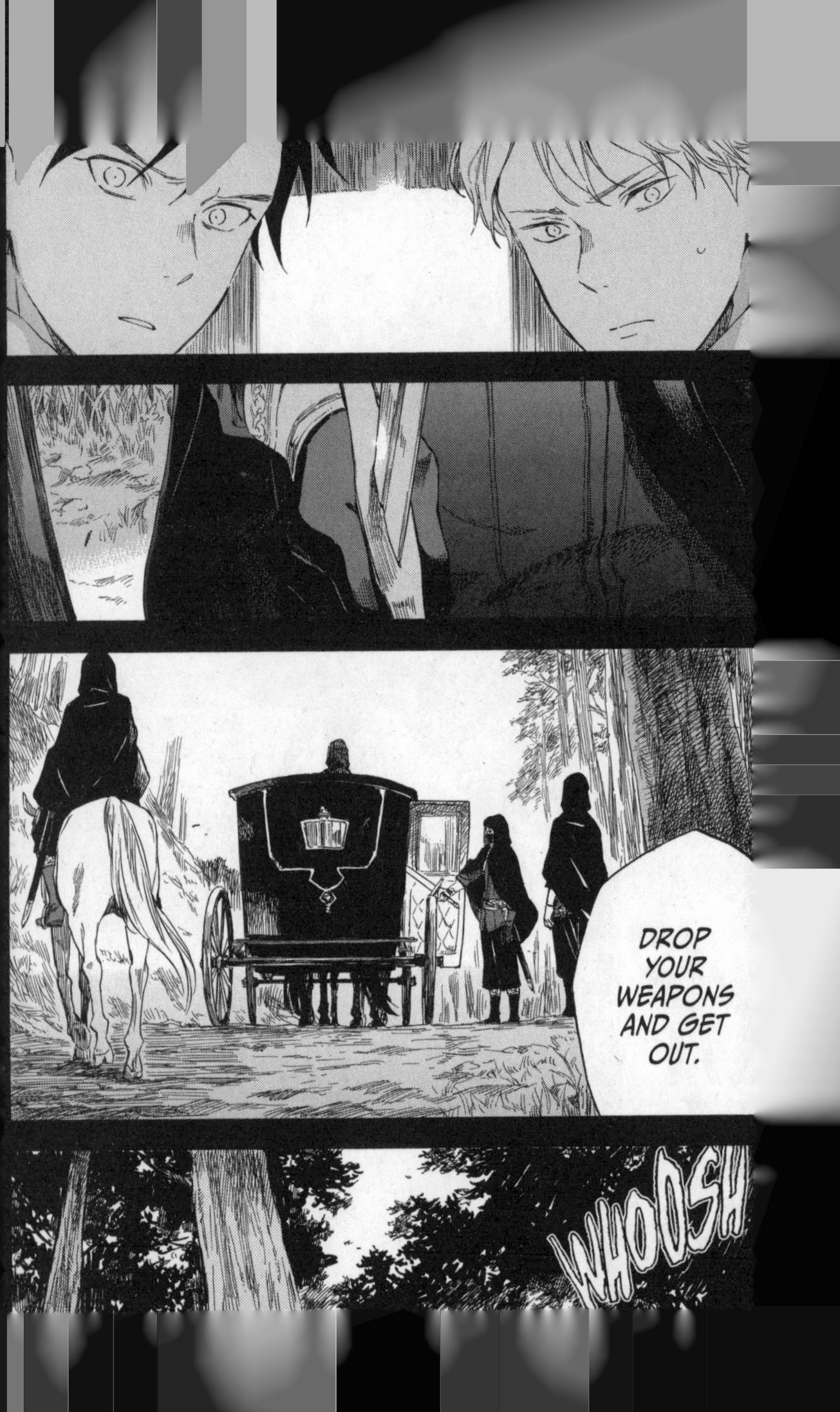
DROP YOUR WEAPONS AND GET OUT.
WHOOSH

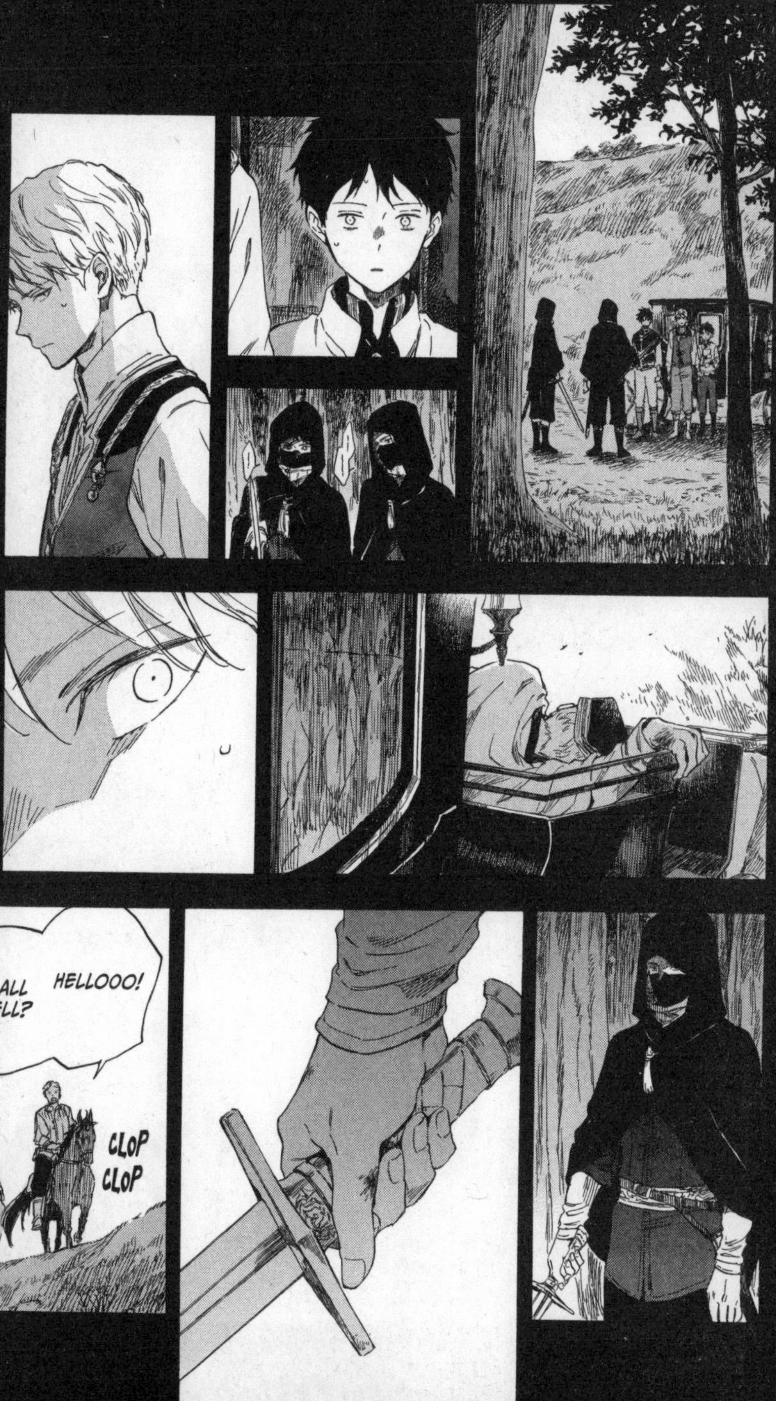
HELLOOO!
IS ALL WELL?
CLOP CLOP

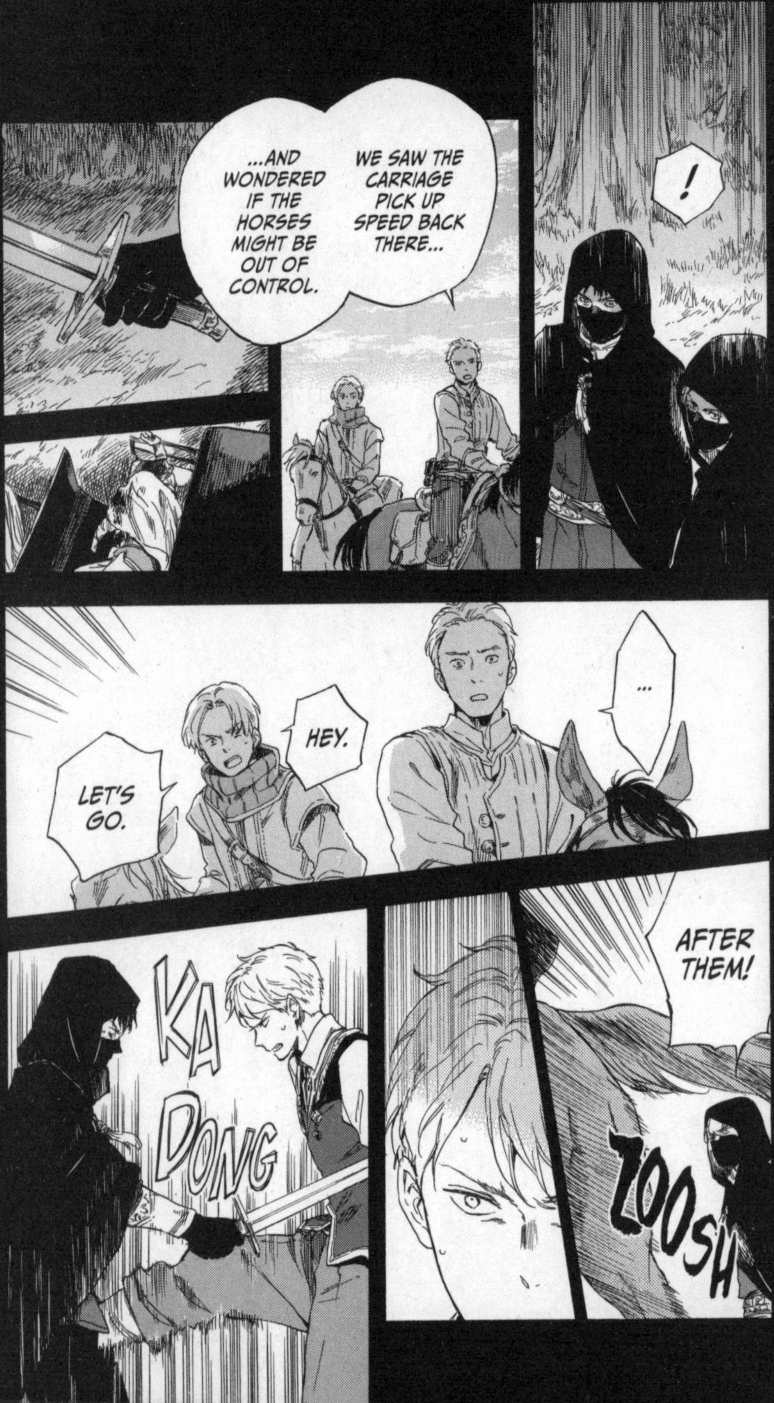
!
WE SAW THE CARRIAGE PICK UP SPEED BACK THERE...
...AND WONDERED IF THE HORSES MIGHT BE OUT OF CONTROL.
...
HEY.
LET'S GO.
AFTER THEM!
ZOOSH
KA DONG

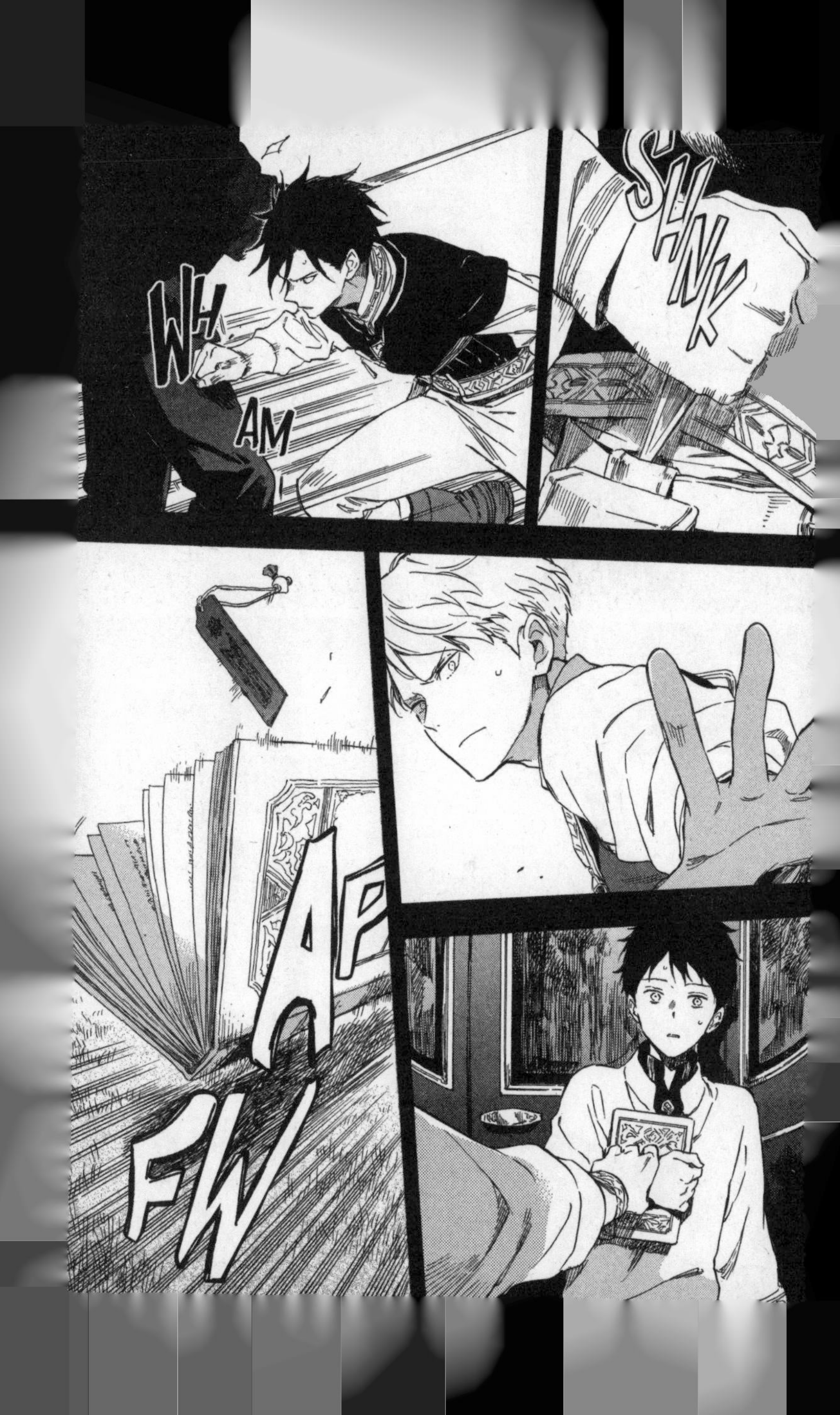
SHNK
WHAM
FWAP

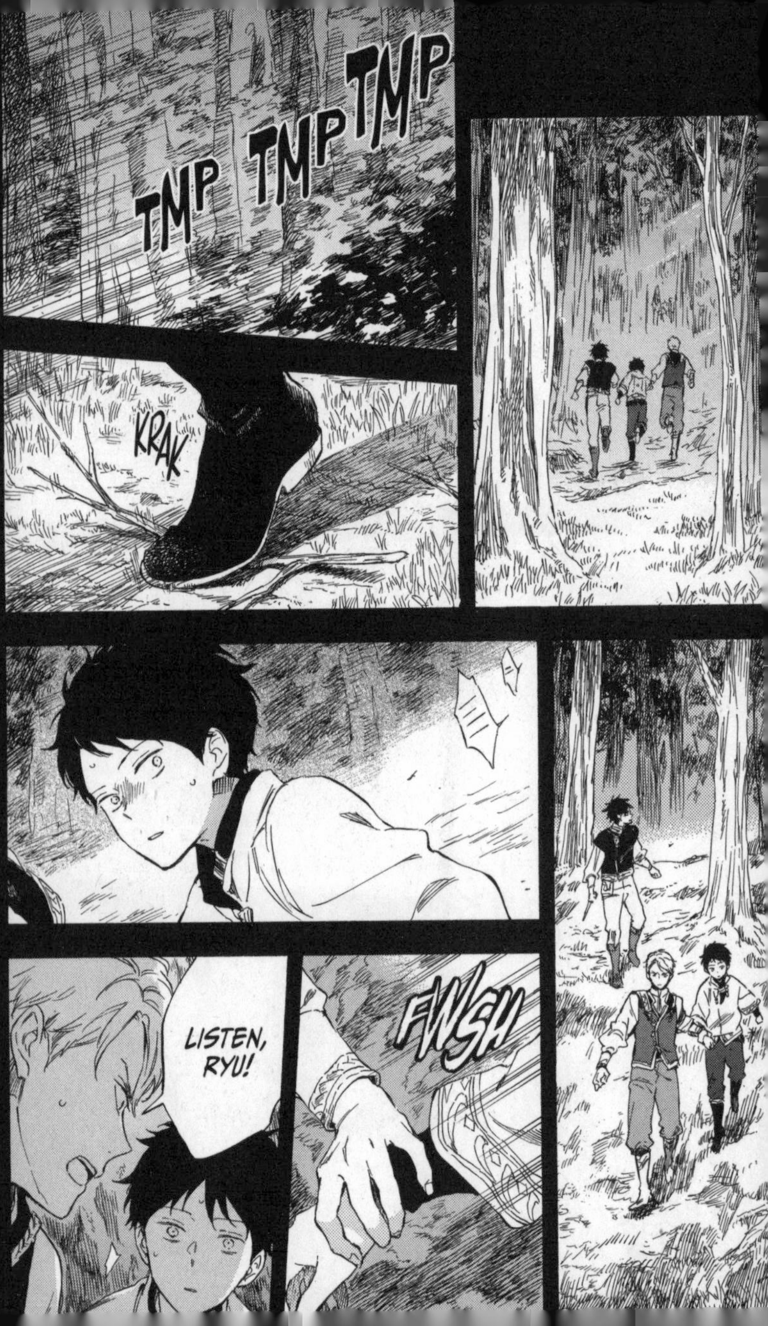
TMP TMP TMP TMP
KRAK
LISTEN, RYU!
FWSH

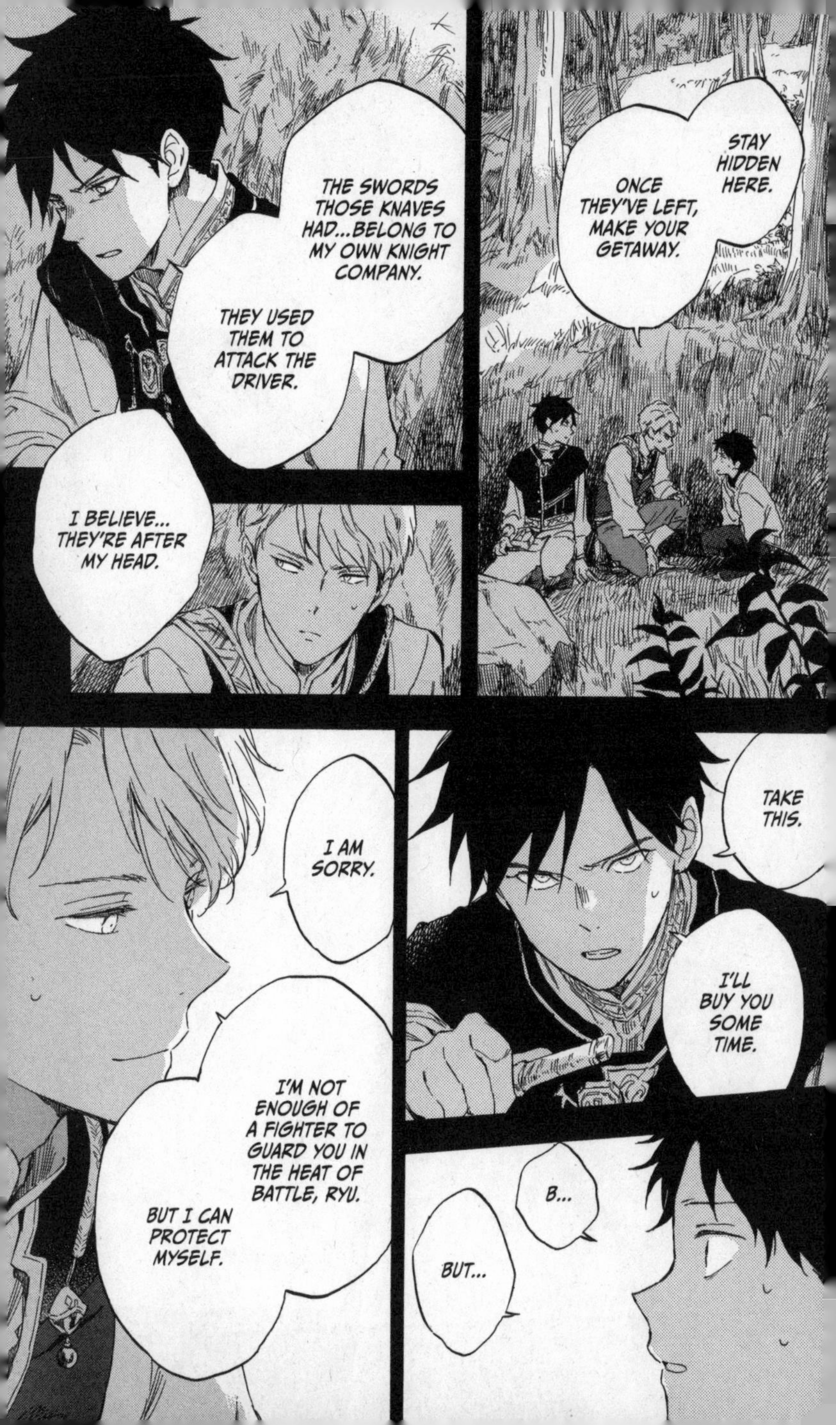
STAY HIDDEN HERE.
ONCE THEY'VE LEFT, MAKE YOUR GETAWAY.
THE SWORDS THOSE KNAVES HAD...BELONG TO MY OWN KNIGHT COMPANY.
THEY USED THEM TO ATTACK THE DRIVER.
I BELIEVE... THEY'RE AFTER MY HEAD.
TAKE THIS.
I'LL BUY YOU SOME TIME.
B...
BUT...
I AM SORRY.
I'M NOT ENOUGH OF A FIGHTER TO GUARD YOU IN THE HEAT OF BATTLE, RYU.
BUT I CAN PROTECT MYSELF.

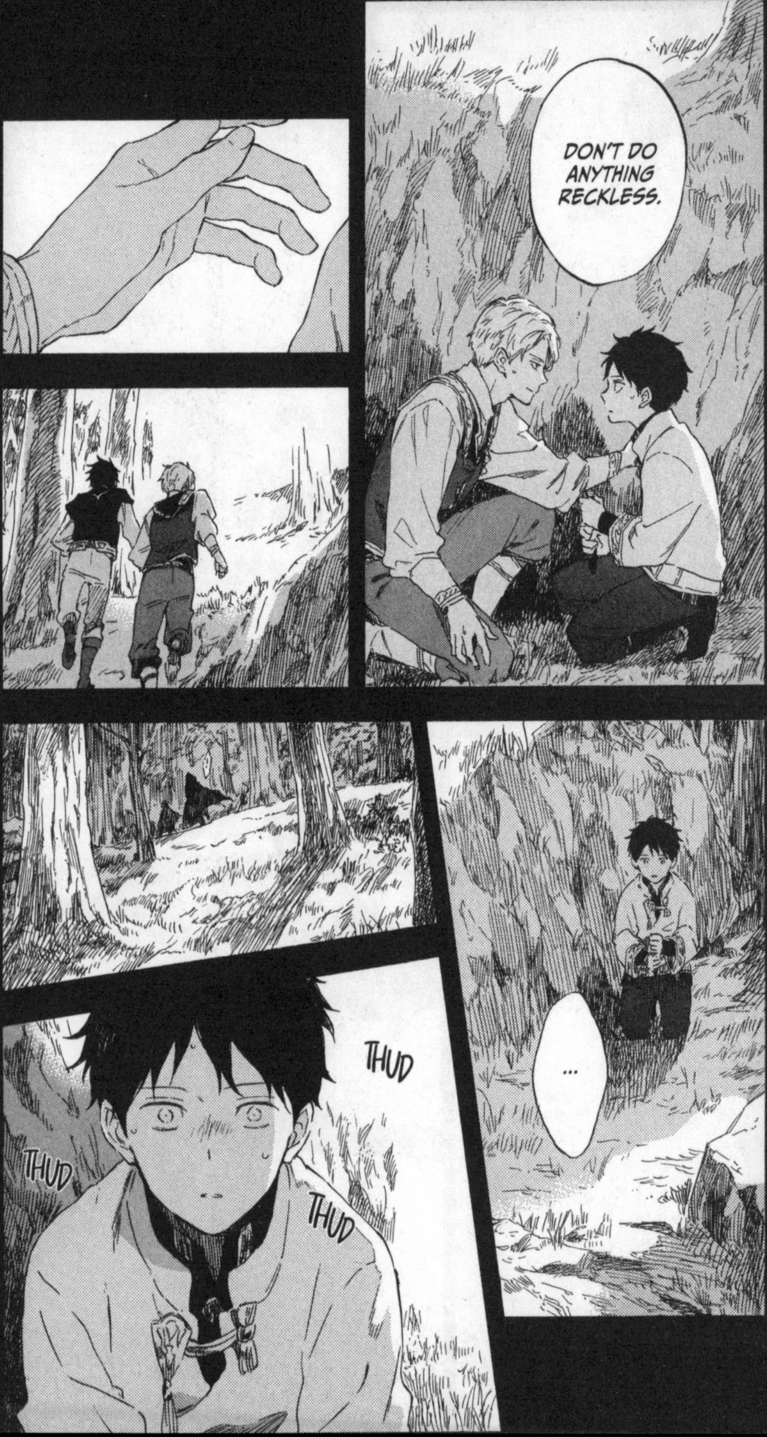
DON'T DO ANYTHING RECKLESS.
...
THUD
THUD
THUD

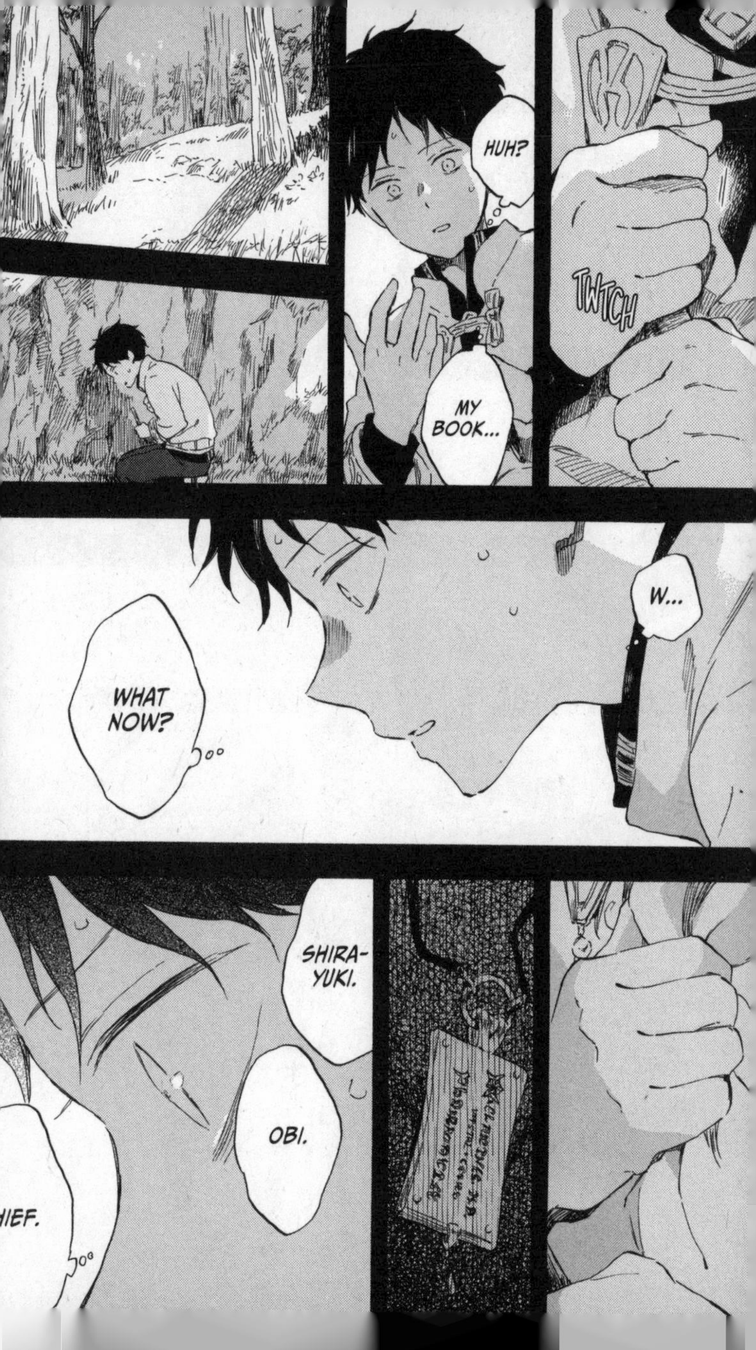
TWTCH
HUH?
MY BOOK...
W...
WHAT NOW?
SHIRA-YUKI.
OBI.
IEF.

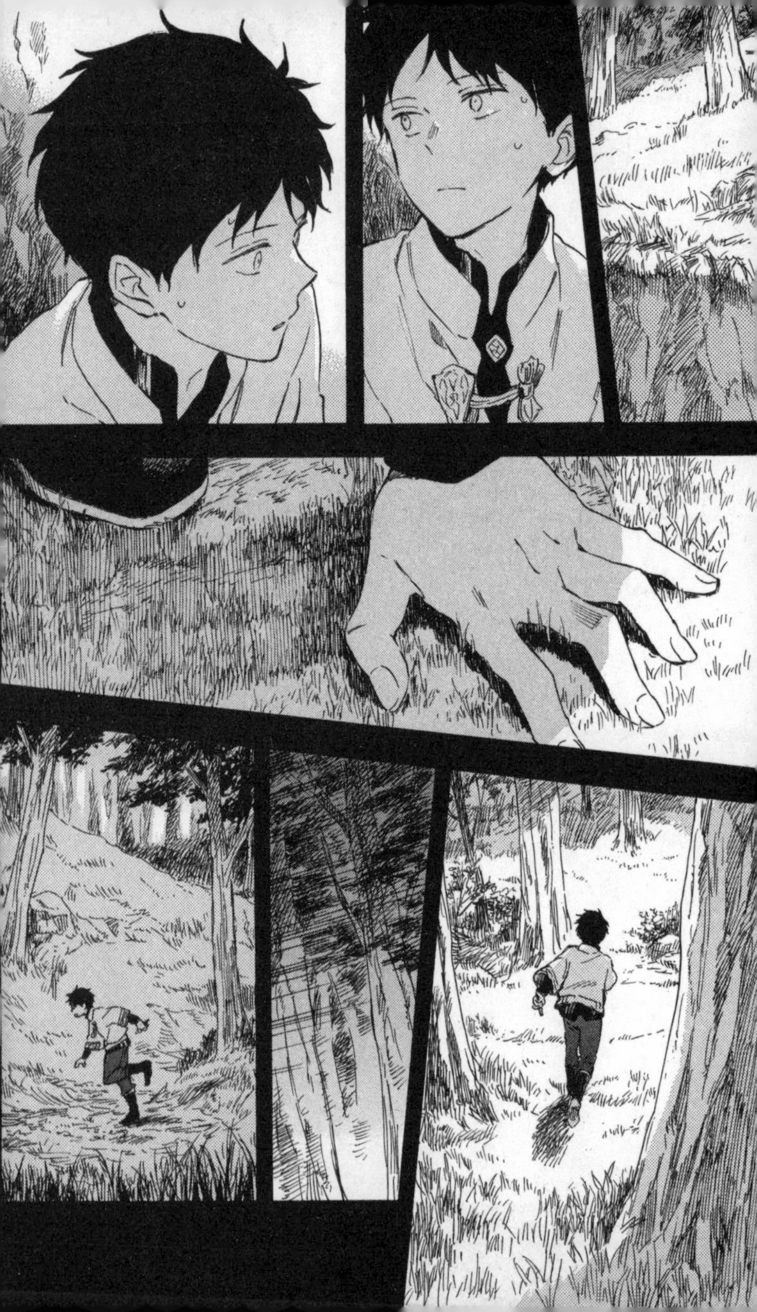

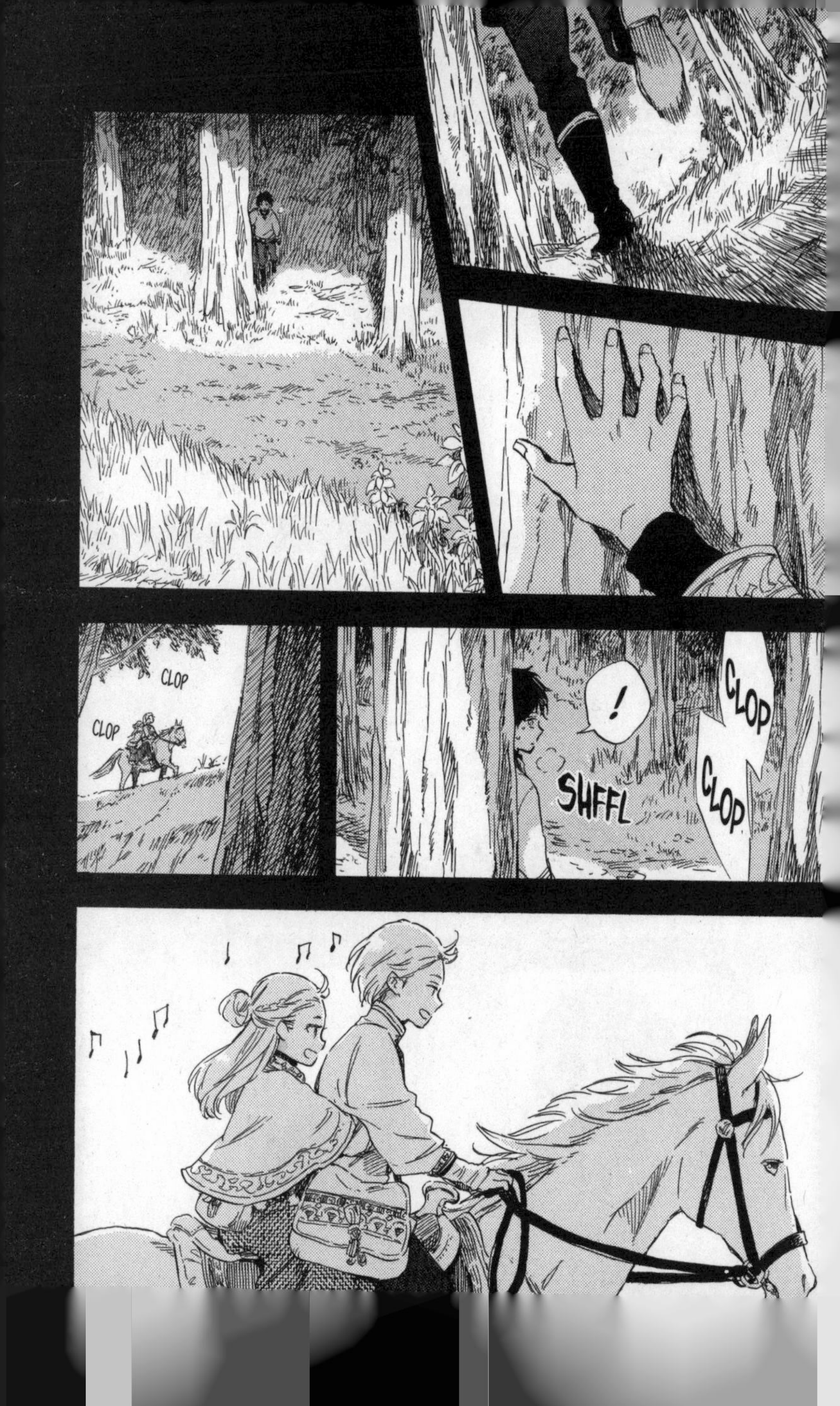
CLOP
CLOP
!
SHFFL
CLOP
CLOP

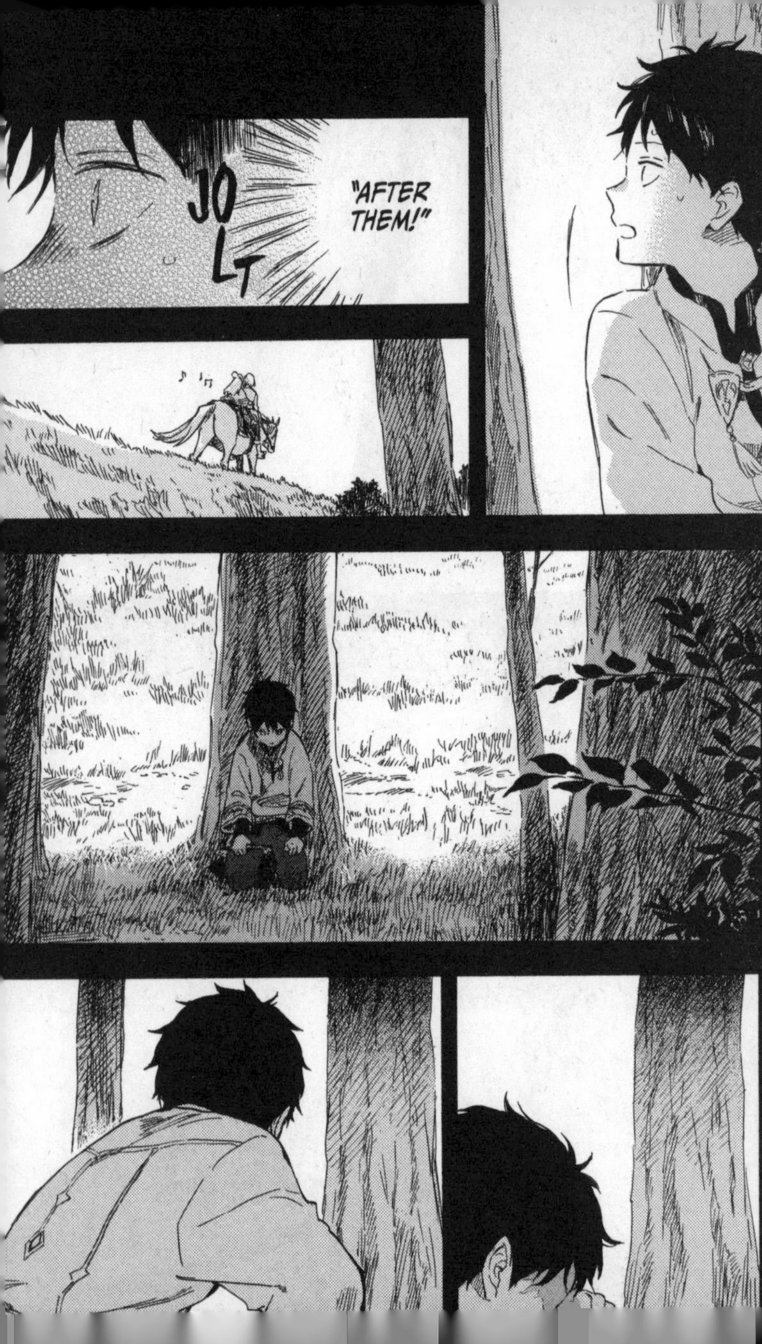
"AFTER THEM!"
JOLT

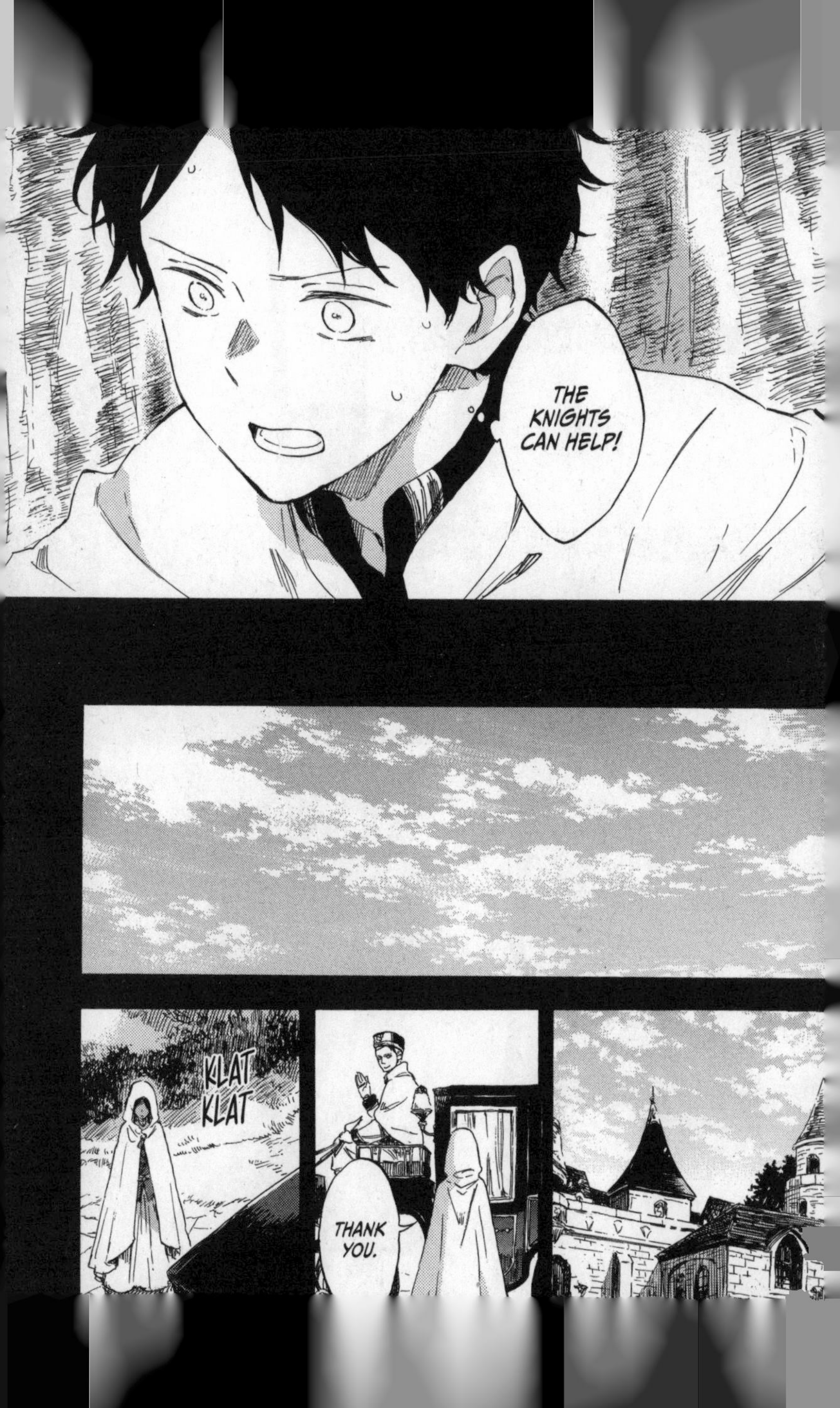
THE KNIGHTS CAN HELP!
THANK YOU.
KLAT KLAT

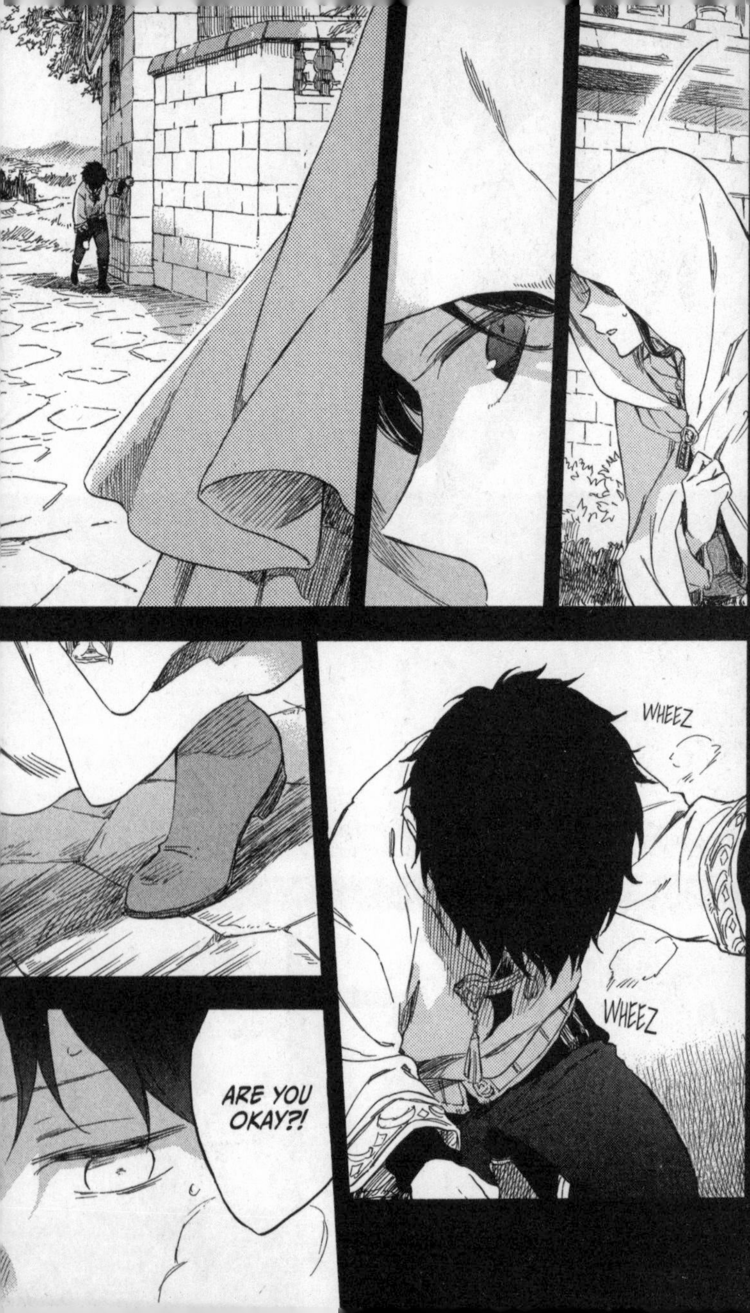
WHEEZ
WHEEZ
ARE YOU OKAY?!

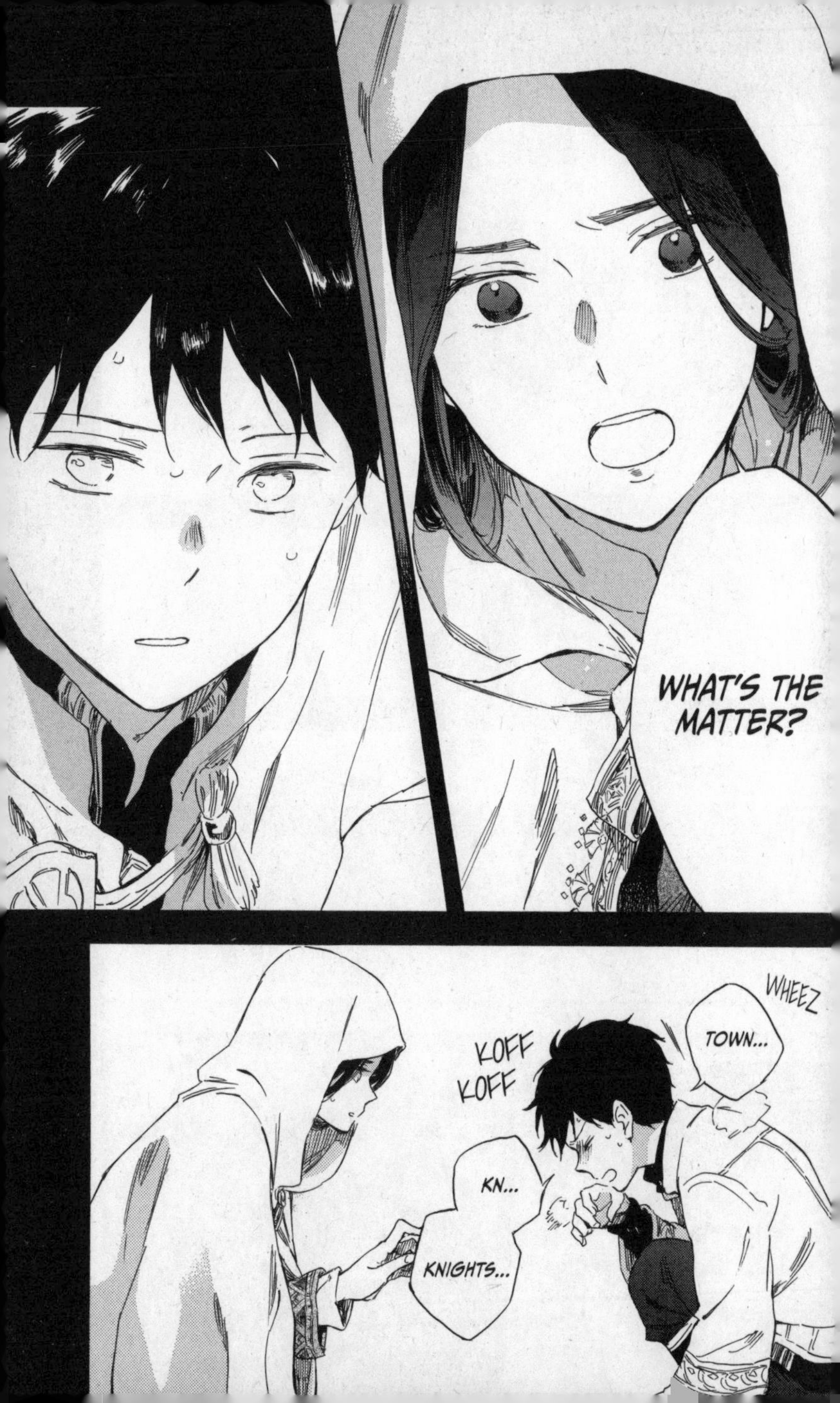
WHAT'S THE MATTER?
WHEEZ
TOWN...
KOFF KOFF
KN...
KNIGHTS...

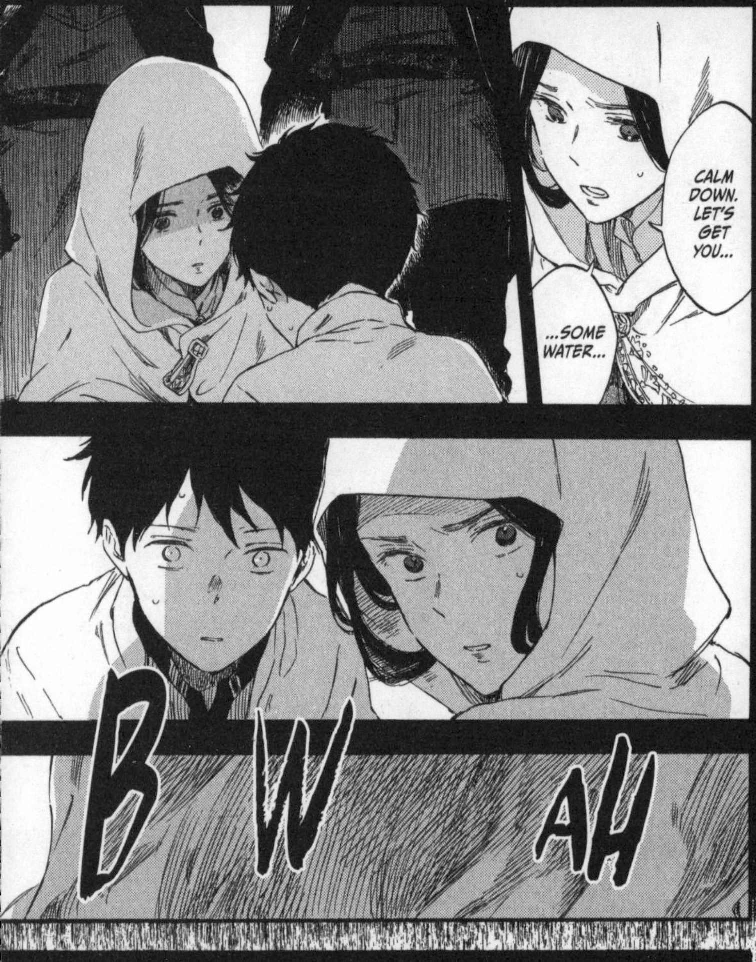
CALM DOWN. LET'S GET YOU...
...SOME WATER...
BWAH

Snow White with the Red Hair
Vol. 24: End

Wirant Happenings

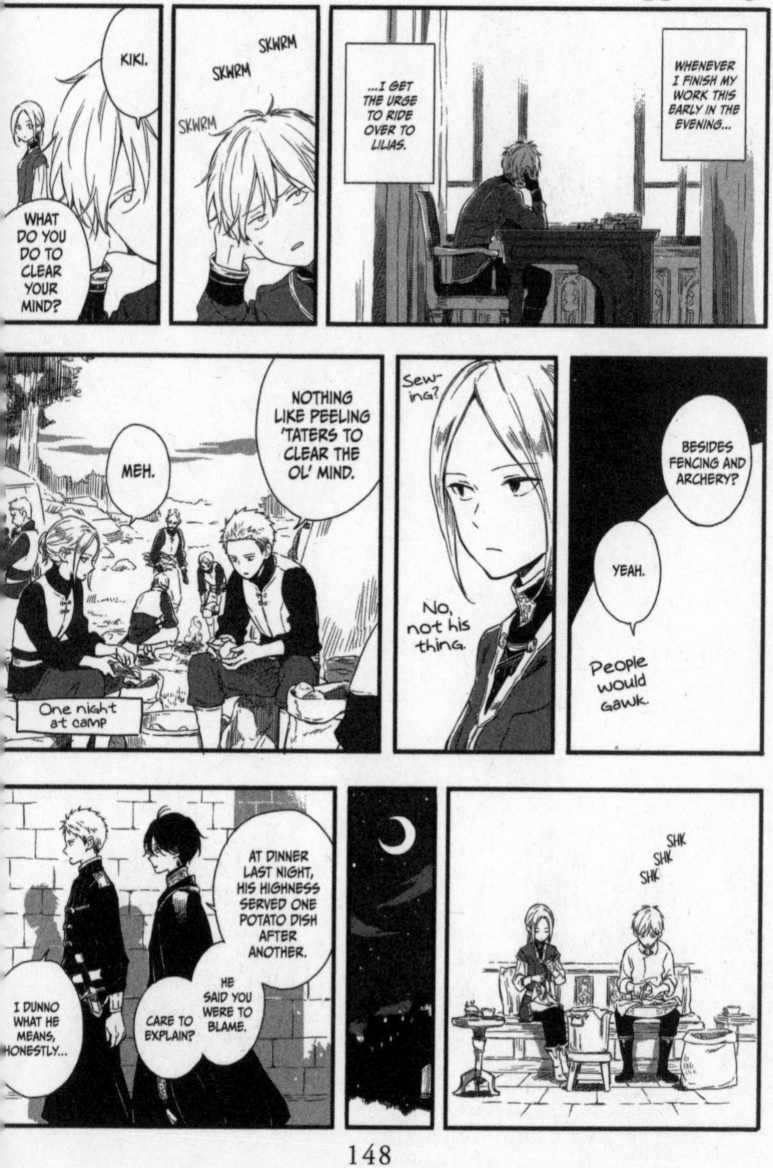
WHENEVER I FINISH MY WORK THIS EARLY IN THE EVENING...
...I GET THE URGE TO RIDE OVER TO LILIAS.
SKWRM
SKWRM
SKWRM
KIKI.
WHAT DO YOU DO TO CLEAR YOUR MIND?
BESIDES FENCING AND ARCHERY?
YEAH.
People would gawk.
Sew-ing?
No, not his thing.
NOTHING LIKE PEELING 'TATERS TO CLEAR THE OL' MIND.
MEH.
One night at camp
SHK
SHK
SHK
AT DINNER LAST NIGHT, HIS HIGHNESS SERVED ONE POTATO DISH AFTER ANOTHER.
HE SAID YOU WERE TO BLAME.
CARE TO EXPLAIN?
I DUNNO WHAT HE MEANS, HONESTLY...

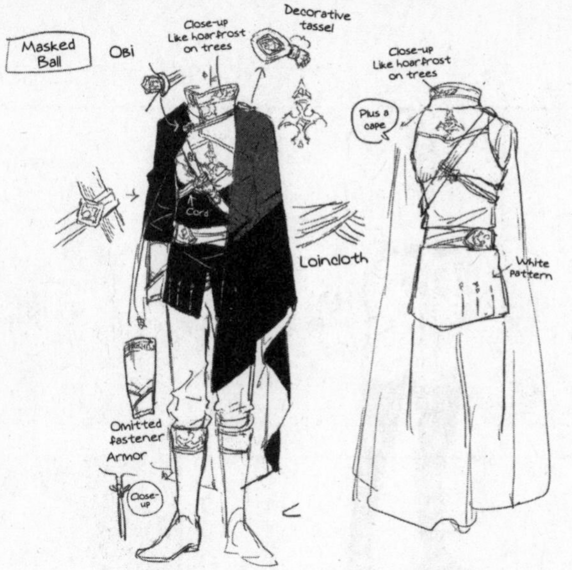
Masked Ball
Obi
Close-up
Like hoarfrost on trees
Decorative tassel
Close-up
Like hoarfrost on trees
Plus a cape
Cord
Loincloth
White pattern
Omitted fastener
Armor
Close-up

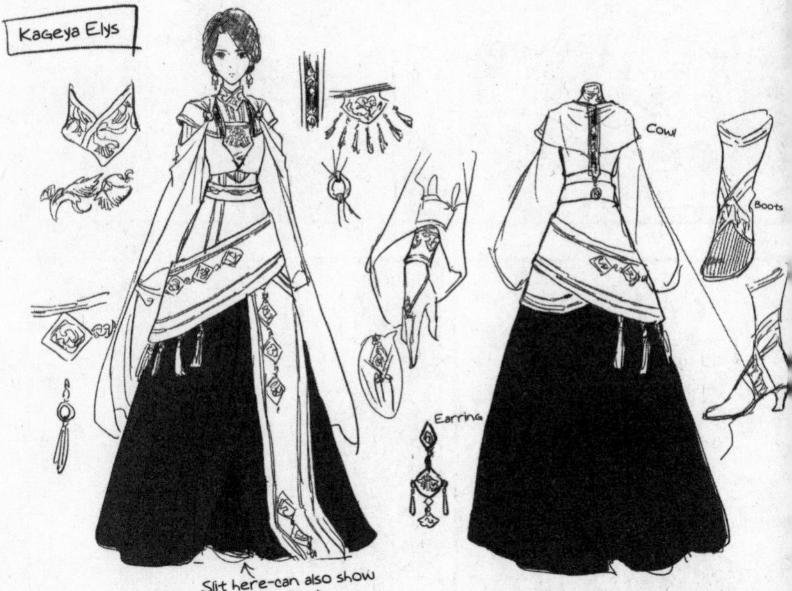
KaGeya Elys
Cowl
Boots
Earring
Slit here-can also show her feet

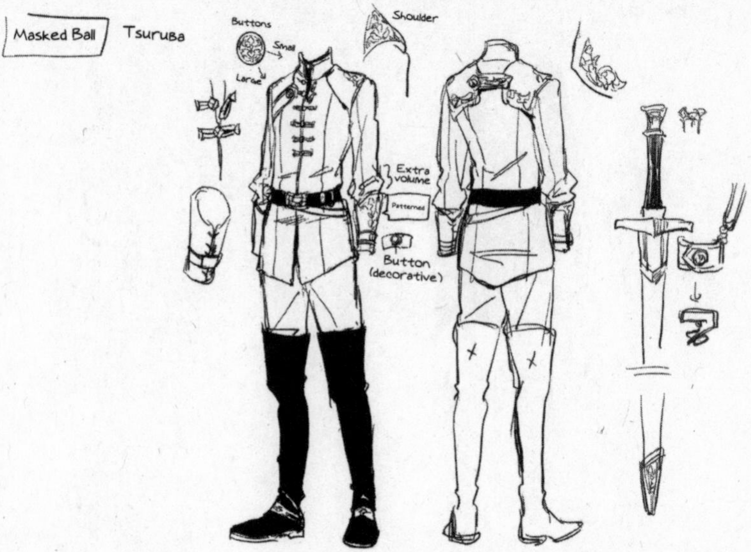

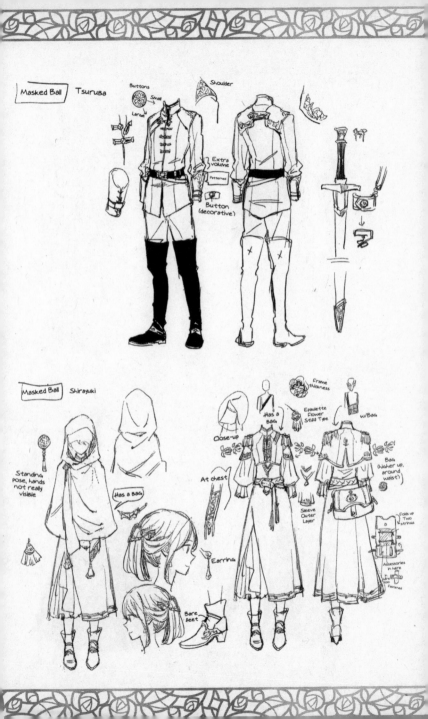

Masked Ball
Tsuruba
Buttons
Small
Large
Shoulder
Extra volume
Patterned
Button (decorative)

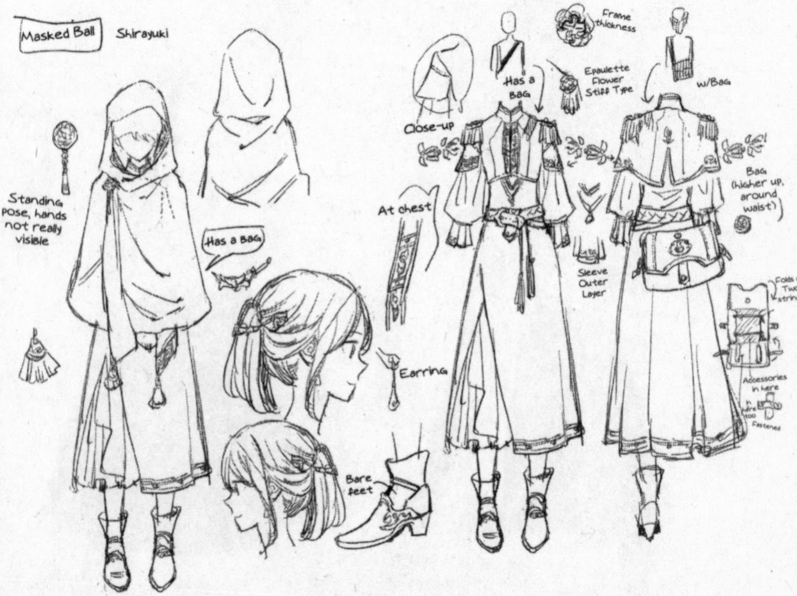

Masked Ball
Shirayuki
Standing pose, hands not really visible
Has a BAG
Close-up
Has a BAG
Frame thickness
Epaulette Flower Stiff Type
w/Bag
At chest
Sleeve Outer Layer
Bag (higher up, around waist)
Folds up Two strings
Earring
Accessories in here
In here too
Fastened
Bare feet

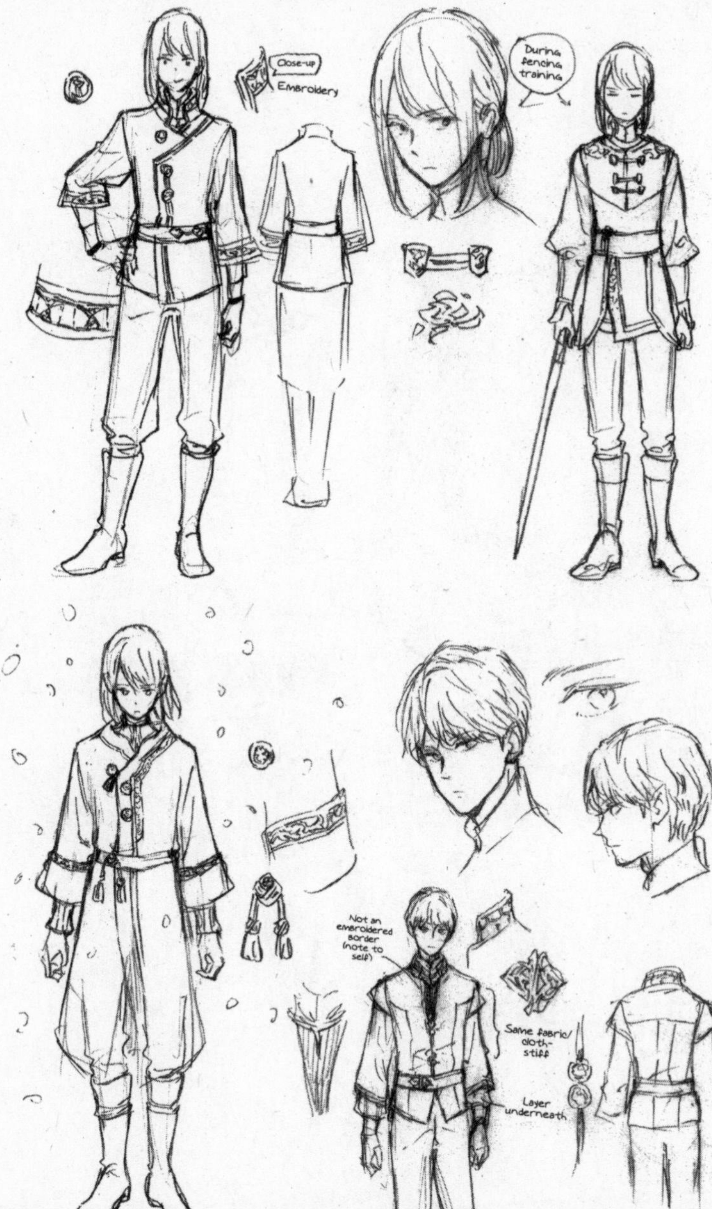
Close-up
Embroidery
During fencing training
Not an embroidered border (note to self)
Same fabric/ cloth-stiff
Layer underneath

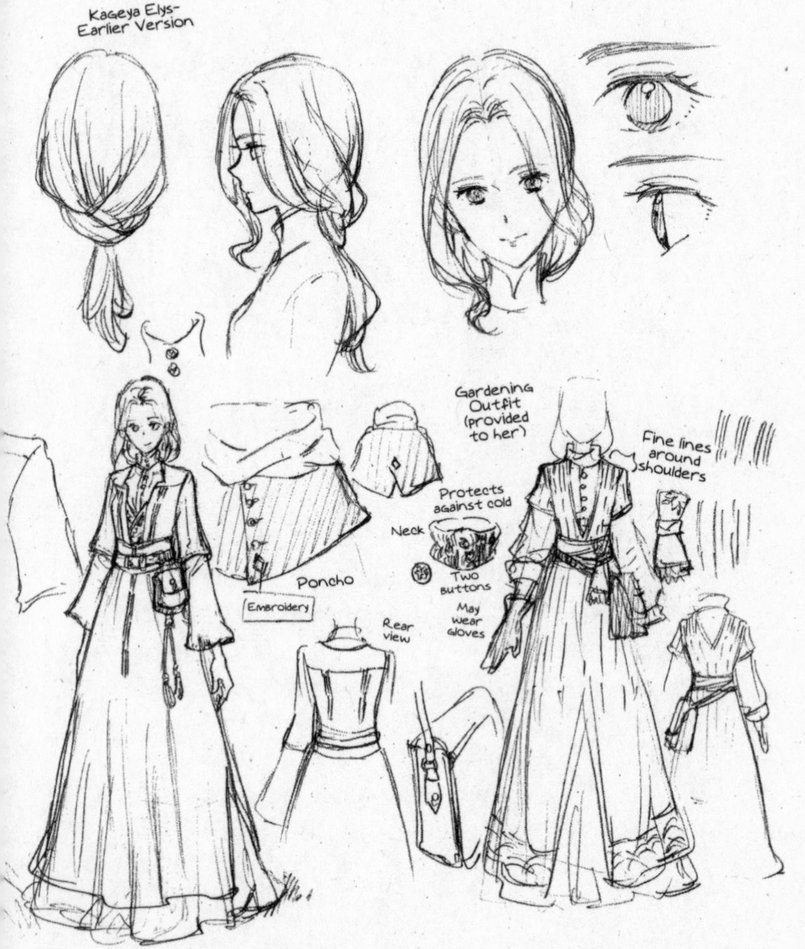

Kageya Elys-
Earlier Version
Gardening
Outfit
(provided
to her)
Fine lines
around
shoulders
Protects
against cold
Neck
Two
buttons
Poncho
Embroidery
May
wear
gloves
Rear
view

Sorata Akiduki was born on March 21 and is
an accomplished shojo manga author. She made her
debut in January 2002 with a one-shot titled "Utopia."
Her previous works include *Vahlia no Hanamuko*
(Vahlia's Bridegroom), *Seishun Kouryakubon* (Youth
Strategy Guide), and *Natsu Yasumi Zero Zero Nichime*
(00 Days of Summer Vacation). *Snow White with
the Red Hair* began serialization in August 2006 in
LaLa DX in Japan and has since moved to *LaLa*.

Snow White
with the Red Hair

24

SHOJO BEAT EDITION

STORY AND ART BY
Sorata Akiduki

TRANSLATION **Caleb Cook**
TOUCH-UP ART & LETTERING **Brandon Bovia**
DESIGN **Alice Lewis**
EDITOR **Karla Clark**

Akagami no Shirayukihime by Sorata Akiduki
© Sorata Akiduki 2021
All rights reserved.
First published in Japan in 2021 by HAKUSENSHA, Inc., Tokyo.
English language translation rights arranged with HAKUSENSHA, Inc., Tokyo.

The stories, characters, and incidents mentioned
in this publication are entirely fictional.

Printed in Canada

Published by VIZ Media, LLC
P.O. Box 77010
San Francisco, CA 94107

10 9 8 7 6 5 4 3 2 1
First printing, April 2023

viz.com

shojobeat.com

Kamisama Kiss

Story and art by **Julietta Suzuki**

What's a newly fledged godling to do?

Nanami Momozono is alone and homeless after her dad skips town to evade his gambling debts and the debt collectors kick her out of her apartment. So when a man she's just saved from a dog offers her his home, she jumps at the opportunity. But it turns out that his place is a shrine, and Nanami has unwittingly taken over his job as a local deity!

Takane & Hana

STORY AND ART BY
Yuki Shiwasu

After her older sister refuses to go to an arranged marriage meeting with Takane Saibara, the heir to a vast business fortune, high schooler Hana Nonomura agrees to be her stand-in to save face for the family. But when Takane and Hana pair up, get ready for some sparks to fly between these two utter opposites!

shojobeat.com

Natsume's BOOK of FRIENDS

STORY and ART by
Yuki Midorikawa

Make Some Unusual New Friends

The power to see hidden spirits has always felt like a curse to troubled high schooler Takashi Natsume. But he's about to discover he inherited a lot more than just the Sight from his mysterious grandmother!

Available at your local bookstore or comic store

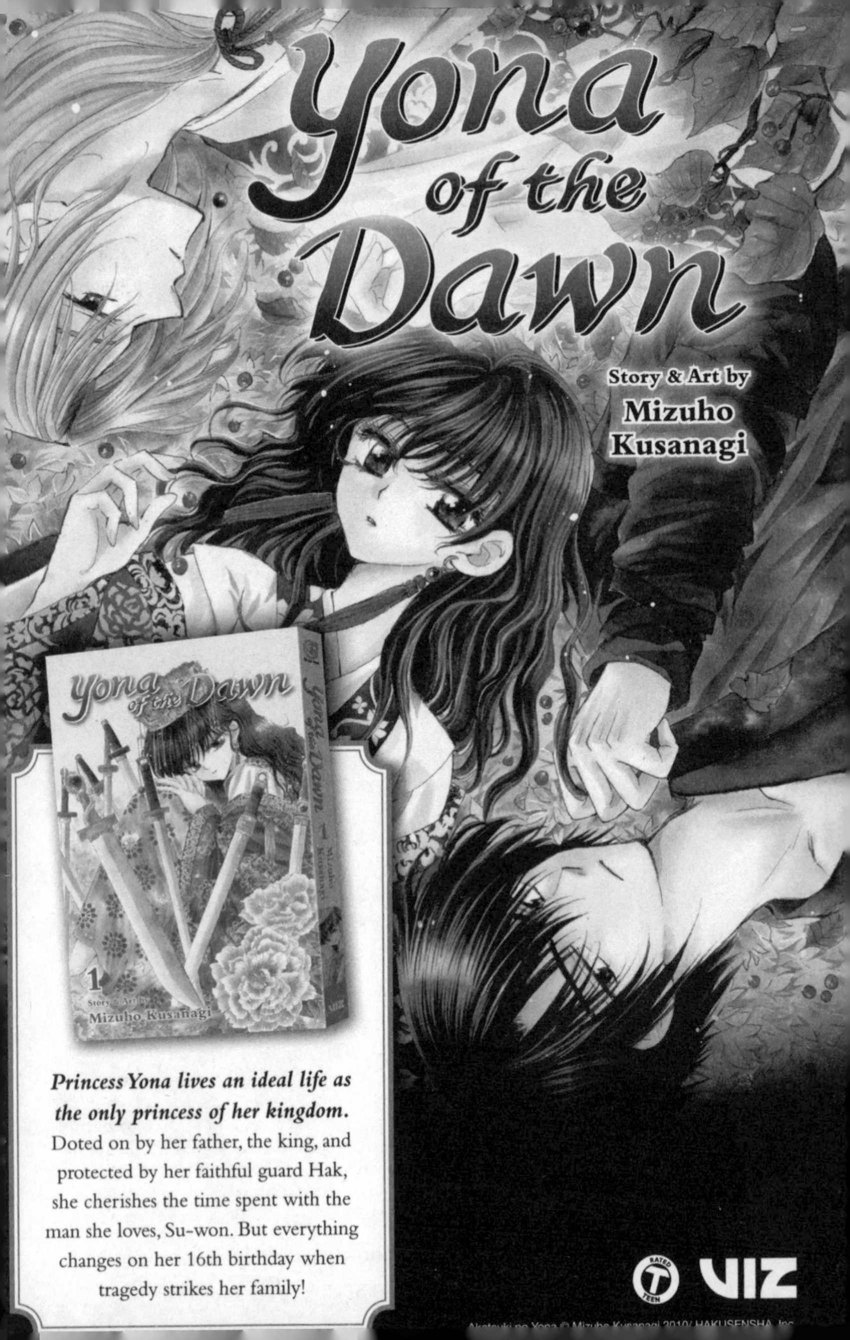

yona
of the
Dawn

Story & Art by
Mizuho Kusanagi

Princess Yona lives an ideal life as the only princess of her kingdom. Doted on by her father, the king, and protected by her faithful guard Hak, she cherishes the time spent with the man she loves, Su-won. But everything changes on her 16th birthday when tragedy strikes her family!

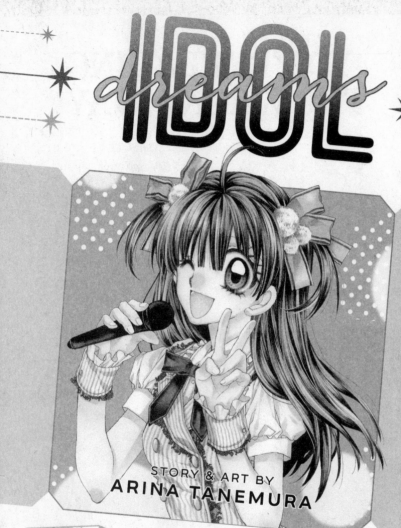

IDOL dreams

STORY & ART BY
ARINA TANEMURA

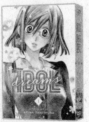

At age 31, office worker Chikage Deguchi feels she missed her chances at love and success. When word gets out that she's a virgin, Chikage is humiliated and wishes she could turn back time to when she was still young and popular. She takes an experimental drug that changes her appearance back to when she was 15. Now Chikage is determined to pursue everything she missed out on all those years ago—including becoming a star!

Shojo Beat VIZ RATED T TEEN

YOU'RE READING THE WRONG WAY!

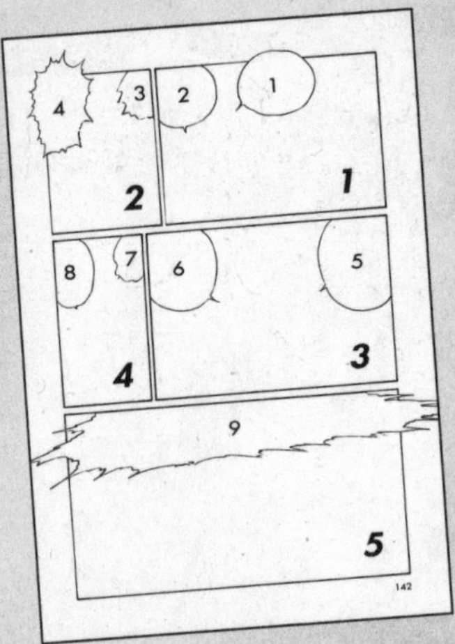

Snow White with the Red Hair reads from right to left, starting in the upper-right corner. Japanese is read from right to left, meaning that action, sound effects, and word-balloon order are completely reversed from English order.

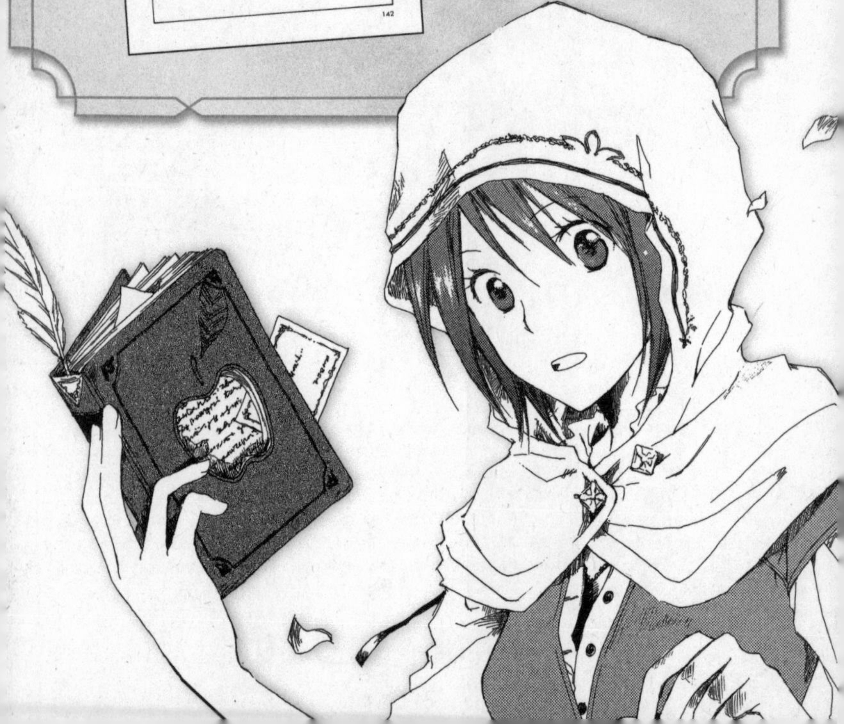